REFORM AND

IN THE ELEVENTH CENTURY

Manchester University Press

MANCHESTER MEDIEVAL STUDIES

SERIES EDITOR Dr S. H. Rigby

SERIES ADVISORS Professor John Hatcher
Professor J. H. Moran Cruz

The study of medieval Europe is being transformed as old orthodoxies
are challenged, new methods embraced and fresh fields of inquiry
opened up. The adoption of inter-disciplinary perspectives and the
challenge of economic, social and cultural theory are forcing medievalists
to ask new questions and to see familiar topics in a fresh light.

The aim of this series is to combine the scholarship traditionally
associated with medieval studies with an awareness of more recent
issues and approaches in a form accessible to the non-specialist reader.

ALREADY PUBLISHED IN THE SERIES

The commercialisation of English society, 1000–1500
Richard H. Britnell

Picturing women in late medieval and Renaissance art
Christa Grössinger

The politics of carnival
Christopher Humphrey

Medieval law in context
Anthony Musson

Chaucer in context
S. H. Rigby

Medieval maidens
Kim M. Phillips

MANCHESTER MEDIEVAL STUDIES

REFORM AND PAPACY
IN THE ELEVENTH CENTURY

SPIRITUALITY AND SOCIAL CHANGE

Kathleen G. Cushing

Manchester University Press

Manchester and New York

distributed exclusively in the USA by Palgrave

Published by Manchester University Press
Oxford Road, Manchester M13 9NR, UK
and Room 400, 175 Fifth Avenue, New York, NY 10010, USA
www.manchesteruniversitypress.co.uk

Distributed exclusively in the USA
by Palgrave, 175 Fifth Avenue, New York, NY 10010, USA

Distributed exclusively in Canada
by UBC Press, University of British Columbia, 2029 West Mall,
Vancouver, BC, Canada V6T 1Z2

British Library Cataloguing-in-Publication Data
A catalogue record for this book is available from the British Library

Library of Congress Cataloging-in-Publication Data applied for

ISBN 0 7190 5833 3 *hardback*
EAN 978 0 7190 5833 2
ISBN 0 7190 5834 1 *paperback*
EAN 978 0 7190 5834 9

First published 2005

15 14 13 12 11 10 09 08 07 06 05   10 9 8 7 6 5 4 3 2 1

Typeset in Monotype Bulmer
by Koinonia, Manchester
Printed in Great Britain
by Bell & Bain Ltd, Glasgow

For Paul, Judy and Frank

with whom distance is a relative thing

CONTENTS

ACKNOWLEDGEMENTS *page* ix

LIST OF ABBREVIATIONS xi

CHRONOLOGICAL LIST OF POPES –
TENTH AND ELEVENTH CENTURIES xii

TABLE OF DATES xiv

INTRODUCTION 1

1 Western Europe and the Latin Church around the year 1000 7

Doctrine and belief 7
Localization of power 9
The organization of the Church 12
Rome and the papacy 17
Economic, intellectual and social change 24
Conclusion 26

2 Understanding reform in the eleventh century 29

3 The 'peace of God' 39

4 'Reforming' the papacy 55

The changing nature of papal authority 55
The transformation of the papacy 65
Papal government 81
Conclusion 86

5 Reform in practice 91

Material renewal 91
Simony and clerical chastity 95
Implementing reform 100

Lay investiture 105
Conclusion 107

6 The rhetoric of reform 111

Purity and pollution 111
The rhetoric against simony 117
The rhetoric against clerical marriage 120
The 'pollution complex' 125
The problem of lay investiture 128
Blurring the lines 130

7 Hierarchy and social control 139

CONCLUSION 160

SELECT BIBLIOGRAPHY 162
INDEX 169

ACKNOWLEDGEMENTS

Addressing the topics of reform and papacy in the space of two hundred or so pages is, inevitably, a challenge. Individual readers will invariably wonder at the exclusion of some material which they would deem to be critical, while others may question the inclusion of topics which they would consider to be peripheral. It needs to be stressed that it was never my intention to write an exhaustive narrative history of reform and the papacy in the eleventh century. Rather, in keeping with the aims of the Manchester University Press series, Manchester Medieval Studies, I have sought to explore reform and the papacy from the perspectives of religious and social change in a period of considerable transformation, with special attention devoted to the rhetoric used by the reformers both to prescribe and justify that change.

My thoughts and approaches to the many problems of understanding eleventh-century reform have been shaped and influenced by both my reading of countless scholars, only some of whose works are listed in the bibliography, and by my discussions over any number of years with many others, all of whom cannot be recognized here. It goes without saying that my greatest debt is still owed to my late supervisor, Karl Leyser. It is important first of all, however, to thank my series editor, Steve Rigby, whose painstaking correction of the typescript has been invaluable, to say nothing of his overall comments and suggestions. I should also like to express my deep gratitude to the anonymous reader for the care and attention with which she/he approached the typescript; his/her suggestions have been of tremendous help. I must also single out Glyn Redworth for his meticulously close reading of the typescript; he has unfailingly helped and challenged me to clarify both my interpretations of eleventh-century reform and my exposition of the material. I should also like to thank the editors and production team at Manchester University Press for their patience and assistance. It is equally important that I recognize my parents and Frank for their unfailing, if somewhat prejudicial, confidence in my abilities.

More specifically, I would also like to thank: Virginia Brown, Isabelle Cochelin, Kate Cooper, John Cowdrey, Jennifer Harris, Dave Hay, Henrietta Leyser, Conrad Leyser, Henry Mayr-Harting, Maureen Miller, Bob Moore, Sandy Murray, Jinty Nelson, William North, Lesley Smith, Roger Reynolds and Fred Unwalla. I should also like to thank my colleagues in the School of History at Keele, especially Ann Hughes, Christopher Harrison, Ian Atherton,

Robin Studd and Peter Jackson, as well as the students at Keele who have endured my special subject on the 'Gregorian Revolution', and who have pressed me constantly to clarify (and explain) my thinking on this extraordinarily complicated topic. Special thanks are owed to my colleague, Philip Morgan, who frequently reminds me of my predilection for making the obvious complicated. It is my hope and belief that, in the following pages, I have made the complicated much more obvious.

ABBREVIATIONS

Ep. vag.	*The Epistolae Vagantes of Pope Gregory VII*, ed. H. E. J. Cowdrey (Oxford, 1972)
JEH	*Journal of Ecclesiastical History*
Mansi	*Sacrorum conciliorum nova et amplissima collectio*, ed. G. D. Mansi, 57 vols (Paris and Arnhem, 1901–27)
Medieval Purity and Piety	*Medieval Purity and Piety: Essays on Medieval Clerical Celibacy and Religious Reform*, ed. M. Frassetto (New York, 1998)
MGH	Monumenta Germaniae Historica
BDK	*Briefe der deutschen Kaiserzeit*
Const.	*Constitutiones et acta publica imperatorum et regum*
Ep. sel.	*Epistolae selectae*
LdL	*Libelli de lite imperatorum et pontificum saeculis XI. et XII. conscriptis*
SS	*Scriptores*
SSRG	*Scriptores rerum Gemanicarum in usum scholarum ex monumenti recusi*
Peace of God	*The Peace of God: Social Violence and Religious Response in France around the year 1000*, ed. T. Head and R. Landes (Ithaca, NY, 1992)
PL	Patrologia cursus completus, series Latina, ed. J. P. Migne, 183 vols (Paris, 1841–64)
PP	*Past and Present*
Reg.	*Registrum Gregorii VII.*, ed. E. Caspar (MGH, *Ep. sel.*, t. 2, 2 vols; Berlin, 1920–3); English trans. by H. E. J. Cowdrey, *The Register of Pope Gregory VII, 1073–1085: An English Translation* (Oxford, 2002)
Reindel	*Die Briefe des Petrus Damiani*, ed. K. Reindel (MGH, *BDK*, 4: 1–4; Munich, 1983–93); English trans. by O. J. Blum, *The Letters of Peter Damian*, 4 vols (The Fathers of the Church, Medieval Continuation; Washington, DC, 1989–99)
TRHS	*Transactions of the Royal Historical Society*

CHRONOLOGICAL LIST OF POPES
— TENTH AND ELEVENTH CENTURIES

John X	Mar./Apr. 914–deposed May 928; d. 929
Leo VI	May–Dec. 928
Stephen VII	Dec. 928–Feb. 931
John XI	Feb./Mar. 931–Dec. 935/Jan. 936
Leo VII	Jan. 936–July 939
Stephen VIII	July 939–Oct. 942
Marinus II	Oct. 942–May 946
Agapitus II	May 946–Dec. 955
John XII	Dec. 955–May 964
Leo VIII	Dec. 963–Mar. 965
Benedict V	May 964–deposed June 964; d. 966
John XIII	Oct. 965–Sept. 972
Benedict VI	Jan. 973–July 974
Boniface VII (anti-pope)	June–July 974
Benedict VII	Oct. 974–July 983
John XIV	Dec. 983–Aug. 984
John XV	Aug. 985–Mar. 996
Gregory V	May 996–Feb. 999
John XVI (anti-pope)	Feb. 997–May 998
Silvester II	Apr. 999–May 1003
John XVII	May–Nov. 1003
John XVIII	Dec. 1003–June/July 1009
Sergius IV	July 1009–May 1012
Benedict VIII	May 1012–Apr. 1024
Gregory VI (anti-pope)	May–Dec. 1012
John XIX	Apr. 1024–Oct. 1032
Benedict IX	Oct. 1032–May 1045;
	Nov. 1047–July 1048; d. 1055/56
Silvester III (anti-pope)	Jan.–Mar. 1045; d. 1063
Gregory VI	May 1045–deposed Dec. 1046; d. 1047
Clement II	Dec. 1046–Oct. 1047
Damasus II	July–Aug. 1048
Leo IX	Feb. 1049–Apr. 1054
Victor II	Apr. 1055–July 1057
Stephen IX	Aug. 1057–Mar. 1058

Benedict X (anti-pope)	Apr. 1058–Jan. 1059; d. after 1073
Nicholas II	Dec. 1058–July 1061
Alexander II	Sept. 1061–Apr. 1073
Honorius II (anti-pope)	Oct. 1061–May 1064; d. 1071/72
Gregory VII	Apr. 1073–May 1085
Clement III (anti-pope)	June 1080; Mar. 1084–Sept. 1100
Victor III	May 1086; May–Sept. 1087
Urban II	Mar. 1088–July 1099
Paschal II	Aug. 1099–Jan. 1118

TABLE OF DATES

430	Death of St Augustine of Hippo
c.480–c.550	St Benedict of Nursia
590-604	Pontificate of Gregory the Great
800	Imperial Coronation of Charlemagne
814	Death of Charlemagne
810s	Benedict of Aniane's promotion of the Rule of St Benedict for monasteries
843	Treaty of Verdun – partition of Charlemagne's empire
910	Foundation of Cluny
923	Vikings in Normandy, Magyars in Western Europe
936-73	Reign of Otto I of Germany (emperor from 960)
963	Deposition of John XII
975	Peace gathering at Le Puy
987	Accession of Hugh Capet
989	Peace Council at Charroux
994	Peace Councils at Limoges and Anse
1000	Peace Council at Poitiers
1012	Elevation of Benedict VIII (beginning of Tusculan-controlled papacy)
1014	Peace Council at Poitiers; Council of Ravenna (Henry II and Benedict VIII)
1022	Council of Pavia (Henry II and Benedict VIII)
1027	Peace Council at Elne-Toulouges
1028	Peace Council at Charroux
1029/30	Peace Council at Poitiers
1031	Peace Councils at Limoges and Bourges
1038	Formation of peace league at Bourges
1039	Foundation of Vallombrosa
1046	Synod of Sutri – deposition of Gregory VI
1049	Elevation of Leo IX; Councils of Rome, Rheims and Mainz
1050	Council of Coyaca
c.1050	Humbert of Silva-Candida, *Three Books against the Simoniacs*
1054	Breakdown of relations with Eastern Church in Constantinople
1056	Councils of Compostella and Toulouse
1056–1106	Reign of Henry IV of Germany

c.1057–75	Patarenes active in Milan
1059	Lateran Council in Rome; papal election decree; Peter Damian, *De parentalae gradibus*
1059-91	Norman Conquest of Sicily
1063	Council of Tours
1064–67	Vallombrosan struggle against Peter Mezzabarba, Bishop of Florence
1066	Norman Conquest of England
1068	Council of Gerona
1073–85	Pontificate of Gregory VII
1073	Saxon rising against Henry IV
1075	*Dictatus papae*; Papal privilege for Patarene priest Liprand
1076	Synod of Worms – deposition of Gregory VII by Henry IV and the German bishops; first excommunication of Henry IV; burning of the priest Ramihrd
1077	Canossa
1078	First prohibition of lay investiture
1080	Second excommunication of Henry IV; second prohibition of lay investiture; Synod of Brixen; deposition of Gregory VII; election of anti-pope Clement III
1095	Council of Clermont, launching of First Crusade
1122	Concordat of Worms

INTRODUCTION

Historians have long recognized that it is unwise to try to find a secular definition of European society for the period we know as the 'middle ages'. As Richard Southern pointed out, 'the identification of the Church with the whole of organized society is the fundamental feature which distinguishes the Middle Ages from earlier and later periods of history'.[1] While it is useful, often even necessary, to consider them separately, the medieval Church and medieval society were intertwined, and membership of the Church was crucial in determining an individual's place in society.[2]

Although the equation of Church and society can by and large be used to describe the condition of earlier medieval Europe as well, it is the argument of this book that during the course of the eleventh century the symbiosis of Church and society became more pronounced. This, of course, was a consequence of the movement for ecclesiastical reform. Indeed, as it will be argued, the attempt to improve standards in religious life had a revolutionary impact on eleventh-century European society. Although these efforts emerged initially at local levels in the later tenth century, and were promoted by local clergy and lay powers, they increasingly were directed in the eleventh century by a newly-ascendant Church hierarchy, and especially a reinvigorated Roman papacy, that sought to promote reform both in an attempt to return to the apostolic ideals of the early Church and as a reaction to far-ranging political, economic and social changes. Yet in the process of promoting reform, the Church would ultimately begin both to delineate and impress a unique identity for the Latin West, that of the *societas christiana*.

The attempt to both define and understand reform in the later tenth and eleventh centuries is thus the chief ambition of this book. This endeavour, however, is especially complicated by the fact that when eleventh-century contemporaries wrote about the aspirations, changes and improvements that they sought to effect in religious life – and within the personnel and institutional frameworks through which those objectives were to be pursued – they seldom used words like 'reform' (*reformare*). They thought instead in terms of renewal, renovation (*renovatio*) and restoration (*restauratio*).[3] Defining and understanding reform, thus, is made difficult not just by the distance of that world from our own, but also by the different cultural and even linguistic assumptions of later tenth- and eleventh-century writers compared to those of modern historians.

At the same time, as Dominique Iogna-Prat has recently cautioned, it is important that historians working on medieval topics, especially the Church, recognize that our task is not 'religious history' but rather 'social history'.[4] Inasmuch as it is important, where possible, to try to gauge medieval society's attachment to religious values, we can often do little more than assess how these intersected with the enactment of belief in accordance with prescriptive rules of an institution, that is, the Church. Moreover, our specific time-frame and place – the Latin West during the later tenth and eleventh centuries – offers an additional challenge. This was, after all, a time when the production and dissemination of ideas was the exclusive province of a very small elite – educated clerics and monks – and their writings and accounts inevitably leave us with only one side of the story. Even more important, the changes in religious life described in such accounts may often be evidence merely of aspirations to effect change rather than real change.

This book looks to address what some historians have called 'the religious revolution of the eleventh century'. It does so by exploring how reform and the papacy developed in the eleventh century, and how these changes affected the rules by which medieval society functioned. On the one hand, it examines the papacy as an institution within the context of the society of which it was a part. On the other, it considers the reform movement against the backdrop of other critical developments in eleventh-century Europe: the so-called castellan revolution and the rise of seigniorial or banal lordship, the move from a gift to a profit economy with incipient urbanization, the 'peace' movement and the emergence of the crowd as a force in Western society.

Particular attention will be paid to the question of whether the 'peace of God' movement was a social revolution that progressively blurred into and merged with the papal-sponsored movement for reform, which was gathering pace from the middle of the century, or whether these forces were deliberately compacted by the reformers in their efforts to promote their vision for Christian society. Throughout the eleventh century, there was increasing emphasis in contemporary sources on ideas of purity and pollution, of cleansing the sacred from contamination by the secular – images and rhetoric which had the function of delineating and thereby more sharply enforcing spheres of human activity. By exploring such changes, this book considers the role of the papacy as a social institution that not only articulated a distinctive ordering on earth but also, in the midst of its attempts to reform itself, sanctioned the hegemony of the powerful over the poor while protesting against it.

Assessing reform and the papacy from the perspectives of social and religious change must inevitably take account of recent and even ongoing debates about how to characterize the eleventh century as a whole. Although chapter 2 will be devoted to a survey of the historiography, it is useful here briefly to discuss what is perhaps the most contentious historiographical debate: that surrounding the 'feudal revolution' and the by now almost synonymous *mutation de l'an mil* or 'transformation of the year 1000'. Taking their cue from Marc Bloch's *Feudal Society*, this interpretation was developed by French medievalists such as Jean-François Lemarignier, Georges Duby, Pierre Bonnassie, Jean-Paul Poly, Eric Bournazel and Guy Bois, who characterized the eleventh century as the time when European civilization was created.[5]

In broad terms, the *mutationnistes* hold that, around the year 1000, European society – and especially French society – suddenly experienced a far-reaching transformation that included the proliferation of castles, banal lordship and 'evil customs' (*malae consuetudines*), the progressive reduction of a free peasantry to serfdom, major changes in class structure, the reorganization of noble kin groups and familial strategies, changes in the character of the nobility, and corresponding shifts in marriage patterns and cultural outlooks. More recently, this interpretation has been underpinned by work on the 'peace of God' movement, which, according to historians such as Richard Landes, Johannes Fried and Thomas Head, not only provides evidence of wide-ranging 'transformation' around the year 1000, but also serves as both 'a testimony to violence and a reaction against it'.[6]

This overall view, however, is far from universally accepted. Indeed, the issue of *mutation* has become so embroiled in debate that participants may never agree precisely what it is, much less what constitutes a convincing defence or refutation of it. Dominique Barthelémy, in particular, has challenged the claims made by Duby, Bois, Landes and others for the complete collapse of Carolingian institutions at the end of the tenth century and the breakdown of all public order. He suggests, through an analysis of the sources chiefly for the Vendôme, that rather than abrupt transformation, there was much continuity from the ninth to the early twelfth centuries and that those changes that did take place were extremely gradual.[7] This view is in many ways supported by Stephen White, whose work on the processes of dispute settlement draws attention to the need to focus on horizontal relations between individuals of roughly the same social status as a better measure of social change than vertical relation-ships.[8]

Other historians such as Thomas Bisson, however, continue to see the viability of the thesis of transformation especially for *c.*980–*c.*1030, arguing that historians have failed to understand the nature of lordship or appreciate the problem of violence in this period. Bisson in particular offers a useful conceptual framework for furthering the whole debate by suggesting that 'revolution' – which he argues is by implication seldom finished – may in the end be a better word than *mutation*, which, at least in scientific usage, implies an instantaneous transformation.[9] Furthermore, the entire 'transformation–feudal revolution' debate, unsurprisingly, has continued to focus attention on the appropriateness of using the construct of 'feudalism' to describe patterns of land tenure, lordship and social relations around the turn of the millennium.[10]

For all the loose ends surrounding the mutation/revolution debates, they have nonetheless immeasurably helped us to understand what was happening in the eleventh century. Yet, the debates about the nature, the timing and even the existence of 'transformation' or 'revolution' can be taken much further because, somewhat surprisingly, apart from the impor-tant work of Robert I. Moore, very little account has been taken of the eleventh-century reform movement.[11] It is the ambition of this book to do just that.

While the book is chronologically structured, it also proceeds thematically. Chapter 1 provides the historical background and context, addressing the state of the Latin Church and western Europe around the year 1000, the social functions of religion, and the beginnings of localized reform initiatives. Chapter 2 focuses on the issue of how we are to understand reform in the eleventh century, its implications and the past historiography of the subject. Chapter 3 looks at the late tenth- and earlier eleventh-century movement known as the 'peace of God', a movement that has often been characterized as a precursor to the papal-sponsored move-ment that developed strength especially after 1049, but whose intrinsic reformist nature has to date perhaps been insufficiently emphasized. Chapter 4 focuses on the Roman papacy itself, and explores the develop-ment both of papal authority and the institutional apparatus through which reform objectives were increasingly pursued. At the same time, it addresses the transformation of the papacy throughout the eleventh century from a venerated if often somewhat powerless institution into one capable both of defining the *societas christiana* and maintaining its outlines. Chapter 5 returns to the explicit topic of reform, analysing its context and the evolution of tactics for eradicating what came to be the three critical issues: simony (the practice of buying or selling church office), married priests and concubinage, and control of the Church by laymen. Chapter 6 focuses on the rhetoric used by the reformers in order to persuade the clergy to accept their dicta. Chapter 7 then explores the role of reform in redefining the behaviour and cultural traditions of the lay aristocracy. These issues are then drawn together in the conclusion.

In the end, by placing both the papacy and reform in their social contexts, this book looks to achieve two fundamental objectives: on the one hand, a deeper understanding of why the papacy developed in the way that it did during the eleventh century; and, on the other, why the vision of reform that was adopted by popes from Leo IX onwards came to be articulated in the specific way that it was. Understanding and defining reform in the eleventh century will thus enable us to appreciate better the transformation of western European society into the *societas christiana*.

Notes

1 R. W. Southern, *Western Society and the Church in the Middle Ages* (Harmondsworth, Middx, 1970), 16.

2 Ibid., 17.

3 See G. B. Ladner, 'Terms and Ideas of Renewal', in R. L. Benson and G. Constable, eds, *Renaissance and Renewal in the Twelfth Century* (Cambridge, MA, 1982; repr. Toronto, 1991), 1–33. Cf. G. Constable, *The Reformation of the Twelfth Century* (Cambridge, 1996).

4 D. Iogna-Prat, *Order and Exclusion: Cluny and Christendom face Heresy, Judaism and Islam (1000–1150)* (Ithaca, NY, 2003), 4.

5 M. Bloch, *Feudal Society*, trans. L. A. Manyon (Chicago, 1961); G. Duby, *La société aux XIe et XIIe siècles dans la région mâconnaise* (Paris, 1953); G. Duby, *The Chivalrous Society*, trans. C. Postan (Berkeley, CA, 1977); J.-F. Lemarignier, 'La dislocation du *pagus* et le problème des *consuetudines* (Xe–XIe siècles)', in *Mélanges d'histoire dédiés à la mémoire de Louis Halphen* (Paris, 1951), 401–10 ; idem, *Le gouvernement royal aux premier temps capétiens (987–1108)* (Paris, 1965); P. Bonnassie, *From Slavery to Feudalism in South-Western Europe* (Cambridge, 1991); J.-P. Poly and E. Bournazel, *The Feudal Transformation, 900–1200* (New York, 1991).

6 This view is challenged by D. Barthelémy, 'Le paix de Dieu dans son contexte (989–1041)', *Cahiers de civilisation médiévale*, 40 (1997), 3–35.

7 D. Barthelémy, *La société dans le comté de Vendôme: de l'an mil au XIV siècle* (Paris, 1993), excerpt translated as 'The Year 1000 Without Abrupt or Radical Transformation', in L. K. Little and B. Rosenwein, eds, *Debating the Middle Ages: Issues and Readings* (Oxford, 1998), 134–47; D. Barthelémy, *La mutation de l'an mil a-t-elle eu lieu? Servage et chevalrie dans la France des Xe et XIe siècles* (Paris,

1997). Barthelémy also argues that documentary change may be more apparent than real and that the declining use of 'allod' (as land held outright) and the greater preponderance of 'fief' or '*beneficium*' (land held by tenure or service from a lord) do not support the progressive reduction of a free peasantry to servile status.

8   S. White, 'Feuding and Peace-Making in the Touraine Around the Year 1100', *Traditio*, 42 (1986), 195-263; and S. White, 'The Politics of Exchange: Gifts, Fiefs and Feudalism', and 'From Peace to Power: The Study of Disputes in Medieval France', in E. Cohen and M. de Jong, eds, *Medieval Transformations: Texts, Power and Gifts in Context* (Leiden, 2001), 169-88, 203-18.

9   T. Bisson, 'The Feudal Revolution', *PP*, 152 (1996), 6-42. See responses by D. Barthelémy and S. White in *PP*, 152 (1996), 196-205, 205-23; T. Reuter and C. Wickham, *PP*, 153 (1997), 179-95, 196-208, and reply by Bisson, 208-25. Cf. Bisson, 'Medieval Lordship', *Speculum*, 70 (1995), 743-59.

10 Or, for the middle ages as a whole: see E. A. R. Brown, 'The Tyranny of a Construct: Feudalism and Historians in Medieval Europe', *American Historical Review*, 79 (1974), 1063-88; reprinted in Little and Rosenwein, eds, *Debating the Middle Ages*, 148-69; S. Reynolds, *Fiefs and Vassals: The Medieval Evidence Reinterpreted* (Oxford, 1991).

11 For example, R. I. Moore, *The First European Revolution, c.970-1215* (Oxford, 2000); 'Property, Marriage and the Eleventh-Century Revolution: A Context for Early Medieval Communism', in M. Frassetto, ed., *Medieval Purity and Piety: Essays on Medieval Clerical Celibacy and Religious Reform* (New York, 1998), 179-208; 'Heresy, Repression and Social Change in the Age of the Gregorian Reform', in S. L. Waugh and P. D. Diehl, eds, *Christendom and its Discontents: Exclusion, Persecution and Rebellion, 1000-1500* (Cambridge, 1996), 19-46; and perhaps, most especially, 'Family, Community and Cult on the Eve of the Gregorian Reform', *TRHS*, 5th series, 30 (1980), 49-69.

1

Western Europe and the Latin Church around the year 1000

A ROUND the year 1000, the Latin Church in many ways defined western Europe. Through a string of chapels, churches, monasteries and clergy extending from Ireland into eastern Europe and beyond the Elbe and Saale Rivers, from the Scandinavian countries to the northern Iberian peninsula, and especially in the European heartlands of Italy, France and the German Empire, the Latin Church was beginning physically to dominate the landscape of western Europe. It also began the immense task of trying to reshape the thought patterns of its many peoples. Led by the Roman pontiff who, as the heir to the apostle Peter held the powers of binding and loosing on earth and in heaven, the Church offered a 'universal' religious belief structure, a code of practice, as well as a social framework for the whole of society. Paradoxically, the Latin Church was itself to be transformed and defined in its attempts to consolidate its hold over the different peoples of western Europe.

Doctrine and belief

In medieval society, the Church fulfilled any number of religious and social roles. Inextricably intertwined, these functions reinforced the increasing centrality of the Church and Christianity in medieval society, a centrality that cannot be underestimated. In his *History, Religion and Anti-Semitism*, Gavin Langmuir made the important distinction between 'religion', which he defined as a system of beliefs prescribed by ecclesiastical authorities, and 'religiosity', which he characterized as the format in which individuals construct a spiritually satisfying re-enactment of that religion.[1] This distinction is vital for understanding the Church's impact in both religious and social terms in earlier medieval European society, even if it must be acknowledged that 'religion' itself is an eighteenth-century concept.

For, in this interpretation, 'religion' implies a formally instituted set of beliefs which are uniformly disseminated, whereas 'religiosity' refers to the way the Church's teaching was practised and this varied with the traditions of local communities. Clearly both of these characterizations are relevant for the Church and Christianity in earlier medieval Europe, if only because they force us to set aside the idea of the medieval Church as some all-powerful and uniform institution in existence from the time of the Resurrection, with the christianization of western Europe as a progressive (even instantly successful) process emanating from Rome that uniformly eradicated pagan belief systems. Nothing could be farther from the truth. The 'official' acceptance of Christianity by the Frankish, Germanic and Anglo-Saxon royal families and aristocrats in the late sixth century was only the first step in a much more complicated process of replacing traditional behaviour, values and beliefs by Christian ones; a process whose repercussions were still being felt in the eleventh century and well beyond. This development, moreover, was a reciprocal one.

As Christianity was accepted by sixth-century kings such as Clovis of Francia or Aethelbert of Kent and their aristocrats, the local languages, symbols and social usages of those cultures strongly affected the way in which the Christian faith was practised in these regions. This was a price of which the Church itself was aware and even encouraged as can be seen from the letter of Pope Gregory I (590–604) to the missionary, Mellitus, regarding the conversion of the English peoples, in which he advised, among other things, that temples of the idols among that people should on no account be destroyed.[2] For the Frankish, Anglo-Saxon and Germanic kings and their aristocrats who turned to Christianity (and 'persuaded' their peoples to do likewise), their native religions had been 'instrumental': the gods were expected to be powerful enough to reward their worshippers, for example, with fertility, victory in war or even wealth. Their relations with the Christian God, whom they were persuaded was more powerful, were equally 'instrumental' as was their expression of that religion through donations and foundations of churches and monasteries.

The Christian God was pleased, or so they were led to believe, by dignified and impressive services conducted in appropriate buildings by learned, sober and – ideally – celibate secular clergy or monks. The offer of money or the donation of land, even prayers, especially if they were offered up vicariously (that is, by priests or monks), not only meant earthly glory but crucially also improved the donor's chances of entering heaven. This was the case not only for the kings and great nobles who sponsored monasteries and built churches, but even for simple peasants whose donation of wax for candles or other votives illuminated the altar of their local church. In many ways the medieval Church became as 'instrumental' as the religions it allegedly replaced, even though its rituals and practices were always said to be concerned with ensuring that Christians were blessed with salvation. But the rituals and codes of practice of the Church did not only serve a purpose in the afterlife. On earth, its deeply ritualistic form of religion provided 'magic' – diversion, as well as meaning – in to a seemingly arbitrary, often terrifying physical world, where violence, death and the unaccountable actions of the elements were the norm.

Localization of power

Despite the universality ostensibly afforded by the Church and the Christian religion, western Europe remained essentially a world characterized by regionalism and limited horizons around the year 1000.[3] Apart from kings or educated clergy and monks, most individuals probably never travelled much beyond their birthplace or local village; their lives were precarious and focused on the unending effort to sustain, clothe and feed themselves. While most people were undoubtedly aware that they were the emperor's or the king's subjects, their understanding of this probably took a local form, that is, as the subject of the immediate duke, count, bishop or abbot. This decidedly restricted, even introspective, outlook was reflected in contemporary chroniclers, who, while noting the great events of their time, inevitably focused their attention on the local repercussions of these great happenings, or else on more immediate events such as feuds or natural disasters such as crop failures which, invariably, were understood in terms of moral failings. Where the outside world touched most places, apart from the mustering of the host or the passing of armies, it was most often – at least in the ninth and tenth centuries – in the form of invaders, be they Muslims, Vikings, Magyars or Slavs.

Despite this local preoccupation and the sheer effort for survival, the kingdoms and regions of western or Latin Europe had a number of common social and cultural features, notwithstanding the diversity of their terrain, local customs and ethnic makeup. Around the year 1000, Latin Europe was essentially a world of peasant communities, which relied on farming, tending flocks and hunting, legal or otherwise. Over these communities stood a small aristocracy of both clergy and laymen and women. The laity existed in complicated and diverse 'systems' of vertical and horizontal alliances, their relations shaped by personal loyalties to kings, other rulers and extended kin – loyalties that could nonetheless overlap or even be rejected. The clergy – meaning here both the secular clergy, such as bishops, priests and deacons, and the regular clergy, that is those living under a *regula* or rule, such as nuns and monks – also operated within often conflicting networks of various institutions and hierarchies, which were headed, at least nominally, by the Roman pontiff.

The cultural inheritance of eleventh-century society was a diverse combination of Latin, Germanic and Christian. These elements reflected the heritages and political dimensions of western Europe's Roman, Germanic and Carolingian pasts. Even for the literate, the glory of Rome and the Roman Empire was a distant literary memory. More immediate and still resonant for the learned men of western Europe around the year 1000 was the overlordship of the great late eighth- and early ninth-century Frankish king and emperor, Charlemagne, whose empire had stretched over much of western Europe. The Carolingian empire had afforded the West a semblance of political stability, not least through its promotion of ecclesiastical reform, its emphasis on Latin as the political and cultural *lingua franca*, and its advocacy of monastic uniformity through its preference for the Rule of St Benedict. After Charlemagne's death in 814, his empire steadily fell apart during the reign of his son, Louis the Pious, resulting in the creation of three separate entities by 843: the west Frankish, east Frankish and middle kingdoms. The ninth- and tenth-century invasions by the Muslims, Vikings, Magyars and Slavs had contributed to this fragmentation, though historians now speculate about the extent to which the empire crumbled from internal weaknesses rather than from external pressure and incursion.[4]

Nevertheless, the disintegration of the Carolingian empire resulted in the rise of semi-independent territorial principalities, often called duchies, especially in Germany and France. Their increasingly powerful dukes, who had risen to prominence through military service and intermarriage with royal dynasties, used their extended kin network to forge alliances with many of the great monasteries. These had often been endowed by earlier kings and emperors, thus enabling them to challenge the authority of their nominal royal overlords. The Ottonian and later Salian rulers provide a useful example. They rose to prominence first as rulers of the east Frankish kingdom under Henry I (919–36) and Otto I (936–73). After Otto's defeat of the Magyars at the Lechfeld in 955 and his imperial coronation in 962, the Ottonian and later Salian emperors were often remote overlords of powerful and troublesome dukes such as those of

Saxony, Swabia and Bavaria. What successes these emperors had lay in their ability to reward the loyalty of these effectively independent lords, while maintaining a balance of power by relying on close ties with royally endowed monasteries and nunneries, as well as the bishoprics. Much the same was true in the west Frankish kingdom. Here, after displacing the last Carolingian king, Lothar, in 987, the Capetian kings of the late tenth and early eleventh centuries, like their tenth-century Carolingian predecessors, were exceptionally weak both politically and territorially, directly controlling little more than the region around Paris. Even more than the German emperors, the Capetian kings were often at the mercy of their more powerful neighbours such as the Duke of Aquitaine, the Duke of Normandy and the counts of Blois and Champagne. The old middle-kingdom region of Lotharingia, Provence and Burgundy maintained something of an uneasy alliance between the German empire and their Frankish neighbours. Across the Alps in Italy, power was even more fragmented between the remnants of the old Lombard kingdom, the northern Italian cities, the pope and the German emperor. In England, while a degree of political unity had been achieved by the victories over the Danes of Alfred (871–99) and his successors, this was still more apparent than real. Although King Edgar (959–75) reunited most of country under the leadership of the ancient kingdom of Wessex, within a few years of his death renewed Danish attacks led to England's absorption into the North Sea empire of Cnut (1016–35).

The regions and cultures that existed on the borders of western or Latin Europe also strongly influenced its political, religious and cultural life at the beginning of the eleventh century. Contact between the Latin West and Greek East was significant (even after the schism of 1054), and the Byzantine Empire – along with the Eastern Orthodox Church in its eastern Mediterranean and southern Italian outposts – offered a powerful challenge to the West as the custodian of *romanitas* in both political and ecclesiological senses. This was not the only challenge facing Latin Europe. Around the year 1000, much of the Iberian peninsula and all of Sicily were under the far more culturally advanced control of, respectively, the Islamic Umayyad emirate and the Zirid dynasty. Furthermore, in eastern Europe, the Magyars, Poles and Bohemians were only slowly being christianized, as was effectively the case in the Scandinavian countries of northern Europe. The Slavonic peoples of the Baltic region still remained largely unknown entities among whom paganism persisted – in some parts, such as Lithuania, for centuries to come. Although over the course of the eleventh century and beyond, these peripheral regions would increasingly be fully incorporated into the *societas christiana* of medieval Latin Christendom, around the year 1000 they still represented a threat not simply to the political stability of western Europe but especially to the universality of its religion.

The Church, however, faced more immediate problems at the beginning of the eleventh century. The universalist ideals of Christianity provided at best a superficial common identity for the diverse peoples whose allegiance and obedience it uneasily claimed. Political fragmentation and invasion over the course of the proceeding century and a half, along with the development of localized centres of autonomous political power, had not only left many local churches and monasteries either destroyed or derelict. Those that still functioned had become 'localized', as quasi-autonomous units with their own ecclesiastical customs and practices. Lacking the strong centralizing trends of the Carolingian empire, the Church had in some sense come adrift, and reforms were attempted only sporadically under the direction of local authorities and rulers, often with little or no guidance from their metropolitans, let alone Rome. While these initiatives were not insignificant, and, as will be seen, promoted social ties between local nobility and monasteries, their sporadic nature and dependence on the will of individual dukes, counts, abbots or bishops reinforced the problems faced by the Church.

The organization of the Church

The organization of the Church around the year 1000 was already the product of a thousand years of historical development.[5] While the reforms of Charlemagne and Louis the Pious in the late eighth and early ninth centuries, especially those promoted on their behalf by Benedict, Abbot of Aniane (750–821), had sought to introduce uniformity throughout western Christendom both in monastic and secular observance, variations and diversity of practice continued as the rule rather than the exception, even if the issue of reform and uniformity had been raised on a wider scale than before. One of the problems which the Church faced in the year 1000 was that it was often organized around competing local institutions or power structures, be they rural churches, local monasteries or private chapels. The same was true for the leaders of the Church, with bishops (in theory at least) answering to archbishops who in turn might be dependent upon or owing allegiance to secular rulers or extended kin. In fact there was a plethora of clerical offices, each with allegedly separate but in practice overlapping functions.

The seven levels of holy orders had evolved over the years to represent the various roles fulfilled by Christ on earth.[6] The highest order was that of bishop – with the pope as bishop of Rome at the head – followed by priests, deacons, subdeacons, acolytes, doorkeepers and exorcists. Also included among Church personnel were monks (though generally not in priestly orders at this time) as well as cloistered nuns and other vowesses, such as those widows who had promised not to remarry. Secular rulers, and especially the emperor, were also integral and even essential parts of the Church around the year 1000, even though they lacked any sacramental power such as presiding at the mass or ordaining priests. Usually the Church's greatest donors, kings and emperors were also the catalyst for the foundation of new bishoprics as, for instance, at Magdeburg and Bamberg. They also endowed or continued to endow royal monasteries and collegial canonries, of which they were often members. Christian sovereigns convened and presided over Church councils, and even appointed bishops and abbots as well as investing them with their temporal properties. They also provided the indispensable material and military support without which the Church could hardly protect itself. Of course, the precise extent of royal authority varied from region to region. In Francia in particular, the Capetian kings struggled with the dukes and counts to retain influence over the Church, which is one of the reasons why the French kings who descended from Hugh Capet were amongst the most generous of church patrons and often relied on their sacral position to bolster their political status.

For the vast bulk of the population, the local church was the fundamental institution for the observance of the Christian faith. Its exact nature around the year 1000 varied greatly across western Christendom and encompassed various private churches, baptismal churches, and small chapels, the functions of each of which were only slowly defined during the course of eleventh century and beyond. Either in church or chapel, most people came face to face with the Church in the form of the local priest, whose abilities, like the different types of churches, varied greatly. Broadly speaking, the priest was responsible to his diocesan bishop for making his church a suitable place for the liturgy, saying the mass and administering the other sacraments such as hearing confessions, as well as conducting burials, receiving tithes and generally providing pastoral care for his parishioners. Perhaps on the very rare occasion he might be educated enough to hold a school.

The parish priest thus was extraordinarily influential, the representative in the local 'little community', as Moore put it, 'of the large, of the bishop and his authority, of the city and its culture'.[7] Documentary evidence of his role and activities in the earlier middle ages is scarce. We know even less about the local traditions, practices and customs of religious life – Christian, proto-Christian or otherwise – which inevitably shaped his interaction with his flock. More often than not, the local priest may have been barely adequate for his duties, though this impression may reflect the rhetoric of later church reformers. Perhaps having only a rudimentary knowledge of Latin, little formal theological training, often married with a family, the local priest may effectively have presided over a congregation that had little (perhaps no) theological understanding, but one that worshipped in a largely ritualistic way through the following of the Church's liturgical year.

In jurisdictional terms at least, the most important player in the Church's organization at this time was the bishop. Not only was he normally endowed with considerable secular wealth, but his office carried many duties even if bishops did not always live up to what was expected of them. As the spiritual head of his diocese and with legal authority over the clergy, he also had a wide range of sacramental tasks that included consecrating churches, altars, the chrism and other liturgical objects, as well as ordaining priests, making visitations, and holding diocesan councils. He was also responsible for safeguarding ecclesiastical property and the rights pertaining to it, ensuring as well wherever possible its augmentation. A bishop was almost invariably a member of the local or regional aristocracy, generally appointed for family connections as for the intellectual and administrative abilities required of a bishop, who was clearly important in temporal as well as religious matters.

Consequently, a bishop's lifestyle was on the whole much the same as his aristocratic counterparts' in the world as far as hunting, feasting, even bearing weapons and fighting was concerned. The sentiments expressed by Archbishop Manasses of Rheims (1069–80) were probably ones shared by a great many tenth- and eleventh-century bishops. He was reported to have said that 'the archbishopric would be a fine thing, if only one did not have to sing Mass for it'.[8] Indeed, a bishop was so enmeshed in secular politics that, not least in the German Empire, he was often expected to be a royal counsellor, as well as being expected to contribute men to the ruler's armies. In a world where the secular and the divine had yet to be separated by the reformers of the eleventh century, this was the price to be paid for being the guardian or steward of any number of important royal estates which were so often entrusted to a bishop's safekeeping.[9]

In the year 1000, bishops often had wives or concubines. This did not necessarily contravene canon law, as they were required only to abstain from sexual relations. This was if they had married before their elevation to the episcopacy; afterwards a bishop could not marry. For example, the anonymous *Life* of the Vallombrosan monk, John Gualbertus, written *c.*1115, in an entirely matter-of-fact way discusses the fact that Alberga, the wife of the earlier eleventh-century bishop, Hildebrand of Florence, sat at her husband's side during a church council. Although the *Life* certainly depicts Alberga as being castigated by Abbot Guarinus of Settimo, she was reprimanded not for her existence as the bishop's wife, but for speaking out in the council, presumably in defiance of St Paul's order that women should be silent in church.[10] Regarding Pope Leo IX's reform attempts at the Council of Rheims in 1049, the Anglo-Norman chronicler Orderic Vitalis commented how 'clerics were ready enough to give up bearing arms, but even now were loathe to part with their mistresses or to live chaste lives'.[11] Both examples underline only too well the difficulties that would be faced by the later eleventh-century church reformers in their efforts not only to promote clerical celibacy, but also to separate the clergy from the worldly habits of their secular counterparts.

Perhaps the most spiritually vital elements in the Church around the year 1000 were those 'communities specially endowed and set apart for the full, lifelong, and irrevocable practice of the Christian life at a level of excellence judged to be impossible outside such a community' – that is to say, the monasteries.[12] The great religious houses were a point of contact for every part of society, having an impact on the lives of peasants, artisans and farmers, as well as lords, bishops and occasionally even popes. Like the Church, monasticism had developed over many centuries, originating in Palestine and Egypt with the so-called Desert Fathers at the end of the third century. Although this eremitical model continued to influence western observance, particularly in the later eleventh century, it was the communal lifestyle advocated by St Benedict of Nursia (*c.*480–550), in the Rule associated with his name, that set the standard for monastic obser-vance in the West. His Rule prescribed the main officials and their duties, the reception of monks and the three principal monastic activities – divine service (*opus divina*), the study of scripture (*opus lectio*) and manual labour (*opus manum*). It was a detailed yet flexible guide that could be adapted to suit the needs of individual communities, which probably accounts for its widespread dissemination.

Given a renewed lease of life with Benedict of Aniane's imperially inspired reforms in 817, the Rule of St Benedict generally became the standard observance (with local variations) not just in the Carolingian empire but also beyond. Even so, the disruption caused by Magyar, Saracen and Norse invasions was to leave many religious houses either vacant, even derelict, or simply unable to impose the necessary discipline. Monastic reform movements sprang up independently in a number of places in the tenth century, for instance in Brogne near Namur in the 920s, in Gorze near Metz in the 930s, and in England under Dunstan, Aethelwold and Oswald in the late 950s and 960s. At first, the reforms that took place in Gorze were particularly influential, thanks to the enthusiastic patronage of several bishops and German princes. Nonetheless, it was the foundation of the Burgundian monastery of SS Peter and Paul at Cluny in 910 by Duke William of Aquitaine, and the subsequent dissemination of the Cluniac ideal under abbots Odilo (994–1048) and Hugh (1049–1109), that had by far the strongest influence until the advent of the Cistercians a century later. Elaborating the liturgy at the expense of manual labour, Cluny became a model of purity and order, albeit aristocratic, that appealed to high Church officials and the lay nobility alike.

The case of monasteries in the Latin West reminds us of the importance of functionality in medieval religion. Great and small religious houses did not simply pray to God in isolation from worldly concerns, for a monastery simultaneously had any number of social functions. These might include the provision of alms, the care of the sick and providing a home for the younger children of the nobility, who in being offered up as oblates were guaranteed a lifestyle commensurate with their social standing. If they became abbot or abbess, they might even bring power and influence back to their family and kin. Child oblations, like donations of land, were simultaneously of religious and social significance, being of tremendous importance to familial strategies. As Karl Leyser has shown for tenth-century Ottonian Saxony, connections with nunneries helped to protect the family's property. For instance, by shifting the burden of safeguarding unmarried daughters, girls and widows, it lessened the chances for alienation of land through marriage, just as endowments of land helped to check the perennial partition of familial property and the splintering of estates, though the land given away still retained value in the form of stewardships or advocacies given back to the family. Ironically, these endowments also tended to protect women's inheritances, as such women were not exposed to the dangers of childbirth and often outlived other heirs.[13]

A family's social standing was often intimately linked over several generations with a local monastery as the donation of land brought with it long-rumbling disputes as well as prestige, as with the eleventh-century Giroie family and the Benedictine house of St Evroul.[14] The alienation of land or the oblation of children was not the only type of association that linked the cloister and the nobility. Confraternities, which were a type of associate membership, also provided ways for leading members of the aristocracy to link themselves to local religious houses, great or small.

All of this is not to deny that religious functions were paramount. At least in theory, the monks' unceasing rounds of prayer offered an example of spiritual perfection to which, it was maintained, ordinary Christians living in the world could not hope to aspire. Monastic prayers also offered Christian society a hope of salvation in a precarious and often unfathomable world. Monks, after all, were the original 'soldiers of Christ' (*militia Christi*), battling demons on behalf of the rest of Christian society, and their prayers for the dead were deemed to be especially efficacious. This, after all, was a society where the dead did not cease to be members of the human community and their ongoing remembrance played a vital role in the lives of the living, who owed their deceased relatives important religious obligations.[15] For the wealthy in particular, these took the form of liturgical remembrance in prayers or masses for the dead just as much as the preservation of the name, reputation and deeds of the departed.

Monasteries, in fact, increasingly became critical mediators between the living and the dead. Not only because the ascetic lives of the monks were thought to lend greater weight to the efficacy of their prayers, but because of the stability associated with religious houses, they were the best placed to ensure continuity of memory long after all the immediate relatives were dead.[16] Cluny in particular claimed a level of purity that would be exploited and appropriated by the later reformers, something which its earlier eleventh-century abbot, Odilo, specifically used as a justification for Cluny's irrevocable possession of lands donated.[17] It is in this context that we should understand his institution in the 1030s of the feast of All Souls. To deflect criticism that the monastery served the needs of only the aristocracy, prayers for all the souls in the afterlife were offered up every November, even for those who had been unable to endow the monastery or receive a final resting place within its hallowed confines. For medieval society at all levels, being associated with monasteries and especially their patron saint(s) mattered as much in the next world as in this one.[18]

Rome and the papacy

At the head of these multifaceted and complicated hierarchies of religious institutions was the revered bishop of Rome – the pope – who, as the successor to the Apostle Peter, was deemed to hold the powers of binding and loosing on earth and in heaven. While the development of papal authority and the transformation of the papacy in the eleventh century will be the subject of Chapter 4, it is worthwhile reminding ourselves how far even Christianity in Rome had become localized. Indeed, in many ways the papacy around the year 1000 was just another centre of local power in a western Europe where power emanated from many localized centres.

Medieval Rome derived its pre-eminence from the fact that the Apostles Peter and Paul had decided to journey to the capital of the then greatest empire on earth, where both were subsequently martyred, reputedly on the same day. Over the course of the following two centuries and beyond, spiritual and secular power increasingly combined to establish Rome's Christian paramount status, which – after the fall of the empire – was all that remained of Rome's former glory, at least in the West. By the year 1000, the city drew its material wealth from its place at the centre of the Christian world, and the city earned its living from what can be called a religious 'tourist trade'. Although the penitents, supplicants and pilgrims who came *ad limina apostolorum* (to the doorstep of the Apostles) all required food, housing and pastoral care, the city nonetheless was a far cry from what it had been when it was the political heart of the Roman Empire. Both in terms of its population and physical size, Rome had been reduced from its former glory to effectively a provincial backwater, with a population probably of 25,000–30,000 inhabitants, down from a peak of nearly 500,000 in the fourth century. Moreover, by the eleventh century, the inhabited part of Rome was substantially smaller than the uninhabited sections and occupied only a very small proportion of the area within the Aurelian walls.[19]

Despite centuries of political decline, the organization of the Church in Rome had nonetheless developed an immensely elaborate liturgical life with its own peculiar grades of churches and officials. The city's liturgical life was chiefly but not exclusively focused on the great patriarchal churches on opposite sides of the city: St John Lateran, the cathedral church with its administrative palace assigned to the pope as bishop of Rome, and the great Constantinian basilica, St Peter's, which contained the *confessio* or tomb of Peter and as such was the principal destination for pilgrims. The other patriarchal basilicas – Santa Maria Maggiore, San Lorenzo and St Paul's Without the Walls – also had distinctive roles in the religious life of the city, especially for great festivals.[20]

As in the Church beyond Rome, there were many clerical offices, each with allegedly separate but in practice overlapping ceremonial and administrative functions. These included deacons and subdeacons, who read the

Gospels and lections at the Lateran and other basilicas. The Roman Church also had a whole host of other minor orders and quasi-secular officials – generally laymen in minor orders – who served in the Lateran palace and the papal household.[21] All of these individuals were at least in theory ultimately answerable to the pope, to whom they generally, if not always, owed their positions. As such, a brief examination of their offices, duties and the roles they played in the religious life of the city is important for understanding the complicated structure over which the pope presided, as well as the extent and limitations of his own power around the year 1000.

The higher orders in the Roman Church, however, were somewhat different than those found elsewhere in western Europe. Although the hierarchical organization of the clergy and the churches in Rome was only given precise definition from the later eleventh onwards with the definitive emergence of the College of Cardinals, its structure had a much longer history. Above the minor orders were the cardinal-deacons, whose many duties included liturgical and administrative tasks as well as pastoral care. Above this level were the cardinal-priests, who were attached to the so-called titular churches, which derived from the old *tituli* that characterized the division of the early Church in Rome before and after Christianity became the religion of the empire. Their chief duties were to say the mass and other services in the patriarchal basilicas, although they also had other roles within the ecclesiastical organization of the city. The highest ecclesiastical level was that of the cardinal-bishops, who presided over the seven suburbicarian Sees – the churches in the vicinity of Rome: Ostia, Palestrina, Porto, Albano, Silva-Candida, Velletri and Labiacum.[22] The role of the cardinal-bishops before the mid-eleventh century was chiefly a liturgical one, although for centuries the cardinal-bishops of Ostia, Porto and Albano had had the privilege of consecrating the new pope, from which, as will be seen, they were increasingly to derive a role in his election. The cardinal-bishops were responsible in turn (a weekly rota) for liturgical duties at the principal altar in the Lateran basilica; apart from the pope, they alone had access to it for the celebration of the mass.

At least for Rome, we can have some idea of how religious life was organized on an almost daily basis around the year 1000. Liturgical observance in Rome did not take place only at the basilicas, though it generally revolved around the pope, which meant that its liturgical life was unlike that anywhere else in western Europe. The city's ceremonial life was based on an ancient sequence that followed a yearly cycle of 'stations', which is to say, churches within or just outside the city where the principal mass of the day was held. By the later eleventh century there were at least 85 stations, with most taking place between Advent and Pentecost. Although evidence is sketchy for the eleventh century, from texts such as the ancient *Ordo Romanus I*, and pontificals such as the *Romano-German Pontifical*, as well as twelfth-century guides, we can be reasonably certain how it functioned.[23] On stational days, the pope met the clergy and people at an assembly point known as the *collecta*. Here, prayers were said before the procession made its way to that day's stational church. Unless absent from Rome or unavailable (in which case a deputy would stand in), the pope would celebrate Mass in a basilica or other major church together with the suburbicarian bishops, representatives of the Roman clergy, and laity from all regions. Lay participation, it seems, was a strong feature, with various quasi-religious and secular officials attached to the Lateran taking part. On major festivals, there would be a solemn procession from the Lateran through the principal streets of the city. At the greater festivals such as Easter or Pentecost, the solemn papal coronations took place (some 18 times per year) and the papal *laudes* were chanted during the mass. These stations and the *laudes* reinforced the pope's position as the spiritual and, at least to some extent, political head of the city. Just as important, though, the *laudes* and ritual served to mark out the grandeur, and hence the superiority, of the bishop of Rome over other bishops, even if in practical terms the pope only intermittently extended his authority beyond the city.

Regardless of Rome's continuing liturgical glories, the private lives of some of the popes between the mid-tenth century and 1046 often served to undermine what pretensions they had to an effective headship of the Church. In fact, the papacy's poor reputation in modern historiography goes back to the widely circulated reports made in the mid-tenth century by the bishop and historian, Liudprand of Cremona, and the canon, Flodoard of Rheims, who are responsible for many scandalous tales.[24] Like many contemporary medieval authors commenting on Roman affairs, Liudprand and Flodoard wrote chiefly for a northern European audience, which evidently was prepared to believe that the Romans – and perhaps especially their popes – were ineffectual, morally corrupt, untrustworthy and capable of anything.

Both contemporary and modern historians often point to the example of Pope John XII (955–964), who has been seen as a symbol of all that was wrong with the papacy in the tenth and early eleventh centuries. The bastard son of Alberic II of the house of Theophylact, prince of Rome (932–54), and grandson of Marozia (924–32) who ruled Rome with an iron fist in the early part of the century, John XII in many ways was probably not an untypical (if less than ideal) spiritual head of western Christendom.

His accession to the apostolic see was more than a little irregular (arranged, against canon law, in his predecessor's lifetime) and his pontificate was reputedly characterized by scandal, bribery, political intrigue, revolt and deposition. He even reportedly turned the Lateran palace into a brothel. John XII has been seen by contemporary and modern historians alike as one of the more dire examples of a papacy occupied by unworthy pontiffs and dominated by the politics of aristocratic Roman families.

Many other examples can easily be found of popes who owed their promotions and their positions, or at least their downfalls, to the intrigue of Roman noble families. This is the case with John X (914–dep. 928). His strong leadership as Archbishop of Ravenna had commended him in the first place to a Roman aristocracy threatened by Muslim attacks. Later his sense of independence led to his deposition and imprisonment in Castel Sant'Angelo in Rome, where he died in 929, allegedly suffocated with a pillow. Popes Leo VI (May–Dec. 928) and Stephen VII (928–31) were effectively stopgap appointments by Marozia, pending the time when her son Theophylact was able to succeed to the apostolic throne. Theophylact (John XI) himself was to be undermined by his half-brother Alberic, who reportedly treated him as his personal slave, placing him under house arrest in the Lateran Palace with nothing to do except say mass. After his death in 936, there followed a series of popes who owed their promotion to Alberic, a number of whom lost his favour, such as Stephen VIII (939–42) who was imprisoned and tortured, and ultimately died of his wounds. While the German emperor Otto I's control over Rome after the deposition of John XII in 963 introduced some order, questions remained over the legitimacy of his successor Leo VIII (963–65), not least because John lived on for another year but also on the grounds of Leo's hasty promotion from layman to pope (through all the ecclesiastical orders) in a single day. While the pontificate of Benedict VII (974–83) did much to restore dignity to the Apostolic See through his promotion of monastic reform and his insistence that disputes be referred to Rome for papal arbitration, with his death – and that of the emperor in 983 – the papacy was once more subsumed in Roman politics. Just a few years later, in 991, many French bishops refused to submit to John XV (985–96) on the grounds that the pope had lost all moral authority.

These and other scandalous reports of the private or political lives of popes, however entertaining, not only misjudge the later tenth- and early eleventh-century papacy (and as a consequence overvalue their later eleventh-century successors), but also fail to take into account the structures and conventions (some of which were local) that provided the context for the pontiffs' rule in the tenth and early eleventh centuries. It cannot be denied that aristocratic Roman families such as the house of Theophylact or the Crescentians, who respectively controlled appointment to the papacy from the 920s and after *c.*975, and especially the Tusculans, who themselves held the papacy from 1012 to 1046, often fulfilled the worst expectations of contemporary chroniclers by using the papacy as a means of obtaining and consolidating political power.[25] In this, however, they were by no means different in their behaviour from aristocratic families in other Italian towns, or elsewhere in western Europe, who tried to develop power networks and dominate their cities and the environs either by controlling the election of the bishop or by retaining that office for family members.

The difference in Rome, however, was that the bishop concerned was also the pope, the head of western Christendom. As a consequence, the feuding, the political intrigue and the scandal inevitably occurred in full view of western European *literati* rather than in customary, and hence decent, provincial obscurity. Moreover, the rewards in Rome were that much larger: even if the pope's authority to intervene directly throughout western Europe in the tenth and earlier eleventh centuries was often limited, the papacy had access to considerable wealth and power, even if those claims were not fully realized. Keeping the papacy in the family so to speak was thus not only desirable, but also profitable both for the family in question as well as the papacy itself. Later reformers, however, in an effort to distinguish themselves, were to characterize these lay entanglements as the root of all evils that not only invariably entailed the enslavement of the Church, but also reinforced a lack of differentiation between the clerical and secular worlds that, if unchecked, could ultimately compromise the headship of the Church.[26]

However much contemporaries – and, even more so, later reformers – saw the tenth- and earlier eleventh-century papacy as being morally corrupt, it is important to recognize that, in the Latin Church, Rome and the institution of the papacy were indisputably at the apex of spiritual power. The Eternal City guarded the tombs of the apostles Peter and Paul, as well as the relics of some of the earliest martyrs, who were believed to be literally present and actively working on behalf of petitioners. The saints, the sites associated with their martyrdoms and (especially) their relics were important means of contact between this world and the next, and thus were tangible manifestations of spiritual power. St Peter, above all, who worked on behalf of and through the pope, drew the Christian world towards Rome in a never-ending pilgrimage. As Richard Southern noted, he was the universal figure in an otherwise local world.[27]

Almost a century ago, Duchesne described the pope of the tenth and early eleventh centuries as 'the high-priest of the Roman pilgrimage, the dispenser of benedictions, privileges, and anathemas.'[28] This is a vital point. Even if the morals of some popes were not all that could be desired by contemporaries, it is more than evident that the papacy as an institution not only continued to function but was in fact esteemed. For instance, between 896 and 1046, the papacy issued numerous papal privileges or other documents granting rights to property or other incomes such as tolls, or else exemption from certain taxes and control by local religious authorities throughout western Europe.[29] In contrast to the accounts of chroniclers, these documents reveal the papacy to be a vibrant and respected institution, as they not only show that there was an increasing demand for papal privileges with nearly as many for 996–1046 as for the entire preceding century, but they also provide evidence of a growing awareness on the part of local individuals and ecclesiastical institutions throughout Latin Europe of the need for some central religious authority.

Partly this was a symptom of the vast increase in monasteries and newly founded churches. As these grew in number from the second half of the tenth century, especially after 1000, and their rights and possessions became increasingly valuable as well as contested, the need for central confirmation of existing privileges along with sanctions for new ones became ever more essential. For instance, the elevation of the monastery of Magdeburg to an archbishopric in 962 requested by Otto I, or the foundation of the bishopric of Bamberg in 1007 by Henry II, the confirmation of Cluny's immunity from episcopal control in 1021–23, or the translation of the bishopric of Zeitz to Naumberg in 1028 would have been utterly meaningless without papal validation.[30] Along with the growing conferral of *pallia* (the stole that was the symbol of office) upon archbishops and occasionally on favoured bishops, these papal privileges served to form essential bonds in an increasingly expanding Latin Church, over which presided the indispensable figure of the Bishop of Rome.

These privileges, however, also reveal that the tenth- and early eleventh-century papacy was an accommodating entity, more than prepared to provide what Karl Leyser aptly termed 'a customer's service'.[31] Indeed, the majority of these privileges show that the papacy was prepared to approve the requests of petitioners, provided that they were, or at least seemed to be, suitably sponsored or else could not be denied. The telling phrase 'as you requested from us' (*qui postulasti a nobis*) that is found in the majority of the privileges from these centuries is a clear acknowledgement by the pope that he was not acting spontaneously but rather in response to an external request, however much its reiterated use could also be taken a sign that the papacy was reminding the recipient that he or she had felt obliged to approach the pope.

Nevertheless, these documents also demonstrate that the papacy during the tenth and earlier eleventh centuries was an essentially passive institution, fixed in Rome, where individuals came for sanction, privileges, guidance and increasingly, it must be noted, judgment. As will be seen, the development of the papacy into a force seizing the initiative to extend its authority over the western Church and Christian society as a whole characterizes the transformation of the Apostolic See during the course of the eleventh century. However much aristocratic Roman families (and others) would continue to seek to control election to the papacy, the pope increasingly needed to be as efficient and effective as the institution over which he presided in order to extend his authority beyond the city walls. The 'Roman family' could of course never be entirely disregarded, but the balance of power was slowly shifting as eleventh-century popes began to concentrate on the wider western European family of the *societas christiana*.

Economic, intellectual and social change

It was not, however, just the Church and the papacy that were to undergo transformation in the eleventh century. Indeed, the overall development of western Europe during the eleventh century has often been described as a lifting of a state of siege. As the effects of the ninth- and tenth-century invasions of the Magyars, Slavs, Norse and Muslims began to recede, western European society slowly emerged from the chaos of a disintegrating Carolingian world order. For the first time in centuries there was an opportunity for stability and consolidation.[32] Indeed, for contemporaries such as the Cluniac chronicler Rodulf Glaber, 'it seemed as if the world were shaking itself free, shrugging off the burden of the past'.[33]

With the slow beginnings of the first substantial growth in population in centuries came the start of agricultural advances, which would increasingly bring hitherto unused land under cultivation through clearance and the wider use of ploughs. Along with the increasing prevalence of a monetary economy, the planting of cereal crops, surplus produce and more reliable transport began to stimulate growth both in local and in longer-distance trade. As a consequence, towns slowly became a stronger feature of life in the eleventh century, with calls for communal autonomy appearing – as early as the 1060s in the case of Le Mans.

At the same time, there was a noticeable flowering of intellectual life beyond the traditional confines of monasteries, whose most important function in intellectual terms – apart from the practical studies of grammar and writing, chronology and music (which were essential parts of Benedictine monastic organization) – had been the preservation of texts. This is not to suggest that monastic intellectual activity was, or would continue to be, negligible. Rather, it was that the scholarly achievements of monastic scholars tended to remain latent, or even just localized. The emergence of cathedral schools as premier centres of learning, and the increasing appearance of gifted scholars such as Gerbert of Aurillac, Fulbert of Chartres, Anselm of Laon, Lanfranc of Bec, Berengar of Tours, Otloh of St Emmeram, Peter Abelard, William of Champeaux and Gottshalk of Aachen, who were not solely associated with the cloister or monastic theology, revealed the beginnings of an important intellectual revival.[34]

The interests and reputations of these and other scholars in rhetoric, dialectic, logic and philosophy would draw peripatetic students from all across western Europe to the new centres of learning, especially those in northern France, such as Tours, Laon, Chartres and Paris, and also in northern Italy at Bologna and Pavia, though it is clear that there was a more continuous tradition of autonomous schools in Italy. Although the scope of the intellectual activity of cathedral schools can perhaps be exaggerated in the eleventh century, they had a number of advantages over their monastic counterparts, not least of which was their location in urban centres, which facilitated communication and exchange. All these developments point to the fact that, during the course of the eleventh century, Latin Europe was seemingly becoming richer, more sophisticated and less localized.

This is not to suggest that the political fragmentation and violence that characterized the disintegration of the Carolingian world had suddenly disappeared. Contemporary sources in fact reveal that violence and anarchy (or at least the perception of them) continued and even increased. Rather, for the first time in centuries, there was an opportunity for consolidation and reform. This meant that the status quo, in both political and religious life, would increasingly no longer be tolerated; the cultural assumptions of the Carolingian world were being tested and found wanting. For many, the safe passing of the millennial anniversaries of Christ's birth and passion offered a promise, but also a terrible challenge. This was especially the case for the Church, whose personnel came increasingly to recognize the need to undertake and promote reform themselves.

Of course, there had been calls for reform before the turn of the millennium. Tenth-century reforms of monastic life – such as the Cluniac, Gorzean and English initiatives – clearly recognized the need to improve standards in religious life. In the secular Church, as will be seen in more detail in Chapter 3, there were also many attempts to promote better standards of priestly conduct as part of the promotion of peace at ecclesiastical councils as early as 989. Yet, by and large, before the year 1000, the 'unreformed' Church – despite its married priests and bishops, and its many instances of lax, worldly or corrupt clergy – nevertheless still managed to meet the needs of Latin European society. That it was able to do so does not imply that 'clean hands' no longer mattered to kings, great nobles or even bishops and abbots. Religion remained as 'instrumental' to the religious and secular nobility of the early eleventh century as it had been to their Carolingian and Frankish predecessors, and it is clear from the documentation of their benefactions to monasteries or churches that they continued to expect high standards, often even prescribing rules of conduct for new religious houses. Yet, like the efforts to improve standards at the early peace councils, these remained essentially localized reforms, whose success and maintenance depended on the will of the immediate abbot, bishop, ruler or lord. This, however, was to change on account of both spiritual and economic necessity.

Conclusion

Around the year 1000, the Latin Church, although supported by centuries of tradition and ideals, was grappling with changing socio-political, economic and cultural realities. It thus, perhaps inevitably, took on the task of censuring the old order and promoting a new vision both for itself and for Christian society, first on local levels, and increasingly throughout Latin Europe. Local reform initiatives that had been appropriate for later tenth- and earlier eleventh-century society were no longer sufficient: the Latin Church and increasingly the Roman papacy would both harness and set limits to the social and political changes, further defining, as a consequence, both itself and western European society in the process.

Notes

1 G. Langmuir, *History, Religion and Anti-Semitism* (Berkeley, 1990), esp. chs. 7, 9, 10.

2 See Bede, *A History of the English Church and People*, 1.30, trans. L. Sherley-Price (Harmondsworth, Middx, 1955), 86–7.

3 K. J. Leyser, 'Concepts of Europe in the Early and High Middle Ages' *PP*, 137 (1992), 25–47.

4 See P. Godman and R. Collins, *Charlemagne's Heir: New Perspectives on the Reign of Louis the Pious (814–840)* (Oxford, 1990); J. L. Nelson, *Charles the Bald*

(London, 1992) and literature cited there; and S. MacLean, *Kingship and Politics in the Late Ninth Century: Charles the Fat and the End of the Carolingian Empire* (Cambridge, 2003).

5 For more details, see J. H. Lynch, *The Medieval Church: A Brief History* (London and New York, 1992); G. Tellenbach, *The Church in Western Europe from the Ninth to the early Twelfth Century* (Cambridge, 1993); and F. D. Logan, *A History of the Church in the Middle Ages* (London, 2002).

6 There was, however, considerable debate about the precise number of orders, with some suggesting that bishops were a higher, eighth order and that a lector should also be added; others suggested six, by omitting one of the lesser orders. See R. E. Reynolds, ' "At Sixes and Sevens" – and Eights and Nines: The Sacred Mathematics of Sacred Orders in the Early Middle Ages', *Speculum*, 54 (1979), 669–84; reprinted in idem, *Clerics in the Early Middle Ages: Hierarchy and Image* (Aldershot, Hants., 1999). Cf. S. H. Rigby, *English Society in the Later Middle Ages* (Basingstoke, Hants., 1995), 208.

7 Moore, *First European Revolution*, 60.

8 Guibert of Nogent, *Memoirs*, 1.11, ed. J. F. Benton, *Self and Society in Medieval France: The Memoirs of Abbot Guibert of Nogent* (New York, 1970), 59.

9 See T. Reuter, 'The "Imperial Church System" of the Ottonian and Salian Rulers: A Reconsideration', *JEH*, 33 (1982), 347–74; and I. S. Robinson, *Henry IV of Germany, 1056–1106* (Cambridge, 1999), 6–7, 114–15.

10 *Vita Iohannis Gualberti auctore discipulo eius anonymo*, 2 (MGH, SS 30/2), 1105; cf. R. I. Moore, 'Family, Community and Cult on the eve of the Gregorian reform', *TRHS*, 5th ser., 30 (1980), 49–69.

11 *The Ecclesiastical History of Orderic Vitalis*, 5.12, ed. and trans. M. Chibnall, 6 vols (Oxford, 1969–80), 3.120.

12 Southern, *Western Society and the Church in the Middle Ages*, 214. For more details on the following, see C. H. Lawrence, *Medieval Monasticism*, 3rd edn (London and New York, 2001).

13 K. J. Leyser, *Rule and Conflict in an Early Medieval Society: Ottonian Saxony* (London and Rio Grande, 1975), 63–70.

14 See Moore, *First European Revolution*, 71–5.

15 P. Geary, *Living with the Dead in the Middle Ages* (Ithaca, NY, 1994), 77–92.

16 D. Iogna-Prat, 'The Dead in the Celestial Bookkeeping of the Cluniac Monks around the year 1000', in L. K. Little and B. Rosenwein, eds, *Debating the Middle Ages: Issues and Reading* (Oxford, 1998), 340–62.

17 Ibid., esp. 361–2; cf. Moore, *First European Revolution*, 86–8.

18 B. H. Rosenwein, *To Be the Neighbor of St Peter: The Social Meaning of Cluny's Property* (Ithaca, NY, 1989).

19 See R. Krautheimer, *Rome: Profile of a City, 312–1308* (Princeton, NJ, 1980), 242ff, with maps of medieval Rome and the *abitato*; R. Coates-Stephens, 'Housing in Early Medieval Rome, 500–1000AD', *Papers of the British School at Rome*, 64 (1996), 339–59. See also C. Wickham, 'The Romans According to Their Malign Custom: Rome in Italy in Later Ninth and Tenth Centuries', in J. M. H. Smith, ed., *Early Medieval Rome and the Christian West: Essays in Honour of Donald*

Bullough (Leiden, 2000), 151–66.

20   Other key pilgrimage centres in the eleventh century included San Sebastiano to the south on the via Appia and Sant'Agnese to the north-east on the via Nomentana.

21   These included the *vestararius* (in charge of the papal vestments and papal treasure), the *vicedominus* (the majordomo), the *arcarius* (financial officer), the *primus defensor* (military position), the *nomenculator* (orator), the *protoscrinarius* (a sort of chief notary) and the *sacellarius* (literally the 'bag man' who originally carried the offerings, or papal paymaster).

22   In the later eleventh century, Labiacum was transferred to Tusculum, Velletri was united with Ostia, and Sabina was added as the seventh see.

23   For an overview, see C. Vogel, *Medieval Liturgy: An Introduction to the Sources* (Washington, DC, 1986). Cf. R. E. Reynolds, 'The Organization, Law and Liturgy of the Western Church, 700–900', in *The New Cambridge Medieval History*, vol. 2: *c.*700–900, ed. R. McKitterick (Cambridge, 1995), 587–621; and H. E. J. Cowdrey, *Pope Gregory VII, 1073–1085* (Oxford, 1998), 10–16.

24   Liudprand of Cremona, *Liber de rebus Gestis Ottonis*, c. 4ff in *Die Werke Liudprands von Cremona*, ed. J. Becker (MGH, *SSRG*, 41; Leipzig, 1915), 160ff; English trans. by F. A. Wright, *The Works of Liudprand of Cremona* (London, 1930), 216ff; Flodoard, *Les annales de Flodoard*, a. 923, ed. P. Lauer (Paris, 1905), 54–5, 179.

25   On the Tusculan popes, see below, Ch. 4.

26   See below, Ch. 5.

27   R. W. Southern, *The Making of the Middle Ages* (London, 1953), 138.

28   L. Duchesne, *The Beginnings of the Temporal Sovereignty of the Popes* (London, 1908), 271.

29   *Papsturkunden 896–1046*, ed. H. Zimmerman (Veröffentlichungen der Historischen Kommission, 3: Denskschriften, 174, 177, 198; Vienna, 1984–89).

30   Ibid., 1, no. 154, 281–4 (Magdeburg); 2, no. 435, 880–3 (Bamberg); 2, no. 530, 1007–9 (Cluny); 2, no. 581, 1097–8 (Zeitz to Naumberg).

31   K. J. Leyser, review of Zimmerman (as n.29), *JEH*, 39 (1988), 247–8.

32   K. J. Leyser, 'The Ascent of Latin Europe', repr. in his *Communications and Power in Medieval Europe: The Carolingian and Ottonian Centuries* (London, 1992), 215–32.

33   *Rodulfus Glabri Historiarum libri quinque (The Five Books of the Histories)*, ed. and trans. J. France (Oxford, 1989), 3.13, 114–16. Cf. Leyser, 'Ascent of Latin Europe', 219, 231.

34   For more discussion, see M. Haren, *Medieval Thought: The Western Intellectual Tradition from Antiquity to the Thirteenth Century*, 2nd edn (Houndsmills, 1992); and C. S. Jaeger, *The Envy of Angels: Cathedral Schools and Social Ideals in Medieval Europe, 950–1200* (Philadelphia, PA, 1994).

2

Understanding reform
in the eleventh century

ECCLESIA semper reformanda – the Church always requires reform: although this idea was cherished by John Calvin and Protestant reformers in the sixteenth century, it is applicable to the Church in any age. As the mystical body of Christ, it comprised the living and the dead. It was concerned not just with those departed souls who were in, or on their way to, heaven. It was also required to guide those still on earth by providing an institution with all the norms and practices required to fulfil its salvific mission. Given the range of its duties, it is almost inevitable that the Church would perennially need to undertake reform.[1] That said, there have been times in the past, at least from the perspective of hindsight, when cries for Church reform seem to have been especially pronounced, periods that have come to be identified as effectively 'ages of reform' such as the early fourth century, the late sixth century, the Iconoclast period and the sixteenth century, to say nothing of the mid-twentieth century. Yet perhaps none of these periods has so dominated the discourse of reform as that of the eleventh century.

The reasons for this are many and complex. One of the chief factors in the seeming omnipresence of concerns about reform in the eleventh century on the part of modern historians is the increasing abundance of documentation, at least as compared with the earlier middle ages. From the late tenth century onwards, it is evident that there was a tremendous surge in the production of all manner of written records, including charters, chronicles and histories, genealogies, saints' lives, philosophical and theological treatises. Although the better survival of texts from the eleventh century onwards can be deceptive and lead one to underestimate the use, sophistication or prevalence of written records before 1000, there can be no doubt that the increase in record-keeping was a real one and was important in a number of ways. On the one hand, it indicates a greater appreciation of the significance of written records, and especially their preservation, in a world where the written word was becoming more prevalent as a means of exercising power.[2] It is worth emphasizing, though, that the written word did not simply supersede the oral culture of the earlier middle ages. Rather, as Brian Stock and others have argued, a new type of interdependence arose between the two, in which oral discourses remained powerful but ever more subordinate to text.[3]

This had important social and cultural implications as the *literati* began increasingly to define and defend the text – and its interpretation – as their privileged sphere. Although churchmen had long dominated the means of communication since the decline of the Roman Empire, monastic and clerical writers in general were now being called upon to write, copy and use texts and records for more than liturgical purposes or their own personal study, though these naturally continued to be fundamental incentives. Furthermore, these monastic and clerical writers increasingly privileged the text on account of their role not only as interpreters of scripture, but also as custodians of memory. They preserved the memory not simply of their own institutions, but also of their patrons and increasingly the donations made by these individuals.[4] The growth of historical writing in general no doubt influenced the perceptions of these writers, and in particular their awareness of time and visible change, which needed to be explained or at least categorized in order to be understood.[5] Such perceptions were also reinforced as the clergy wove the stories of their own churches or religious houses into the larger framework of the history of salvation, a genre which became increasingly popular around and after the millennia of Christ's birth and passion.

Yet the greater quantities of documents bring us no nearer to understanding the preoccupation with reform that apparently characterizes the eleventh century, though they permit us to follow its slow evolution in reasonable detail. One of the chief problems has been that historians have tended to see reform as some sort of inexorable force uniformly emanating from some centre, either at Rome or at a royal court, and thus as the conscious or deliberately articulated policy of one or even several individuals. It would of course be a travesty to deny the role of individuals in promoting reform, but it is important to remember that reform was a series of processes, spanning several generations, in which the ambitions and methods inevitably changed.

While terms such as 'reform agenda' and 'reform programme' are unavoidable, it is important to avoid envisaging some stable, consistently deliberate and (especially) top-down initiative through which reform was imposed, at least in the eleventh century, whatever may be said of the Carolingian reforms in the ninth century. The almost unending repetition over the course of the eleventh century (and beyond) of prohibitions of simony (the buying or selling of church offices), clerical marriage and other measures should alert us to the need to view reform over the *longue durée* and in the appropriate context. However much reform initiatives may have been promulgated as proscriptive or normative measures, that is, as establishing uniformly binding and enforceable laws, in reality they were prescriptive measures, advocating certain standards of practice. Like much canon law, reform initiatives were thus an idealized vision of what the reformers aspired to achieve for the Church and by extension for Christian society, rather than being immediately binding laws.

But how are we to account for the seemingly widespread interest in promoting Church reform in the eleventh century, reform that was also accompanied by the first sustained reappearance of heresy in the West in some seven centuries? The two are not as unrelated as they might seem to be. Janet Nelson, for one, has argued that before *circa* 1000, European society was served by a generally coherent system of religious beliefs and rituals, and was as a consequence essentially stable.[6] But the sweeping changes in the political and economic structures throughout the later tenth century and beyond (such as those, as will be seen in Chapter 3, that accompanied or prompted the 'peace of God', for instance) and the resulting social instability placed the older religious ideology under pressure. According to Nelson, marginal individuals in the newly-emerging society, of whom there were increasing numbers, faced a 'crisis of theodicy'. She defined this as the problems that arise when individuals experience suffering or alienation that their belief system fails to accommodate. This crisis resulted initially, she suggested, in a reaffirmation, extension and (especially) intensification of the older beliefs and practices.[7]

It cannot be denied that such a process of extension characterized the development of the Church in the eleventh century. This can be seen in the foundation of new monasteries and monastic orders, the multiplication or expansion of liturgical offices and feasts, the promotion of new (or newly-discovered) saints and relics, a greater emphasis on pilgrimage and penitential activity that found its expression both in external acts as well as increasingly internal examination, and most especially some sustained attempts at reform. It is clear from hindsight, however, that this strengthening of the old religious belief structure had serious disadvantages: with the intensification of devotional practices and the promulgation of reform ideals, the result was increasing institutionalization that placed ever greater importance on strict adherence to what the Church identified as correct behaviour. This was in turn exacerbated by the visible attention drawn to the failings of the Church to meet its own lofty ideals of a freely-elected and chaste clergy; the more forcefully such ideals were pronounced, the more conspicuous its shortcomings became. This isolated still further those who had originally felt ill-served by the belief system and who, as a consequence, sought alternatives in the form of heretical groups. For Nelson, it was the failure of the belief system, and especially of its institutional framework to adapt, that accounted for the sustained reappearance of heresy in the West from *circa* 1000.

While in large part concurring with this interpretation, Talal Asad sought to recast Nelson's conclusions from the perspective of social anthropology. He suggested that, as the Church became more able to extend its power, it faced intensifying challenges to its authority as sole custodian of truth as, ironically, there were potentially greater areas exposed to the danger of transgression.[8] For Asad, it was not so much social and economic instability that prompted religious dissatisfaction. Rather it stemmed from the fact that, since the Church was now better equipped to define and guard that truth more precisely, the more its tighter definitions *might* be challenged. The disciplinary strategies increasingly emphasized throughout the eleventh century were logical outcomes of the effort to determine who was and who was not rightly oriented in accordance with the Church's single transcendent truth. Our interest here is not with the emergence of heresy – with which Nelson and Asad were particularly concerned – but their analysis of the intensification and institutionalization of the Church moving progressively towards a more uniform set of disciplinary strategies. Their analysis provides an extremely important context for understanding not only why reform was seen as needed, but also why it may have been pursued in the manner it was.

Interpretations of the nature of the movement for Church reform, the success and failure of its objectives, and even its desirability have had a long and chequered history, beginning even as the reform movement itself was developing in the eleventh century. One early and noteworthy commentator (among many who could be named) was the Ottonian historian Thietmar of Merseburg (975–1018) who viewed monastic reform as rank hypocrisy, and who took offence at critics of the less stringent and more accommodating forms of spiritual life that characterized what we consider as the 'unreformed' Church.[9] Since the eleventh century, characterizations of the reform movement have ebbed and flowed according to partisan and propagandistic need quite as much as historical fashion: for instance, the reformers were often reviled in the pamphlet literature of Tudor England but extolled in counter-Reformation circles and amongst Catholic apologists thereafter. With the rise of constitutional or political history, reform was inserted into the broad 'church versus state' historical debate, which tended to locate eleventh-century reform almost exclusively in the context of the bitter conflict between Pope Gregory VII (1073–85) and the German king and later emperor, Henry IV (1056–1106), over the question of lay investiture and what has been termed 'the right order in the world'.[10]

For the better part of the twentieth century, this historiography has been reinforced by the tendency of historians to divide the reformers into 'moderate reformers' in the earlier part of the eleventh century and 'radical reformers' in the second half. Moderate reformers were seen as those such as Pope Leo IX (1049–54) or Peter Damian (1007–72) who sought to improve standards in religious life in co-operation with royal powers, whilst radical reformers were identified as those such as Humbert of Silva-Candida, Hugh of Die and especially Gregory VII, whose vision of a freely elected and chaste clergy uncontaminated by contact with lay society led them into direct conflict with royal powers with whom they could not compromise. Following the publication between 1924 and 1937 of Augustin Fliche's three-volume work, *La Réforme grégorienne*, this historiographical trend was strengthened as historians increasingly began to identify, and even to equate, the movement for Church reform in the eleventh century almost exclusively with Gregory VII.[11]

This historiography has since been challenged by historians such as Joseph Ryan, John Gilchrist, Ovidio Capitani and Robert Somerville among others, who have shown that the reform movement consisted of more than the pontificate of one individual, that there were often radically different opinions and agendas, and in particular that Gregory VII's 'reforms' had in large part been anticipated by his predecessors.[12] Yet Gregory persists in dominating characterizations both of eleventh-century reform and the eleventh-century reform papacy. Indeed, far from historians having abandoned Fliche's approach, his *réforme grégorienne* has effectively become the 'so-called Gregorian reform', which still in some way privileges Gregory's pontificate as the decisive point of reform.

While these historiographical revisions have been useful, they have perhaps not gone far enough in a number of critical ways. Gregory VII, understandably, is a seductive figure. His importance, his charisma in the Weberian sense, and the substantial sources that we have for his life and career, particularly his *Register*, have rightly commanded historians' interest. The force of his personality and his overwhelming commitment to reform that made him the movement's standard-bearer are nowhere more apparent than in his final encyclical written between July and November 1084 from his exile in Salerno:

> Ever since by God's Providence, mother Church set me upon the apostolic throne, deeply unworthy and, as God is my witness, unwilling though I was, my greatest concern has been that holy Church, the bride of Christ, our lady and mother should return to her true glory and stand free, chaste and catholic.[13]

Gregory is not, however, the entire story of reform in the eleventh century, the history of the eleventh-century papacy, or even of what many historians now refer to as the eleventh-century 'revolution'.

This is not to suggest that his role was negligible. Yet 'Gregorian reform' and even the 'Gregorian revolution' had their antecedents in individuals and events prior to Gregory's tumultuous arrival on the apostolic throne in 1073 and the full working-out of their implications, which were effectively the creation of a new social order, would not be fully apparent until 1215 or even later – at least according to one recent interpretation.[14] At the same time, simply focusing on the prominent reformers with whom Gregory was closely or at least ideologically associated – men such as Leo IX, Nicholas II, Humbert of Silva-Candida, Peter Damian, Alexander II, Bernold of Constance, Anselm of Lucca, Hugh of Die, Lanfranc of Bec, Gerald of Ostia, Bruno of Segni and William of Hirsau – does not give us a full understanding of the complexities of the reform movement, even if the actions of these men, and especially their polemic on the nature of power and on what sort of man ought to exercise authority were critical factors in the eleventh-century revolution.

The chief problem of much earlier scholarly work perhaps lies in the linear and evolutionary attitude with which historians have approached ecclesiastical reform in the eleventh century. The prevailing image is one of inexorable progress, akin to the description of churches spreading across western Europe described by Rodulf Glaber in his *Five Books of the Histories*.[15] Substantiated in large part by the reformers' own polemics, ecclesiastical reform in the eleventh century in the narratives of most historians almost invariably begins with Pope Leo IX (1049–54). Moreover, it is generally depicted as a process that simultaneously involved the suppression of simony, the eradication of clerical marriage and concubinage, the elevation of priestly morals, and the separation of clerics from the visible pollutants of blood, money and weapons until eventually it came to focus on the contentious issue of lay dominance. Other accounts of reform in the eleventh century follow the 'church-versus-state' model and focus almost exclusively on the power politics of the later eleventh-century papacy, the clash with Henry IV and the traditional 'political' concerns of investitures. Although recent work – by Paolo Golinelli, John Howe, Maureen Miller, Robert I. Moore and others, on the regional variations in the implementation of reform and the significance of local reform communities in western Europe – has done much to dispel this chronology, this roseate characterization and especially this narrow focus,[16] there remains a need to question not only what is meant by 'reformer', but also the 'top-down' understanding both of the reform agenda and of the reform papacy which produced these traditional interpretations.

Whatever else may be said of the successes or failures of ecclesiastical reform in the eleventh century, there can be no doubt that among the reformers' most notable achievements was a 'reorientation of loyalties'.[17] In particular, this was the recognition by clerics and monks that their identities lay first and foremost within the ecclesiastical sphere, a sphere increasingly marked out not just by their religious status but also by celibacy, which distinguished them from those who could not live without sex and marriage. Among these figured the 'fighters' (*bellatores*) and the 'workers' (*laboratores*), who – especially in eleventh-century discourse, but also in reality – constituted the other segments of society, and whom the 'prayers' (*oratores*) were more and more desirous of regulating, by defining their married status as inferior. In fact, this distinction was soon developed into a new, tripartite scheme. At least among ecclesiastical circles, the notion was mooted that Christian society was broken up into the virgins, the continent and the married. In a particularly self-serving definition, the reformers used the ideal of celibacy, and correct sexual behaviour in general, to designate those who should exercise the highest authority in society, further reinforcing the separation of the *oratores* from the rest of society.

The question still remains, however, of loyalty to whom or to what? Loyalty to the ideals of clerical purity that had been repeatedly set out in canon law since the fourth century and that in the age of eleventh-century reform were to be made reality? Or loyalty to the ecclesiastical institutions, hierarchy and normative mechanisms through which these ideals were to be promoted? For reform in the eleventh century was concerned not only with religious ideals but also with normative channels of power.

Indeed, reform in the eleventh century was not solely about the overt issues of simony, clerical unchastity, ecclesiastical property and freedom from lay control, though the reformers were insistent that ecclesiastics were to be unmarried and celibate, that they were to shed neither human nor animal blood, and that they were expressly forbidden from trafficking in the Holy Spirit by selling ecclesiastical office. Reform was also about setting boundaries, both for and between different parts of society. It was chiefly (and initially) an exercise in clerical discipline, but it was also, or at least eventually became, an attempt to construct a new social order, one based on firm distinctions between ecclesiastical and lay spheres, and within the ecclesiastical hierarchy itself. Those clergy, both monastic and secular, as well as the laymen of every rank over whom they attempted to set themselves, who did not respect the new and increasingly enforced dispensations of status and condition became in the eleventh century 'matter out of place', dangerous anomalies who contravened social order.[18] Indeed, the exercise of power in the eleventh century, as R. I. Moore has suggested, became increasingly conditional on the performance of specific roles, each of which was defined by a particular code of moral and especially sexual conduct. This discourse, as Moore rightly suggests, underlies the entire transformation of European society during this period.[19]

The papacy, at least from the middle part of the eleventh century, took a prominent part in these developments, but its initiatives owed much to earlier social, political and religious change as well as the actions of local religious authorities. The anachronistic focus of many historians solely on the reform papacy, and especially the pontificate of Gregory VII, has not only obscured these earlier developments but in large sense has also failed to take into account the very nature and cultural context of reform efforts in the eleventh century. It is thus of considerable importance that attention be devoted both to the transformation of the papacy throughout the entire eleventh century and also the context of the changing society in which the reforming movement and papacy both existed and developed. For far too long, these respective threads have been approached in isolation from one another.

Indeed, it is not just papal historiography that divides at 1049 with the elevation of Pope Leo IX. Rather, the historiography of the entire eleventh century in many ways remains divided between those historians, like the *mutationnistes*, who focus on socio-economic history, especially in France before 1050, and those who concentrate on the ecclesiastical and political history of the post-1050 reform papacy. Trying to draw both threads together is no small challenge, for the issue of how to understand the nature and the timing of those changes – the wide-ranging social, political, intellectual, cultural and economic changes of the eleventh century that formed the backdrop to the reform movement and influenced its objectives – remains contentious, as was discussed in the Introduction. But it is only by taking these interpretations and their modifications into account that we can begin to have anything like a real understanding of the religious and social revolution(s) that took place in eleventh-century Europe.

Thus, while considering the nature and evolution of the reform movement and the transformation of the papacy in the eleventh century – both of which left indelible marks on the society in which they developed – we need to be sensitive to how social changes challenged, intersected with and were harnessed by the reformers in the pursuit of their objectives. As will be seen in Chapter 3 on the 'peace of God', in some ways itself another instance where social and religious elements have been addressed in isolation from one another, the historiographical frameworks of *mutation*, 'revolution' and especially reform are not only useful but essential for an understanding of social and religious change in eleventh-century Europe.

Notes

1 D. Callahan, '*Ecclesia Semper Reformanda*: Clerical Celibacy and Reform in the Church', in M. Frassetto, ed., *Medieval Purity and Piety*, 377–88.

2 M. T. Clanchy, *From Memory to Written Record: England, 1066–1307*, 2nd edn (Oxford, 1993); cf. P. Geary, *Phantoms of Remembrance: Memory and Oblivion at the End of the First Millennium* (Princeton, NJ, 1994), 3–22.

3 B. Stock, *The Implications of Literacy: Written Language and Models of Interpretation in the Eleventh and Twelfth Centuries* (Princeton, NJ, 1983), esp. 30–87.

4 This is not to deny the significant and ongoing role played by women as custodians of family memory: see E. van Houts, *Memory and Gender in Medieval Europe, 900–1200* (Basingstoke, Hants., 1999). Cf. Geary, *Phantoms of Remembrance*, 48–80.

5 G. Constable, 'Past and Present in the Eleventh and Twelfth Centuries: Perceptions of Time and Change', in *L'Europa dei secoli XI e XII fra novità e tradizione sviluppi di una cultura* (Miscellanea di centro di studi medioevali, 12; Milan, 1989), 135–70; repr. in his *Culture and Spirituality in Medieval Europe* (Aldershot, Hants., 1996).

6 J. L. Nelson, 'Society, Theodicy and the Origins of Heresy', *Studies in Church History*, 8 (1972), 65–77. Cf. the response of T. Asad, 'Medieval Heresy: An Anthropological View', *Social History*, 11 (1986), 345–60.

7 Nelson, 'Society, Theodicy', 65–77.

8 Asad, 'Medieval Heresy', 345–60.

9 *Ottonian Germany: The Chronicon of Thietmar of Merseburg*, 6.21, 7.25, ed. and trans. D. A. Warner (Manchester, 1998), 251–2, 323–4.

10 The phrase comes from G. Tellenbach, *Church, State and Christian Society at the*

37

Time of the Investiture Contest, trans. R. F. Bennett (Oxford, 1940), who should not be understood solely as a 'church–state' historian as his *The Church in Western Europe from the Ninth to the Early Twelfth Century* (Cambridge, 1993) shows. For more detailed discussion of the historiography of reform, see U.-R. Blumenthal, *Gregor VII. Papst zwischen Canossa und Kirchenreform* (Darmstadt, 2001).

11   A. Fliche, *La réforme grégorienne*, 3 vols (Spicilegium sacrum Lovaniense, études et documents, fasc. 6, 9, 13; Paris, 1924–37).

12   For example, O. Capitani, 'Esiste un'età gregoriana? Considerazione sulle tendenze di una storiografia medievistica', *Rivista di storia e letteratura religiosa*, 1 (1965), 454–81 ; J. T. Gilchrist, 'Was there a Gregorian Reform Movement in the Eleventh Century?' *Canadian Catholic Historical Association, Study Sessions*, 37 (1970), 1–10 ; now repr. in his *Canon Law in the Age of Reform, Eleventh and Twelfth Centuries* (Variorum, Collected Studies Series, CS406; Aldershot, Hants., 1993); J. J. Ryan, *St Peter Damiani and His Canonical Sources: A Preliminary Study in the Antecedents of the Gregorian Reform* (Toronto, 1956); R. Somerville, 'The Councils of Pope Gregory VII', in *La riforma gregoriana e 'Europa'* (Studi Gregoriani, 13; Rome, 1989), 123–49.

13   *The Epistolae Vagantes of Pope Gregory VII*, ed. H. E. J. Cowdrey (Oxford, 1972), n.54, 130.

14   Moore, *First European Revolution*, esp. 160ff.

15   Rodulf Glaber, *Historiarum libri quinque*, 3.13, 114–16.

16   For example, P. Golinelli, *'Indiscreta sanctitas': studi sui rapporti tra culti, poteri e società nel pieno medioevo* (Istituto Storico italiano per il medio evo, studi storici, fasc. 197–8; Rome, 1988); J. Howe, *Church Reform and Social Change in Eleventh-Century Italy* (Philadelphia, PA, 1997); M. Miller, *The Formation of a Medieval Church: Ecclesiastical Change in Verona, 950–1150* (Ithaca, NY, 1993); R. I. Moore, 'Property, Marriage and the Eleventh-Century Revolution: A Context for Early Medieval Communism', in *Medieval Purity and Piety*, 179–208; R. I. Moore, 'Postscript: The Peace of God and the Social Revolution', in T. Head and R. Landes, eds, *The Peace of God: Social Violence and Religious Response in France around the year 1000* (Ithaca, NY, 1992), 308–26; R. I. Moore, 'Family, Community and Cult', *TRHS*, 5th series, 30 (1980), 49–69. On the underestimation of the 'pre-reform' papacy, see also K. G. Cushing, *Papacy and Law in the Gregorian Revolution: The Canonistic Work of Anselm of Lucca* (Oxford, 1998), 11–18.

17   M. Miller, 'Clerical Identity and Reform: Notarial Descriptions of the Secular Clergy in the Po Valley, 750–1200', in *Medieval Purity and Piety*, 305–35.

18   See A. Remensnyder, 'Pollution, Purity and Peace: An Aspect of Social Reform between the late Tenth Century and 1076', in Head and Landes, *Peace of God*, 280–307, esp. 289–90. 'Matter out of place' is the classic phrase from M. Douglas, *Purity and Danger: An Analysis of the Concepts of Pollution and Taboo* (London, 1966).

19   Moore, *First European Revolution*, esp. 65–111.

3

The 'peace of God'

I N 975, Bishop Guy of Le Puy convened a large meeting in a field outside his city with the intention of constraining those secular lords and knights who were responsible for pillaging the churches and attacking the poor of his diocese. Reinforcing his threats of excommunication with the presence of his nephews' armed followers, Guy forced those gathered, both knights (*milites*) and armed peasants, to take an oath swearing to maintain the peace. Acting as he did with secular support rather than with his fellow bishops, Guy was not in a position either to promulgate canons or formally to act with the full force of ecclesiastical sanctions. Yet the gathering at Le Puy, even though it was a strictly local initiative responding to a particular set of circumstances, set important precedents, not least in its promotion of an oath to maintain the peace. As subsequent similar councils held at Charroux in 989 and Limoges in 994 indicate, Guy's fellow bishops in time came to realize the utility of such mass gatherings. Moreover, from 989 onwards, the bishops began to use the relics of the saints as a means of drawing even larger crowds.

The practice of convoking councils to promote peace developed first in the Auvergne and Aquitaine, and then spread to Burgundy at the end of the tenth century. It is usually known as the 'peace of God' movement – though historians have often questioned the appropriateness of that term, given that the councils were independent initiatives responding to local circumstances rather than an organized 'movement', however much they have been used as evidence of the 'feudal revolution'. The councils ostensibly sought to limit lawlessness by threatening with excommunication those who committed certain crimes and by calling on those present to swear mutual oaths to refrain from private fighting. As the account of Letaldus of Micy makes clear, from the time of the Council of Charroux in

989 onwards, two elements were of paramount importance – the assembly of saints' relics and the enthusiastic participation of 'large' crowds of people (*populus*):

> a great crowd of many people gathered there from the Poitou, the Limousin, and neighboring regions. Many bodies of saints were also brought there. The cause of religion was strengthened by their presence, and the impudence of evil people was beaten back. That council – convoked, as it was thought, by divine will – was adorned with frequent miracles through the presence of these saints.[1]

The presence of both kinds of 'witnesses' placed significant pressure on those whom the bishops and abbots were seeking to constrain to peace: the bodies of the saints, not only through their working of miracles but also on account of the sacred quality they afforded to the oaths sworn over them; and the body of the *populus* as witnesses both to the miracles of the saints and the swearing of the oaths.

The councils gained renewed momentum from about 1019–20, when the practice of convening them spread northwards from Burgundy. From this time, the councils increasingly became more organized, promoting longer-term arrangements as is evinced by the formation of peace leagues like that at Bourges around 1038. After this time, peace councils increasingly came under the supervision of both the papacy and secular rulers, rather than simply local lords in whose interest it had been to support the bishops' initiatives, in the form of the more widely known Truce of God (*Treuga Dei*). Unlike the 'peace', the truce of God aimed less at the protection of individuals, places and property and rather sought to constrain warring aristocratic behaviour by limiting the days on which (legitimate) fighting could take place.

The earliest peace council from which actual canons survive was that held in Charroux in 989. Convened by Archbishop Gunbaldus of Bordeaux and attended by bishops Gilbert of Poitiers, Hildegar of Limoges, Frotarius of Périgueux, Abbo of Saintes and Hugh of Angoulême, the council's objective was principally a defensive one: to put an end to the anarchic and criminal activity in the bishops' respective dioceses that had arisen because of the long delay in summoning a council.[2] According to the council's decrees, three specific crimes were to be punished by excommunication.[3] The first two decrees focused on safeguarding the Church's property and personnel: theft of church property and assaults on unarmed clerics were thus resoundingly condemned under penalty of excommunication. The final decree condemned the theft of cattle, oxen, asses, sheep, goats and pigs from peasants or the poor and, according to some interpretations of the sources, also censured other unspecified acts of violence against the poor. The decrees of later councils such as Limoges (994), Poitiers (1000, 1014), and Elne-Toulouges (1027) generally followed the pattern established at Charroux though, as will be seen, with an expanding set of preoccupations, however much they continued to address local questions. It is especially in these councils that we find increasing interest devoted to the issue of what constituted appropriate behaviour among both clergy and laity. Thus at Anse in 994, in addition to making celibacy obligatory for those in higher orders, the clergy were also prohibited from hunting, whereas the council at Le Puy in the same year prohibited clerics from bearing weapons and instructed priests not to accept money or gifts for penance, or for other sacraments. At Poitiers in 1000/14, not only was tonsuring required, but priests and deacons were also required to remain celibate, and were prohibited from keeping women within their houses. Those who did so were to be deposed from clerical and priestly orders – an early, and hence noteworthy, harsh punishment. Furthermore, the reception of priests' sons into holy orders was strictly prohibited. In 1027 at Elne-Toulouges, the prohibition of communion with excommunicates was reiterated and the canons were instructed not to offer masses or prayers for them, or to reconcile them without their superiors' knowledge. Moreover, it is evident that such basic provision and instructions to the clergy were genuinely necessary. At Bourges in 1031, for instance, provisions even had to be made for the celebration of the mass in churches every Sunday.

While some historians have long recognized that there is a connection between the 'peace movement' and church reform, they have tended to treat the increasing appearance of canons demanding celibacy or the free bestowal of sacraments, especially penance, as somehow separate from the 'peace' itself. This division not only unnecessarily complicates the 'peace' of God, but also reinforces the one-sided interpretations of those who separate reform from the peace. While the later peace councils do clearly offer a sense of an increasingly coherent, if varied, concept of 'the peace', at the same time they suggest that 'peace' in its most restricted meaning was not, nor ever had been, the sole objective.

Among the chief difficulties in assessing both the nature and the significance of the 'peace of God' is that of the documentary evidence. Indeed, of some twenty-two peace councils known to have taken place, there are contemporary accounts of just eight of them, and only four for which there are extant conciliar canons. Thus, historians are forced to rely on hagiographical texts, miracle collections such as Bernard of Chartres' *Book of the Miracles of Saint Foy* (*Liber miraculorum sanctae Fidis*) or Andrew of Fleury's *Miracles of St Benedict* (*Miracula sancti Benedicti*), accounts of the translation of saints' relics to and from the councils such as that of Letaldus of Micy, charter evidence and oaths, as well as passing references from chroniclers such as Rodulf Glaber and Adhemar of Chabannes.[4] However valuable the descriptions in these accounts may be, they provide only incidental discussions of the 'peace of God' embedded within other discourses or objectives. We shall return to this below. It is useful, however, first to review in more detail both traditional and revisionist interpretations of this so-called movement in order to have a better understanding of its connection with eleventh-century reform as well as its repercussions for eleventh-century society.

Traditionally, the 'peace of God' has been seen as something of a 'war on war', in other words, as a reaction to the disorder, whether real or perceived, that resulted from the disintegration of the Carolingian Empire during the later ninth and especially tenth centuries. Central to this understanding is an acceptance of the collapse of Carolingian public order and justice, and as a consequence, the proliferation of new, violent and arbitrary lordships exercising the powers known as the ban (justice and rights) and imposing 'evil customs' (*malae consuetudines*) that increasingly threatened ecclesiastical property and burdened the peasantry.[5] These, clearly, are key elements of the 'feudal revolution' argument.

The 'peace' was thus effectively seen by historians as a reaction by the *pauperes*, meaning the politically powerless rather than the economic poor (in other words, the Church together with the peasantry), against the lawlessness of the *potentes* or powerful, that is, the new castellans and knights who took political and economic advantage of the breakdown of public order. This supposedly produced some sort of compact amongst the 'poor', who sought in turn to bring the power of the saints, the ecclesiastical sanction of anathema and the force of public indignation to bear on the rising castellan class in an effort, ultimately, to influence them constructively. Such interpretations rely heavily on accounts of anarchy and chaos in texts written chiefly (though not exclusively) by monks, whose own agendas more often than not may have led them to exaggerate both the extent and the nature of the violence.[6]

This point of view was in many ways supported by Erdmann, who saw the 'peace' as an attempt by the Church to insert the European warrior classes more securely within the framework of Christian society. This was to be achieved not just by prohibiting or setting limits to their fighting, but also by directing their militaristic inclinations against the enemies of the peace. The objectives of this redirection, or so Erdmann believed, would be extended to include the enemies of Christendom first with the *militia* or *fideles sancti Petri* and later in the crusades, where war became not only a legitimate but even praiseworthy endeavour.[7]

More recently though, historians such as Hans-Werner Goetz, R. I. Moore, Janet Nelson and others have argued that, far from being simply a reaction to the breakdown of order or 'feudal anarchy, the 'peace of God' did not constitute an attack on the warrior aristocracy. In fact, it is clear that princes and seigniorial powers often took an active part in convoking councils and peace leagues.[8] Moreover, when we take into account regional variations, the continuities between the 'peace' and earlier judicial institutions, the varied nature of ecclesiastical action and response, and the role of the saints and their miracles as revealed in the incidental documentary evidence, it becomes clear that there was an intersection of interest, chiefly to do with property and the power derived from it, between the ecclesiastical and secular hierarchies with regard to the 'peace', one that was perhaps deliberately cultivated. Therefore, far from any simple or single narrative of the powerless (*pauperes*) against the powerful (*potentes*), most historians now tend to emphasize that the 'peace' was one of several quasi-institutional means used by ecclesiastical and secular hierarchies alike to promote, to contain, and especially perhaps to channel both the 'anarchy' and social change that had arisen in the wake of the political fragmentation of the Carolingian Empire.

This intersection of interest can be seen in any number of ways. Although the early phase of the 'peace' was undeniably directed by bishops, soon local secular magnates and increasingly also rulers came to see the value of peace councils, and looked either to associate themselves with such gatherings or (even better) to appropriate them for their own ends. This is apparent at Poitiers *circa* 1030 with the French king, Robert the Pious, who consciously sought to bolster his rather weak political and territorial position by association with the Church and by requesting that peace councils be held throughout his kingdom. Robert undoubtedly used the council to enhance his prestige by associating himself with a 'peace' that he could no longer directly impose in large parts of his kingdom.[9]

More instructive, though, are the ends towards which these councils were convoked, which were far from either uniform or consistent. While the peace councils were initially and clearly aimed at the protection of property, especially ecclesiastical property, and the safety of (unarmed) clerics, as can be seen in the canons from Poitiers (1000/1014) and especially from Elne-Toulouges (1027), their objectives quickly expanded to include issues both of church reform and social mores, for instance, prohibitions of simony, incest, fornication, or communion with excommunicates, and even condemnations of heresy. Even more important, the supposed initial ambitions of these councils now seem far more ambiguous than once was thought. For instance, the idea that the peace councils were especially concerned with disinterestedly protecting the poor and the peasantry seems highly doubtful. At least with respect to Charroux, as Hans-Werner Goetz has shown, there was far less interest evinced by the Church in the peasants themselves than in protecting the ecclesiastical fields and vineyards on which they worked; concern for the peasants extended only as far as protecting them while they brought in the ecclesiastical landlords' harvest.[10]

One of the chief problems with understanding the 'peace of God' is the tendency of historians to use it simultaneously as the cause of social and religious change in the later tenth and earlier eleventh centuries and as the explanation of that change. This is perhaps especially the case with historians such as Landes and Head who, as noted above, have used the 'peace' to underpin a *mutationniste* perspective of transformation, in which the peace councils and the popular enthusiasm generated by them are evidence both of the violence in late tenth- and early eleventh-century society and of the ways that certain sections of society sought to combat that situation. As a consequence, the 'peace' has been seen both as transforming customary social relationships by giving various sections of the *populus* a forum in which to protest against political anarchy and demand higher standards of religious life among the clergy, and at the same time as justifying that transformation. It is not perhaps surprising that in a time of increasing though still meagre documentation the descriptions of processions of relics and clerics among the people, imploring God and the saints to come to their assistance – in a period apparently when 'kingdoms were tottering on their foundations' and the 'cause of religion was beaten back'[11] – have exerted a powerful influence on how historians interpret this period. It was a time when change in any number of spheres – whether gradual or radical – seems especially noticeable.

The real problem is that it is just one small step from this to envisaging the 'peace' as a 'movement' with the inescapable connotations of organization, agenda and delineated leadership. This is problematic in any number of ways. The councils, after all, were localized initiatives, responding to local problems. Although later councils were no doubt indirectly influenced by earlier ones, they can scarcely be seen together as a coherent whole. Moreover, their geographic diffusion, to say nothing of their diversity, weighs strongly against the notion of a 'movement'. The peace councils originated in Aquitaine and the Auvergne, effectively on the fringes of the Capetian kings' authority. These were regions with traditions of reasonably strong ducal and comital power, unlike the descriptions of anarchy and lawlessness in ecclesiastical accounts. Moreover, the characteristic peace councils had little if any impact beyond Francia, whether in Italy, the German empire or England. Although, as indicated above, proclamations of 'peace' did tend to become part of many royal and ecclesiastical councils during the course of the eleventh century, the idea that southern French society was somehow more prone to violence and political disorder than other regions of Latin Christendom is untenable.

Most worrying, perhaps, is the way that modern historians' views of a 'peace of God' presuppose some idyllic past when, to echo Janet Nelson, God was in heaven, Carolingian emperors were securely on the throne, public justice was ubiquitous, church lands were completely secure and there were neither unjust exactions nor 'evil customs'.[12] Such a view is clearly false. In fact, as Nelson and others have shown, all the political abuses condemned in peace councils around the year 1000 had been denounced two centuries earlier, although not eradicated. To assume otherwise is both to overestimate the machinery of Carolingian administration and to underestimate the uneasy, but necessary interdependence that existed between the Carolingian state and seigniorial power.[13] That levels of violence increased – or at least perceptions thereof – in the wake of, and long after, the Norse, Saracen and Magyar incursions cannot be denied, but it must be emphasized that such outbreaks were regionally restricted and sporadic.[14]

What was far more important was the increased *perception* of disorder by those members of society whose position at this juncture was most ambivalent and in many ways under threat: the clergy. Their effective marshalling of their liminal status – through liturgical cursing, the ritual humiliation of the saints' relics, and perhaps especially the public peace councils – was both a reaction to and a remedy for this perceived disorder, a disorder that they magnified to some extent. Behind this reaction, however, lay an attempt to come to terms with the new realities, and to try to define afresh the changing relationship between the secular donors and the ecclesiastical recipients in an age when gifts of land needed to be granted in perpetuity rather than on a temporary basis.

This is not to suggest that there was some conscious decision on the part of clerics or monks to pursue such an agenda at any given point between 989 and the 1030s. But if we accept the idea that the collapse of public order in the tenth century may have been more apparent than real, we can begin to understand both the nature of the so-called anarchy and the 'peace' as a response to it. At its root, unsurprisingly, was land, and especially the nature of rights over those landed properties. Behind these, though, were equally important shifts in both the nature and cultural significance of gifts.

Throughout the tenth and early eleventh centuries, the Church as a whole had become much more prosperous, but particularly the monasteries. This was chiefly due to donations from the nobility, including the rising castellans, who were fearful of eternal damnation, but who were also looking, in the face of competition, to improve or at least to cement their social position on earth.[15] In exchange for spiritual services such as prayers and masses for the dead, burial within the monasteries' cemeteries, commemoration in the monasteries' liturgical round, and the all-important association with the holy saints who were the monasteries' most important patrons, the nobility conceded their lands, their rights and even the memory of their families to those best placed to secure them a position of prominence in both worlds.[16] Dominique Iogna-Prat has described these exchanges in terms of the sociology of gift and counter-gift, whereby monks 'charged' for the spiritual benefits they provided in exchange for material ones.[17] But such gifts *ad sepulturam* had in the past generally been made *in beneficium* rather than *in proprietatem*. This meant the donor retained certain rights, such as the advocacy of a monastery, rights to hospitality and, most significantly, potential rights of reversion. Reversion meant that the land, rights or other gifts would return to the heirs at the death of the original donor.

We can thus begin to understand the proliferation of charters of confirmation in this period, whether genuine or forged, as the death of a donor could mean financial ruin for the monastery in question, and often brought in its wake protracted disputes as relationships were renegotiated.[18] As rights to land ownership became ever more contested following the fragmentation of the Carolingian Empire, the aristocracy increasingly sought to consolidate their holdings, to move from partible inheritance to primogeniture, and to ensure the reversion of what had been given 'temporarily'. As Moore notes, they were not always scrupulous to take back only what had actually been given.[19] At the same time, the aristocracy sought to increase revenues by taking more from their dependent peasants. By using force, often disguised as the extension of rights of public power and the power of the ban, they progressively reduced independent cultivators to dependency. This also had implications for ecclesiastical (chiefly monastic) landowners who followed the same policy, all the while protesting against the hegemony of the powerful over the poor, with whom they had humbly aligned themselves.

Seen in this light, the 'peace of God' as Moore has argued was more about a realignment of power relationships among the privileged, developing at a time when the preoccupations both of the Church and the new lordships with landed property and their rights or privileges confronted each other, and ultimately intersected. The basic narrative could thus be recast as follows. The 'peace' developed in the first place from an ecclesiastical mobilization of the *populus*, whose need for consistent protection mirrored that of the politically powerless Church. By harnessing the charismatic power of the saints' relics, the Church provided a focal point for popular action, one that was replicated and reinforced in the processions and liturgies. Having thereby mobilized the laity in its efforts to promote peace, bishops and abbots increasingly faced the real issue: the need to stabilize their positions over the longer term *vis-à-vis* the castellans and secular rulers alike.

A good example can be found in the way that the monks of Saint Maxient, in protesting against the evil customs imposed by Count William of Aquitaine's *prevôts*, extracted a new kind of immunity for their property by linking it with the peace stipulations made at Poitiers in 1029/1030.[20] While in this case the monks of St Maxient were the winners, their protest shows that it was not enough simply to defend themselves against attacks, plunder and depredation. Churchmen had to (re)establish not only their claim to direct society in terms of the faith, but also to show why it was in everyone's interest that they be custodians of the aristocracy's material wealth and to some extent its political power. The 'peace' therefore, perhaps inevitably, foreshadowed the outlines of a new social order, where distinctions would be drawn not only among the privileged and the underprivileged, but also between the lay and clerical spheres, with the latter needing to establish its purity and irreproachable conduct to justify its claim to superiority. As will be seen, these were issues that were to lie at the heart of the reform agenda.

In many ways what is most striking about the 'peace of God' has little do with the promotion of 'peace' at all. Rather it is the fact that churchmen were able to begin to persuade the ruling classes to accept their dictates and thereby prove their fitness to exercise power.[21] The beginnings of this reconstruction of the laity can be seen when we look closely at the legislation of some of the councils. Although, as has been seen above, these councils were at first preoccupied with the reform of the moral and sexual behaviour of the clergy alone (apart, that is, from the injunctions to maintain peace), they soon began to address the moral and sexual conduct of the laity in connection with the protection of property. For instance, at the councils of Poitiers in 1000/14, along with the restoration of peace and the discussion of procedures for resolving disputes, laymen were prohibited from presenting gifts to bishops or priests in exchange for penance and confirmation.[22] (The growing interest in such concerns is reflected in the councils of the Salian Church such as those convened by Henry II at Ravenna in 1014 and Pavia in 1022, or the Council of Seligenstadt in 1022 convened by Archbishop Aribo of Mainz, though these are not considered to be 'peace' councils *per se*.)[23]

The Council of Elne-Toulouges in 1027 is a particularly important example. Not only did it formulate detailed provisions regarding the protection of the peace, of unarmed clerics and monks, of those going to and from church, of men accompanying women, of churches and their environs to a thirty-yard radius as well as safeguards for church property in general, the council also banned incestuous marriages within the sixth degree of consanguinity or blood relationship (and those remaining in them were to be excommunicated), and sharply reiterated the centuries-old prohibition of any contact whatsoever with excommunicates, including eating or drinking with them, and even simply greeting them.[24] Interestingly, the council also warned priests not to say mass or prayers for excommunicates and also condemned the unauthorized absolution by canons or priests of those excommunicated for any of these crimes.

How are we to account for the emergence of these and similar strictures? The preamble to the decrees of Elne-Toulouges is instructive:

> They inquired whether the statutes hitherto laid down by the aforesaid bishops were observed. But when they found that all of them were not only trampled underfoot but also forgotten, they strove to renew them in those terms in which they had first been established.[25]

This suggests not simply an expansion of the objectives, but also a shift from 'peace' to the underlying preconditions required for the establishment of God's peace on earth in the new order of things, or, as Amy Remensnyder has put it, a move towards issues of right behaviour and discipline.[26] It needs to be argued, however, that reform issues like these underlay the promotion of 'peace' at the time of even the earliest councils.

From the beginning, it is clear that a penitential spirit was an important characteristic of the promotion of 'peace' and this became increasingly pronounced in the councils following the turn of the millennium of Christ's birth, and also around 1033 with the anniversary of the passion. For instance, when discussing the first council of Limoges in 994, Adhemar of Chabannes mentions that a three-day fast for both clergy and laity was declared in preparation.[27] The Cluniac monk and chronicler Rudolf Glaber gives us further indications of this penitential, but also reformist, quality of the 'peace'. Writing of events in the year 1033 which he took to mark the millennium of Christ's passion, Glaber noted that peace councils had effectively two purposes: 'the reformation of the peace and of the holy faith'.[28] He then went on to describe other disciplinary decisions made by such councils regarding abstention from sex, wine and meat. These, for him, were clearly preconditions of any attempt to restore and maintain a sustained climate of peace – a peace that would be rewarded by abundant harvests, according to his text. His later characterization of the many individuals who returned to their former ways after the safe passing of the millennium as 'dogs returning to their own vomit' underlines the importance attached to right behaviour, the lack of which among both clergy and laity, at least for Glaber, led inevitably to a breakdown of God's peace on earth.

In 1049, Pope Leo IX held his important reforming council at Rheims. Here, for the first time, the peace was universally proclaimed thanks to a papal promulgation. Interestingly however, the proclamation of the peace was just one of a long list of disciplinary canons aimed at the laity as much as the clergy and which prohibited among other things simony, clerics bearing arms, incest, the repudiation of wives, theft, fornication and sodomy.[29] Although Rheims is not traditionally seen as a 'peace' council and there will be more to say about the council in later chapters, it should be understood not as the beginning of reform, as many historians have suggested, but as the culmination of the underlying reform objectives of the 'peace': the beginnings of the reconstruction of the moral landscape of both clergy and laity. The community of interest that the 'peace' had promoted between ecclesiastical and secular leaders, which entailed leaving the Church in undisturbed possession of its acquisitions for which the aristocracy was compensated by other means, meant that all parties were now increasingly obliged to accept the new definitions of their privileged positions.[30]

There can be no coincidence that, alongside such strictures and the expansion of objectives in peace councils and ecclesiastical circles in general, there was renewed emphasis on the tripartite division of society into those who pray (*oratores*), those who fight (*bellatores*) and those who work with their hands (*laboratores*). Although bishops such as Gerard of Cambrai and Adalbero of Laon used the 'three orders' to argue against other bishops' promotion of peace councils – and especially peace leagues, which they believed to be unacceptable arrogations of the power and function of the king – it is clear that their uses of the 'three estates' idea were not simply conservative reactions. Rather, they were attempts to fix, at least rhetorically, a social schema that did not yet exist in reality and whose outline needed definition. Gerard and Adalbero's concern was probably directed chiefly at the *oratores*. For now more than ever, to be a cleric was to be a member of a caste set apart, one which drew its special status from its service at the altar and its unpolluted contact with the sacred, both of which were compromised by involvement with the 'peace'.

Idealized views of society such as those of Adalbero and Gerard probably also reflected a desire to impose order where it was lacking. Indeed, their conservative reactions were probably symptomatic of concerns shared by many individuals at perhaps the most unexpected outcome of the 'peace': that of making the people (*populus*) visible, of giving them a role in the public arena. In fact, it is not unreasonable to see the 'peace' in many ways as the start of what R. I. Moore long ago referred to as the 'appearance of the crowd on the stage of public events', however much the impact of the 'peace' lay chiefly in a realignment of power among the privileged.[31] Defining the 'people' or the 'crowd' in this context, as Moore notes, is a difficult task; the various names under which they are grouped in contemporary sources, however, make it clear that that they were seen as separate from the *milites* or knightly class.[32] Moreover, it is clear that the people were seen as a potent force.

Whatever may be said of the ultimate intentions of churchmen, it is clear that in orchestrating the peace councils, these bishops and abbots not only created but also harnessed public opinion in support of their aims.[33] As a consequence, there can be no doubt that whether consciously or unconsciously, deliberately or haphazardly, the people were raised into a public arena, and as witnesses and even as participants they afforded a principle of legitimacy for the varied objectives of the 'peace' councils. Despite the reappearance of the *populus* in the narratives of the peace movement, it should not be forgotten that their role was often largely rhetorical. It would be a very long time before the populace could exercise a political role independent of their lay or ecclesiastical masters.

The fact that the many peace councils were concerned with defining and defending the social order is especially clear from Andrew of Fleury's description of the activities of the peace league of Bourges.[34] The league had been formed at a council or gathering in Bourges about 1038 by Archbishop Aimon of Bourges. It saw an important innovation to the general pattern of the 'peace' movement. Apparently, Aimon made everyone over the age of fifteen, clergy and laity alike, swear on the relics of the martyr Stephen to maintain the peace among themselves, but also to take up arms against anyone who attacked or stole ecclesiastical property, harmed priests and religious, or in any way threatened the Church. The significance of Andrew's text has long been recognized by historians for its use of the term *milites* to denote mounted warriors who had by then become a recognizable class.[35]

Indeed, Andrew clearly disapproved of a ruse attempted when, during a battle against the enemies of peace, Aimon ordered what Andrew terms as a 'plebian rabble' *(plebiae multitudinis)* to be mounted on asses and mixed amid the knights *(milites)*. The peasants' subsequent terror as battle was joined made them flee in disarray; in the chaos they were set upon not only by the enemy but also by their own side. This was grim justice in Andrew's opinion, since the league and their supporters had earlier refused mercy to the innocent inhabitants of a castle during a siege.[36] Duby in particular saw this disdain as prompted by a desire to protect existing social order from change, and as a reaction against peasants (who interestingly enough in Andrew's *Miracula* are initially *rustici*, only later becoming 'rabble') who usurped the function of their lords at the instigation of their local clergy.[37]

In spite of monastic disapproval shown by writers like Andrew, the ability of the few to mobilize the support of the many would have far-reaching repercussions. This is apparent not only in the nascent communal aspirations that begin to appear from the 1060s at Le Mans (for which the league at Bourges may be a sort of precursor), but especially in the form of the *fideles* (faithful ones) whose 'boycott' of the ministrations of simoniacal and unchaste clergy would become so important to the reformers in Milan with the Pataria and elsewhere in the Latin West. These will be considered in more detail in chapters 5 and 6. Yet giving a voice, or at least a role – albeit chiefly an indirect one as witnesses rather than as agents of change – would also prove dangerous for the Church. For the raising of hope amongst the laity of a more moral and conscientious clergy reflecting God's peace on earth created an atmosphere of expectation that could not ever be fully met. As a consequence, many sections of the *populus* inevitably and ultimately drifted into heterodoxy and heresy.

It is the *populus*, however, that reminds us of the difficulties of assessing the 'peace of God' and its connection with reform. For the 'peace' was clearly more than a 'war on war', or even simply an extended process of dispute resolution initiated by conservative bishops or abbots trying to retain what they had been granted, in the face of either 'new' castellans looking to seize property or the disinherited fighting to take back lands over which they had lost control.[38] This recognition also makes it possible to reject the view that early efforts at reform were adjuncts to the business of the 'peace' or simply the product of bishops seeking to assume a moral high ground by appropriating the standards of monastic holiness. In this view, episcopal promotion of spiritual and moral improvements in the clergy (i.e. reform) was nothing more than an attempt to entrench their separate, higher status as guardians of morality and western society's property. The 'peace of God' was all of these things, but also more. In the end, the 'peace' was not separate from – or merely a forerunner to – the papal-led reform later in the eleventh century, but rather a complicated socio-political realignment. At the same time, it represented a critical stage in the redefining of the Church's role as an arbiter in a society grappling with 'real' concerns about reform, justice and order in the face of the millennial anniversaries of Christ's birth and passion.

Notes

1 Letaldus of Micy, *Delatio corporis s. Juniani ad synodem Karoffensem* (989), trans. in Head and Landes, eds, *Peace of God*, 328–9.

2 Council of Charroux, trans. in *Peace of God*, 327–8.

3 Ibid., 327–8.

4 Not all the key texts are available in translation: *The Book of Saint Foy*, ed./trans. P. Sheingorn (Philadelphia, 1995) – Bernard wrote the first two books of this composite life; *Les miracles de saint Benoit écrits par Adrevald, Aimon, André, Raoul Tortaire et Hugues de Sainte Marie, moines de Fleury*, ed. E. de Certain (Paris, 1858), partial trans. in *Peace of God*, 339–42; Rodulf Glaber, *Hist. Libri V.* (Oxford, 1989); *Chronique de Ademar de Chabannes*, ed. J. Chavanon (Paris, 1897). See *Peace of God* for additional translated material pertaining to the peace, Appendix A, 327–42.

5 The classic view is found in M. Bloch, *Feudal Society*, trans. L. A. Manyon (Chicago, 1961). For a review of scholarship since Bloch, see F. S. Paxton, 'History, Historians and the Peace of God', in *Peace of God*, 21–40.

6 For example, *Gesta episcoporum Cameracensium* (MGH, *SS*, 7), 475, 585; excerpt trans. in *Peace of God*, 334–7.

7 C. Erdmann, *The Origin of the Idea of Crusade*, trans. J. W. Baldwin and W. Goffart (Princeton, NJ, 1977), esp. 57–94.

8 For example, H.-W. Goetz, 'Protection of the Church, Defense of the Law, and

Reform: On the Purposes and Character of the Peace of God, 989–1038', in *Peace of God*, 259–79; Moore, 'Postscript', 308–26; Moore, *First European Revolution*, 7–10, 103–5 *et passim*; J. L. Nelson, review of *The Peace of God* in *Speculum*, 69 (1994), 163–9.

9   For example, peace oath proposed to Robert by Bishop Warin of Beauvais (1023) in *Peace of God*, 332–4. Cf. E. Magnou-Nortier, 'The Enemies of the Peace: Reflections on a Vocabulary, 500–1100', in ibid., 58–79, esp. 71ff; and A. Debord, 'The Castellan Revolution and the Peace of God in Aquitaine', in ibid., esp. 162–3.

10 Goetz, 'Protection of the Church', 259–79.

11 *Gesta episc. Cam.*, 475, 585; *Peace of God*, 334–7. See also the charter from St Maxient in 1032, at 337.

12 Nelson, review of *Peace of God* in *Speculum*, 69 (1994), 163–9.

13 Ibid., 168. Cf. Moore, *First European Revolution*, 39ff; D. Barthélemy, 'La mutation féodale: a-t-elle eu lieu?', *Annales: Economies, sociétés, civilisations*, 47 (1992), 767–77; D. Barthélemy, 'Le paix de Dieu dans son contexte (989–1041)', *Cahiers de civilisation médiévale*, 40 (1997), 3–35, esp. 11ff; and T. Bisson, 'The Feudal Revolution', *PP*, 142 (1994), 6–42, and responses by D. Barthélemy and S. White in *PP*, 152 (1996), 196–205, 205–23, and by T. Reuter and C. Wickham in *PP*, 153 (1997), 177–95, 196–208. Bisson replies to all in *PP*, 155 (1997), 208–25.

14 See T. Bisson, 'Medieval Lordship', *Speculum*, 70 (1995), 743–59, for an interesting reassessment of the problem of violence.

15 Moore, *First European Revolution*, 71ff for discussion of a relevant example, the Giroie family.

16 See P. Geary, *Phantoms of Remembrance* (Princeton, NJ, 1994), 48–81; P. Geary, *Living with the Dead* (Ithaca, NY, 1994), 77–92; B. Rosenwein, *To Be the Neighbor of St Peter* (Ithaca, NY, 1989).

17 D. Iogna-Prat, 'The Celestial Bookkeeping of the Cluniac Monks', in Little and Rosenwein, eds, *Debating the Middle Ages*, 240–62.

18 S. White, 'The Politics of Exchange: Gifts, Fiefs and Feudalism', and 'From Peace to Power: The Study of Disputes in Medieval France', in Cohen and de Jong, *Medieval Transformations*, 169–88, 203–18.

19 Moore, 'Postscript', 310.

20 Debord, 'The Castellan Revolution and the Peace of God in Aquitaine', in *Peace of God*, 135–64, esp. 162–3.

21 Moore, *First European Revolution*, 65–111, esp. 85ff.

22 Council of Poitiers, canons 2–3, trans. in *Peace of God*, 330–1.

23 On Ravenna and Pavia, see below, Ch. 5.

24 Council of Elne-Toulouges, trans. in *Peace of God*, 334–5.

25 Ibid., 334.

26 A. Remensnyder, 'Pollution, Purity and Peace', in *Peace of God*, 280–307.

27 Adhemar, *Chronicon*, 3.35, trans. in *Peace of God*, 329–30.

28 Rodulf Glaber, *Hist. Libri V.*, 4.5.13–17, 194–9. Cf. R. Landes, 'The Fear of an Apocalyptic Year 1000: Augustinian Historiography, Medieval and Modern', *Speculum*, 75 (2000), 97–145.

29 An account of the 1049 council's proceedings and the canons promulgated are

preserved in a text by Anselm, a monk of St Remy, whose account also describes the rededication of the church of St Remy that preceded the council: *Historia dedicationis sancti Remigii apud Remos*, in J. Hourlier, ed., 'Anselme de Saint-Remy: histoire de la dédicace de Saint-Remy', in *La Champagne bénédictine* (Rheims, 1981), 179–297, text 200–60 (with facing Latin and French texts); other editions include J. Mabillon, *Acta sanctorum O.S.B.*, 6.1 (Paris, 1701), 711–27, and *PL* 142.1409–40. This council of Rheims will be discussed in more detail in Ch. 6.

30 Moore, 'Postscript', 322.

31 R. I. Moore, 'Family, Community and Cult', *TRHS*, 5th ser., 30 (1980), 49–69.

32 Ibid., 50–1, 53.

33 L. C. Mackinney, 'The People and Public Opinion in the Eleventh-Century Peace Movement', *Speculum*, 5 (1930), 181–206. Cf. R. Landes, 'Between Aristocracy and Heresy: Popular Participation in the Limousin Peace of God, 994–1033', in *Peace of God*, 184–218.

34 T. Head, 'The Judgment of God: Andrew of Fleury's Account of the Peace League of Bourges', in *Peace of God*, 219–38. By locating Andrew's comments in monastic hagiographic tradition, Head suggests that his chief concern was not so much with peace leagues but rather with the misappropriation of the spiritual power of the saints, over whose relics the league had been formed. He thus points to a heightening undercurrent of competition between the clergy and the *agni immaculati*, or monks, who increasingly privileged themselves over the secular clergy on account both of their celibate lives and their custodianship of the relics, memory and power of saints.

35 G. Duby, *The Three Orders: Feudal Society Imagined* (Chicago, 1980); see also 'The Laity and the Peace of God', in his *The Chivalrous Society*, 123–33.

36 Ibid.

37 Duby, *Three Orders*, 186ff; cf. Duby, 'The Laity and the Peace of God', 127ff.

38 As D. Barthélemy, *L'an mil et la paix de Dieu: La France chrétienne et féodale, 980–1060* (Paris, 1999); cf. review by F. S. Paxton in *Speculum*, 77/1 (2002), 135–7.

4

'Reforming' the papacy

ALTHOUGH there is considerable evidence that standards in religious life and the reform of the Church in general were animating individual ecclesiastical officials and secular rulers from as early as the later tenth century, what galvanized these initiatives and extended reform objectives in the eleventh century was the Roman papacy. Many elements and individuals contributed to the emergence of the papacy as the indisputable leader of the Church – and in many ways leader also of the Latin West – during the course of the eleventh century. Although, as will be seen, the reform, indeed transformation, of the papacy into an effective supranational institution depended on innovation and the harnessing of social change, it owed as much to the reiteration (if not, on occasion, invention) of apostolic traditions, privileges and practices ostensibly going back to the time of the early Church. It was simply that in the eleventh century these claims were now being extended and made tangible, however much the reformers would subordinate the weight of antiquity to a principle of papal discretion when required.

The changing nature of papal authority

The supposed historical establishment of the Church is described in Matthew 16.18–19: 'You are Peter and on this rock I will build my Church and the gates of hell will not prevail against it; and I give you the keys of the kingdom of heaven, and whatsoever you bind on earth shall be bound in heaven, and whatsoever you loose on earth shall be loosed in heaven' (*Tu es Petrus et super hanc petram edificabo ecclesiam meam et portae inferi non prevalebunt adversus eam; et tibi dabo claves regni caelorum, et quodcumque ligaveris super terram, erit ligatum et in caelis, et quodcumque solveris super terram erit solutum et in caelis*). This was understood by early Church writers as the foundation both of the papacy and of papal authority. The nature of this so-called Petrine commission, the granting of the keys, and powers of binding and loosing on earth and in heaven, however, had been a source of much debate in the early Church. Not only had there been various interpretations as to whether the power of the keys was given specifically to Peter or was shared by all the apostles, which some argued was implicit in John 21.15-17, but there was also the troublesome question of whether this power was actually inherited by Peter's successors.[1]

There was, after all, no clear evidence that Peter had directly instituted a successor. Even the chronology of the supposed first three popes was not unequivocally established, with some traditions indicating that Peter had been followed by Linus (*c.*66-*c.*78), then Anacletus (*c.*79-*c.*91) and Clement I (*c.*91-*c.*101), and others suggesting that Clement had been consecrated by Peter as his successor. More worrying, though, was the question of whether a personal commission from Christ, based on Peter's own faith, was somehow transferable. In fact, it was not until the mid-fifth century that Pope Leo I (440-61) definitively formulated the principle that the bishop of Rome, or pope, was Peter's heir, albeit an unworthy one (*indignus haeres beati Petri*).[2] Influenced by Roman law, Leo argued that the pope as Peter's heir, provided that he was properly elected, succeeded to the same legal authority though not to the same personal merit. He thereby made at least tentatively the important distinction between the man and the office, an argument that would later be crucial in legitimizing the actions of even an unworthy pontiff.

Leo's writings were influential in articulating the authority of the pope in other ways. He derived from St Paul his understanding of the Church as *corpus Christi*, or body of Christ. This in turn allowed him to equate the papacy with the *caput* or head, seeing the other churches along with their bishops simply as the *membra* or limbs. This clearly had important implications for the pope's status *vis-à-vis* other bishops. Related to this was Leo's use of the term *plenitudo potestatis* ('fullness of power'), to describe the authority of the pope. Although in the past there has been a tendency to understand this concept in the strongly jurisdictional sense that it would acquire in the thirteenth century (i.e. that only the pope retains the fullness of power given by Christ to Peter), it is likely than Leo understood it in terms of how the authority delegated to a papal legate differed from his own authority, which was full.[3] By the end of the fifth century though, with further articulation of papal pre-eminence in terms of the immunity of the pope from judgment (attributed to Silvester I), such ideas increasingly coalesced and served to bolster a unique jurisdictional position for the pope: the ultimate earthly judge, and thus one who could be judged by God alone.

Other developments contributed both to the elucidation and amplification of papal authority in the early middle ages. From the time of Constantine's acceptance of Christianity after the battle of Milvian Bridge in 312, the Church had evolved in the context of a world delineated by the Roman Empire and ruled by an emperor, whose power had formerly been absolute in both secular and religious matters. With the acceptance of Christianity as the official religion, this balance was henceforth altered: the Roman emperor became not only the special protector of the Church but crucially also her son (*filius*). Moreover, as Ambrose's censure of Emperor Theodosius in 390 made only too clear, the emperor was a son subject to the Church's authority in religious and moral matters. Although the precise nature of the relationship between ecclesiastical (especially papal), and secular authority would not be clarified for centuries (and as a consequence was frequently contested), by the late fifth century Pope Gelasius I (492–96) made what would become perhaps the most important definition of their respective powers.

In his famous letter to Emperor Anastasius during the Acatian schism, Gelasius began by arguing that the world was ruled by two powers: the sacred or consecrated authority of bishops (*auctoritas sacrata pontificum*) and the royal power (*regalis potestas*).[4] These, as Gelasius understood it, were obliged to work in harmony in order to fulfil God's intentions for humanity. Gelasius concluded the letter, however, by stating that the priestly authority was the weightier, as priests would be expected to answer for the souls of all men, even kings, at the Last Judgment. Together with Gelasius' other writings, especially the *Tomus de anathemate vinculo*, as well as his willingness both to wield the spiritual sword of excommunication and to direct the material sword in the Church's interests, the ideas afforded the papacy, in theory at least, a formidable position of authority.

In the mid-fifth century, Leo I called Rome the *caput orbis*, or head of the world, by virtue of its being the seat of St Peter. In reality though, the papal headship of the Church was rather limited, whatever would subsequently be made of the implications of Leo and Gelasius' ideas on the authority of the pope. Indeed in the early Church and for all intents and purposes to *circa* 1000, the pope as Peter's successor was known chiefly as the Bishop of Rome; in fact, the title *papa* was seldom used before the late eleventh century. The pope was effectively the first among equals (*primus inter pares*), meaning among the other bishops, though special esteem was accorded to the Bishop of Rome because the city had been the site of the Apostles' martyrdom. The pontificate of Gregory I (590–604) is instructive here.

Although, like Leo I, he has often been seen as a key figure in the development of what many medieval historians term the 'papal monarchy', Gregory illustrates the theoretically strong, but in practical terms restricted position of the pope in the early Church. Gregory referred to himself as the 'servant of the servants of God' (*servus servorum Dei*), a title adopted by many of his successors particularly from the second half of the eleventh century. This not only underlined his humility, but also reinforced Gregory's understanding both of papal authority and the pope's pastoral role. Gregory clearly was convinced that the pope was the jurisdictional as well as the spiritual head of the Church; yet it is evident from the letters in his *Register* that he understood this chiefly in terms of the Roman Church being the final court of appeal rather than as an executive authority. More important for Gregory was the pontiff's pastoral role, which obliged him to have *cura animarum* (care of souls) for all the churches under his headship. This was not, as has often been argued, a claim for 'absolute' authority.[5] Rather, Gregory understood papal primacy in terms of defending and extending the faith, along with securing ultimate appellate jurisdiction in ecclesiastical matters.

In practical terms, therefore, while the pre-eminence of the bishop of Rome was at least theoretically established as elements of doctrine and canon law, it depended on the individual pope whether this jurisdiction and headship was realized. Most often, the pope's power was like that of any other bishop, though he retained certain unique privileges such as convoking universal councils, creating new dioceses, translating bishops and presiding over imperial coronations. There were occasionally popes such as Gregory I and Nicholas I (858–67) who were effective, able leaders, holding councils, sending legates, and extending the faith in England and Bulgaria, thereby making their spiritual headship a reality beyond Rome. Other popes were at the mercy of local aristocratic factions, or were caught up in the politics of the Carolingian and Ottonian empires, as well as contending with the claims of the kings of Italy, the Byzantine emperor and other powerful rulers.

Although the Donation of Constantine (a ninth-century forgery) appeared to grant political power to the pope in Italy, in the centuries before the eleventh century, the pope remained effectively a spiritual leader, bishop of his city, with little consistent authority beyond its environs. As indicated in Chapter 1, the papacy was effective just one localized centre of power in a Latin West made up of local centres.[6] There was no *sustained* attempt by pre-eleventh-century pontiffs to arrogate to themselves 'political' power as universal leaders, beyond their claims to universality in spiritual terms. Indeed, such a concept would have been meaningless before the reformers of the eleventh century separated the secular and the divine. This is not to suggest that the pope had no authority beyond that of any other bishop. On the contrary, and as is increasingly apparent during the tenth and early eleventh centuries, papal authority was not only being extended but also was beginning to make itself felt. This can be seen most clearly in the increasing confirmations of immunity and grants of papal *tuitio* (protection) for monasteries, as well as in a shifting perception of the papacy among ecclesiastical writers. In the earlier middle ages, grants of *tuitio* (protection) and privileges of immunity or exemption were generally the prerogatives of secular rulers or local bishops.[7] Far from being signs of weakness in terms of ceding privileges to a particular community, as they have often been viewed in the past, such grants of immunity and/or protection were generally the product of a prolonged process of negotiation, one that is not always evident in the final charter. While such grants invariably involved a redistribution of power or, at the least, a repositioning of relationships, ironically they generally benefited the conceder or donor quite as much as the recipient. In this way, though often taking the form of a transfer, and hence loss of property or rights, charters of immunity and protection confirmed the old maxim that the more one gave away, the more one received. To put it another way, the sheer fact of making and receiving a grant acknowledged the implicit authority of the donor.

For the papacy in particular, which had sporadically taken religious institutions under its protection in the earlier middle ages and increasingly did so after the mid-tenth century, issuing privileges was a means not only of cementing alliances but also of establishing its overlordship.[8] Although in practice the papacy often lacked the power to enforce its rulings beyond Rome and its vicinity, the fact that monasteries increasingly bypassed local authorities in favour of Rome is a clear sign of the increasing significance that Rome played in clerical and monastic perceptions through the later tenth and early eleventh centuries. The papacy was thus able to turn to its own advantage a religious house's desire to thwart the interference of the local diocesan bishop or secular lord. Privileges for Fleury and Cluny provide useful examples.

Cluny has long been seen as the unique model of immunity and papal protection on account of its foundation charter in 910, by which Duke William of Aquitaine placed the monastery under the direct protection of the apostles Peter and Paul, and thus of the papacy. In fact, Cluny lagged behind other monasteries, particularly Fleury, in terms of the scale of the exemptions it secured.[9] Fleury had already, quite exceptionally, gained the right to appeal directly to Rome in the eighth century. But by the late tenth century, the ever-resourceful abbot, Abbo of Fleury, realizing the benefits of negotiating with the papacy over exemptions, gained an exceptional charter from Pope Gregory V (996–99) based on one that he had already forged several years earlier. Not only was the right of appeal to Rome reiterated, but the charter also permitted the abbot of Fleury to over-ride the authority of the local bishop in terms of binding and loosing his monks and subordinates, which fell to the abbot alone. Moreover, Gregory V exempted Fleury from interdiction, which meant the monastery's services could continue even when the diocese was under anathema.[10] It was not until 1024 that Cluny began to obtain similar privileged status with grants from Pope John XIX.[11]

Though such changes may not seem dramatic, their cumulative effect was nothing short of revolutionary in elevating both the prestige and power of the papacy. The case of Gerbert of Aurillac is illustrative here. A famed intellectual who had assumed the archbishopric of Rheims after his predecessor Arnulf had been deposed by Hugh Capet and other French bishops for treason, Gerbert fought a losing battle to secure his office, insisting against Pope John XV that episcopal deposition did not require papal sanction. Ironically, on his elevation as Pope Silvester II in 999, Gerbert himself became an intransigent champion of papal authority. Not only did he authorize his former rival Arnulf to resume his duties as arch-bishop of Rheims on the grounds that his deposition had not been approved by Rome, he also acted swiftly against metropolitans who incurred his disapproval. Even though he persisted in his ideas that most ecclesiastical problems could best be resolved by local councils, Silvester nevertheless insisted upon holding regular papal synods and adroitly defended the papacy's rights.[12] His many privileges for monasteries are further indica-tions of the trend towards the extension of papal authority.[13]

These examples, among many that could be given, reveal a new-found respect for Roman authority from the second half of the tenth century. Further evidence of this shift is apparent in the greater prominence now accorded to the Roman papacy by secular rulers. Otto III's diploma of 1001 granting eight counties to the Roman Church noted that: 'We hold Rome to be the head of the world, and acknowledge the Roman Church as the mother of all churches, though by the carelessness and ignorance of its bishops the clarity of its claims has long been obscured.'[14] Although Otto's diploma effectively rejected the broader claims of the papacy to territorial rule in Italy (as based on the Donation of Constantine), this was not, as Reuter suggested, intended to diminish the papacy. In fact, it is clear that Otto saw the rejuvenation of the papacy as an essential part of his plans for the broad renewal of the 'Roman' empire of the Ottonians. Moreover, it is clear that he sought to achieve this in partnership with Pope Silvester II.[15] Similar co-operation would be a key feature in the reign of Otto's successor, Henry II, who clearly looked to work in partnership with Pope Benedict VIII in the promotion of church reform.

In many ways, increasing respect for papal authority from the mid-tenth to the mid-eleventh centuries can be best viewed through the spectrum of two Roman families: the Crescentians and the Tusculans, whose control of the papacy would have important ramifications for both the promotion and the direction of reform. The families were both descended from the same ancestor, Theophylact, whose origins are obscure, but who came to dominate Rome between 904 and 924.[16] In charge of the papal vestments and treasure (*vestararius*) and as chief soldier (*magister militum)* of the Apostolic See, Theophylact combined military authority with financial power in Rome, where civil administration – insofar as it existed – was intimately connected with the Lateran palace. Theophylact's power passed first to his daughter Marozia and then to his grandson Alberic II, whose son Octavian became Pope John XII. Although rule by the house of Theophylact gave rise, as noted above, to all manner of slanderous tales, at the same time it afforded protection and stability both for the Church and the governance of Rome, whose day-to-day workings were only sporadically shaped by the distant German kings and emperors.

From *c.*975, the Crescentian branch exercised control much as Theophylact, Marozia and Alberic II had done, keeping the papal succession closely linked to, or at least supervised by, their family, with a prominent member controlling public affairs. They revived the ancient title of *patricius* to replace the title of 'city prefect' in order to emphasize their role as guardians of the Apostolic See, even though the Crescentians' landed wealth and power base seem to have lain outside the city.[17] Politically astute, they checked the power of their rivals, the Tusculans, and came to terms with the regency government of the German Empress Theophanu and later with the Emperor Otto III. His subsequent residence in Rome from 999 to 1001 nevertheless threatened the family's dominance of the city and they may well have inspired the city's revolt in 1001. Otto's early death in 1002, and the need of his successor, Henry II, to consolidate his hold on the German kingship, left the Romans once more effectively under Crescentian control. By 1012, however, the Crescentians' dominance at Rome ended in a violent political upheaval that saw the elevation of Theophylact – son of Gregory I, Count of Tusculum – as Pope Benedict VIII.[18]

With his brother Romanus as city prefect, one of Benedict's first acts was a military campaign against the strongholds of the Crescentians outside Rome. Succeeded in 1024 by his brother Romanus as Pope John XIX, and in 1032 by their nephew Benedict IX, the Tusculan popes, while keeping the papacy quite clearly in their family, were not financial profiteers. By and large they did not use their control of the papacy to augment their substantial holdings in Tusculum, in the Sabina, north of Rome, or in Rome itself, where their power remained concentrated in certain parts of the city. Indeed, the Tusculans did not claim the *patricius*, and in fact appear to have used their resources both inside and outside Rome to augment church property, thereby extending the power of the papacy.[19]

Although a layman at his election, Benedict VIII was a particularly vigorous pope. He revived papal authority and was a leading figure in Italian ecclesiastical affairs. Avoiding the subservience of previous pontiffs, Benedict worked in close co-operation with Henry II, confirming privileges for the king's foundation at Bamberg and crowning him emperor in 1014.[20] Although particularly concerned with the preservation of ecclesiastical property, Benedict VIII also foreshadowed the reforming efforts of later eleventh-century popes, first at a council in Ravenna and notably at a council in Pavia in 1022 held with Henry II where stringent prohibitions against clerical concubinage were promulgated.[21] Benedict appears to have great personal admiration for Abbot Odilo of Cluny, and on the whole favoured reforming abbeys.[22]

His successor, John XIX, if somewhat less adept than his brother in co-operating with the new king and emperor, Conrad II, was by no means a puppet.[23] Even more closely associated with Odilo of Cluny, John was particularly solicitous of the cause of monastic immunity, on two occasions confirming Cluny's privileges and taking decisive action on the monks' behalf against the encroachments of Bishop Gauzlin of Mâcon, among many other examples.[24] Even their nephew Benedict IX, the report of whose crimes and deviance became ever more squalid as the later reformers grew in power, was – at least for the first twelve years of his pontificate – an adequate and credible, if not perhaps immensely pious, pontiff. Benedict IX presided over a noteworthy early papal bull of canonization for Simon of Trier; he placed Montecassino under papal protection; and after the Emperor Conrad's death in 1044, he restored the patriarchal status of Grado over Aquilea which John XIX had been forced to reverse.[25]

The seemingly unchallengeable power of the Tusculan popes, which had rested to a large degree on balancing and conciliating rival families as much as on their efforts to extend papal authority, was in the end eclipsed by the actions of Benedict IX. By the autumn of 1044, his position was seriously threatened. Benedict saw off the creation of an 'antipope', Silvester III, but by May 1045 he had 'voluntarily' resigned the papacy to the well-respected archpriest John Gratian, who ascended the papal throne as Gregory VI to the evident relief of reform-minded individuals.[26] Accusations of simony against Gregory VI, however, were soon rife, though no immediate moves were made against him. On an expedition to Italy in the autumn of 1046, King Henry III of Germany presided over a synod of Lombard, German and Burgundian bishops at Pavia. Although the precise content of the decrees promulgated is unknown, it seems that there was some sort of prohibition of simony.[27] Henry then travelled to Piacenza and met Gregory VI, apparently receiving the pope honourably.[28] What occurred next remains unclear, but by December the king had clearly been led to believe that there were certain irregularities in Gregory's elevation. Gregory VI, Benedict IX and the antipope, Silvester III, were ordered by Henry to appear at a synod to be held at Sutri. On 20 December, following an examination of the circumstances of his election, Gregory VI (the only one to appear) was pronounced guilty of simony and was deposed. Silvester III, who had long since returned to his bishopric in Sabina, was condemned for 'invading' the apostolic see, was deprived of orders and ordered to retire to a monastery.[29] Three days later in Rome, Benedict was excommunicated as a simonist and Henry III's German candidate, Bishop Suidger of Bamberg, was elevated to the apostolic see as Clement II.

It is usually thought that Henry III's dismissal of three popes and appointment of another marked the turning-point in the restoration of an internationally respected papacy. Such an outcome, however, was by no means inevitable. After all, by what right did a German monarch intervene in the fortunes of the papacy? He was not yet even acknowledged as emperor. Henry III's actions at Sutri and Rome were, after all, those of a secular ruler, albeit a priest–king (*rex–sacerdos*) who disposed of the papacy in much the same way as the houses of Theophylact or Crescentius had. Though chroniclers such as Hermann of Reichenau sought to justify

Henry's high-handed actions by claiming that he was merely the agent of the synod and the popular will, and had anyway deposed a pope who had long been the subject of censure, it was evident that the initiative was the king's. Moreover, the deposition of Gregory VI by a layman was to many a clear infringement of canon law.[30] Others, however, viewed Henry's actions as perfectly acceptable, including some who had previously rejoiced at the elevation of John Gratian as Gregory VI.[31] It is therefore ironic that what many historians see as the launch of the reformed papacy was brought about by the intrusion of a layman in the affairs of the Church.

While the king's actions were on the whole viewed matter-of-factly, they were not entirely unchallenged. In fact, objections to royal intervention in ecclesiastical affairs had been made earlier in Henry's reign. For instance, on his election to the archbishopric of Lyons, Abbot Halinard of St Bénigne in Dijon had refused to offer the customary oath of fealty to Henry III. Halinard justified his refusal by appeal to scripture and canon law on the unsuitability of clerics making 'private' oaths lest they be foresworn.[32] More relevant perhaps was the condemnation by Bishop of Wazo of Liège of Henry III's intervention in the case of Archbishop Widiger of Ravenna, who had been deposed for celebrating Mass in archiepiscopal vestments prior to his consecration as archbishop.[33] Wazo reiterated these condemnations even more vehemently after Sutri, complaining not only that the king had intervened in the papal succession but also that he had had the temerity to stand in judgment over a Roman pontiff, who was to be judged by God alone.[34]

The most strident reaction to the events at Sutri came from an anonymous French author, whose text is known as *De ordinando pontifice* ('On the ordination of the pope').[35] Although it had little subsequent influence, the text remains a vital source for what took place at Sutri, and it is important for several reasons. Largely ignoring the prevalent canonical sources in favour of the then-less-widely-used Pseudo-Isidorian *Decretals*, it denounced Henry III – a Christian king and emperor – as *nequissimus* (the most evil). Even more significant was the author's implicit defence of priestly, and especially papal, authority through his insistence on the immunity of the pope from judgment under most circumstances. Although the author's intended aim was to demonstrate the episcopate's right to proceed against an 'unworthy' pope, in practice he bolstered the papacy's position by denying any such right to an emperor. Although attempts by rulers to appoint and depose popes would by no means end after Sutri, doing so would become increasingly difficult and would entail a very high price.

The transformation of the papacy

The elevation of Bishop Bruno of Toul as Pope Leo IX on 12 February 1049 has long been seen as the decisive moment in the fortunes of both the papacy and the movement for ecclesiastical reform. Although the German popes, Clement II (December 1046–October 1047) and Damasus II (July–August 1048), designated by Henry III after Sutri gave indications of their intentions to pursue reform measures, their pontificates were too brief for any major initiatives. Yet, by taking the names of popes from the apostolic age, they at least signalled a return to the supposedly purer traditions of the early Church.[36] By most contemporary accounts, however, their successor Leo IX was the reformer *par excellence*.

As bishop of Toul, he had been a champion of monastic reform, placing the monasteries of St Evroul, St Mansuy and Moyenmoutier under the oversight of the renowned reformer, William of Volpiano. Leo had also founded a priory at Deuilly and had been a strong advocate of the nunnery at Poussay, founded by his predecessor at Toul, Berthold. When designated by the Emperor Henry III as successor to Damasus II in 1048, Leo reportedly declared that he would not ascend the papal throne unless the clergy and people of Rome unanimously and freely elected him as pope.[37] Even his subsequent journey to Rome was said to have been marked by miraculous events, with Leo apparently hearing the voices of angels.[38] His pontificate has been seen by contemporaries and modern historians alike as an auspicious one and, in many ways, Leo was a model for how the Roman papacy could assume tangible leadership over the universal Church.

It is important, though, to not lose the perspective afforded by a closer examination of Bruno/Leo's early career, which was not necessarily what contemporaries might have expected of a holy, reforming bishop and pope. Born in 1002, Bruno came from a prominent lineage traceable back to the late seventh-century Alsatian Etichonide family.[39] Though his hagiographer predictably claimed royal blood for his parents, for once this was not wishful thinking as he was related, albeit distantly, to the Salian dynasty that would assume the German kingship on the death of the last Ottonian, Henry II. As a younger son, Bruno was inevitably destined for the Church, and at the age of five, he was made an oblate in the cathedral chapter at Toul where he was taken under the bishop's personal supervision. After Henry II's death, Bruno was sent by his family to join the entourage of his kinsman, the new king, Conrad II, who installed him in his *Hofkapelle* or royal chapel, that notable training ground for future imperial bishops.

Bruno accompanied the king on his expedition to Italy in 1025 at the head of troops supplied from Toul, during which he was promoted to bishop of that city when news of the death of the former bishop reached the king. Though the *Life of Leo* described how the clergy petitioned the king for Bruno's appointment (also emphasizing Bruno's protests of unworthiness), the election probably had as much to do with Conrad's political objectives (Toul being an important city on the western frontier) and family connections, and even a possible instance of simony. This context needs to be remembered when considering not just Leo's promotion to the papacy by Henry III in 1048, but also his subsequent demands for a 'free and canonical' election. At least in respect to church appointment, Leo was neither an anti-imperialist nor a revolutionary reformer. It is clear that he in no way rejected or otherwise challenged the emperor's right to designate candidates to vacant sees and abbacies, and in fact he saw lay rulers as indispensable partners in promoting the moral reform of the clergy. For Leo IX, it was simply that the clergy and people must voluntarily 'acclaim' a designated candidate.

Nevertheless, the significance of Leo's pontificate for the future direction of both the papacy and of ecclesiastical reform cannot be under-estimated. His use of papal legates and especially his many reforming councils, both in Rome and north of the Alps, mark the beginnings of the transformation of the papacy from being a significant if essentially passive institution into one which had seized the initiative. Although it must be remembered that attempts to improve standards in religious life had begun long before his elevation, with Leo there are the first clear moves towards establishing a group of similarly reform-minded individuals at Rome itself. These included the future cardinal-bishop of Silva-Candida, Humbert of Moyenmoutier, Archdeacon Frederick of Liège, brother of Duke Godfrey of Lower Lotharingia and later Abbot of Montecassino before becoming Pope Stephen IX (1057–8) after the pontificate of Leo's successor, Victor II (1055–7), and Hugh the White from the monastery of Rémiremont, who served as a papal legate to Spain and later became cardinal-priest of St Clemente. Archbishop Halinard of Lyons, whom Leo had known from his time in Toul, though he seldom visited Rome, remained a constant source of advice after his friend's elevation to the Petrine See, as did the ascetic hermit Peter Damian, who made his presence felt through many letters to the pope and to others, while continuing to reside at Fonte Avellana. Perhaps most significant, Leo also recalled to Rome the young Hildebrand, who had accompanied Gregory VI into exile in Germany after his deposition. Hildebrand was elevated to the rank of archdeacon and was initially placed in charge of the estates of St Paul's without the Walls.

Among the most significant aspects of Leo's pontificate was the emphasis he placed upon reasserting the legislative prerogatives of the papacy. Indeed, apart from Peter Damian, Leo was among the first of the reformers to recognize the advisability of promoting canon law as a means of more successfully pursuing the reformist agenda against simony, clerical marriage and concubinage. For instance, in April 1049 at the first of his reforming councils in Rome, Leo opened the proceedings with a solemn reconfirmation of the canons of the first four ecumenical councils, and then ordered that all the decrees of his predecessors be confirmed and obeyed. Only then, having established the weight of papal authority, did he turn to his own condemnations of simony and other abuses.[40] Although the actual canons are not extant, it is clear that simony was the principal issue. Indeed it seems that Leo initially attempted to depose clergy of every rank who had either obtained their offices by simony or who had knowingly allowed themselves to be ordained by simonists. When it was protested that liturgical services would cease and that society would be left without pastors if such a measure were enacted, Leo apparently agreed to re-promulgate the more moderate decree of Clement II, which had imposed a penance of forty days on those knowingly ordained by simonists.[41] According to Damian, Leo also took stringent measures against clerical concubinage at the Roman council of 1049, even stipulating that wives and concubines of priests were to be declared unfree and become the property of the Lateran palace.[42] Simony, clerical marriage and concubinage would also be the preoccupations of Leo's councils at Rheims and Mainz later that year.

Leo's pontificate, however, ended in disastrous circumstances. After devoting himself almost exclusively to the promotion of his vision of reform for two years, he found himself embroiled in political struggles with the Normans, who had arrived in southern Italy in the 1030s as mercenaries for Lombard and Byzantine princes, and who now, under leaders such as Robert Guiscard and Roger of Aversa, were setting up their own kingdoms at the expense both of the Byzantine principalities and the papal patrimony. Matters came to a head after Leo accepted the overlordship of Benevento at the request of its inhabitants. In 1052, in the midst of negotiations with the Byzantine emperor, and after his plea for assistance from Henry III brought no aid, Leo himself decided to command an army against the Normans, justifying this by their arbitrary violence and persecution of the people. The result was an overwhelming defeat of the papal army at Civitate in June 1053, at which Leo himself was captured by the Normans and subsequently held in captivity until shortly before his death in April 1054. His successor, Victor II, held office from 1055 to 1057, which was far too short a period for much to be accomplished. Yet Henry III's death in 1056 – which left his three-year-old son, Henry IV, as king and heir to the empire – would have far-reaching implications for the papacy, ones that meant that Leo's vision of partnership between pope and emperor in the work of church reform would have to be fundamentally altered.

As was the case with Victor II, the pontificate of Stephen IX (1057–58) was all too brief, though he was the first pope to have been elected since 1045 without consultations having first been made with the German court. That said, he found time to appoint the zealous reformer, Peter Damian, to the cardinal-bishopric of Ostia, and also made Humbert papal chancellor, thereby strongly reinforcing the links of the reform papacy with monastic interests. After all, Pope Stephen had been abbot of the great Benedictine monastery of Montecassino before his elevation. Taken with Hildebrand's promotion by Pope Leo, Stephen's appointments of Humbert and Damian saw to it that the papacy was now closely advised by three of the most committed reformers of the age.

Following the sudden, if not wholly unexpected, death at Florence on 29 March 1058 of Pope Stephen IX, who had been seriously ill for some months, the Tusculan nobility made an attempt to regain the papacy by quickly electing Cardinal-Bishop John of Velletri as Pope Benedict X.[43] Although the reformers refused to accept Benedict, there was no immediate reaction until some time after October when five cardinal-bishops, along with Hildebrand, met in Siena and elected Bishop Gerard of Florence, a Burgundian by birth, as their new pope. Taking the name of Nicholas II, he was not enthroned in Rome until 24 January 1059, and only then through the military assistance of Duke Godfrey of Lower Lotharingia.

The legitimacy of Nicholas II's election was debatable. This left the reformers in an unenviable position, since the election of Benedict X at Rome had at least followed the requirements of canon law (such as they were), even if the customary rights of the emperor and those emerging ones of the cardinal-bishops had been ignored. Furthermore, Benedict himself scarcely presented the image of a wicked usurper. As Cardinal-Bishop of Velletri, he was a well-known figure in Roman ecclesiastical circles and his election probably enjoyed large support. The much delayed election of Nicholas II outside Rome in the presence of a small number of clerics, and the even longer delay in his enthronement, must have seemed rather more irregular, and hence lacking in legitimacy. The situation clearly left the reformers in a quandary, not only revealing a potentially serious lack of agreement among them, but at the same time underlining the inadequacy of existing procedures for papal elections. The result was ultimately a new decree.

The strictures that governed election to the papacy in the earlier middle ages were, to put it mildly, rather loose. Indeed, the canonical norms that existed were chiefly those that regulated the election of *any* bishop, and such ideals were seldom preserved in practice. The procedures for episcopal elections had developed between the fourth and sixth centuries, with Leo I describing a proper election as one that took place in an atmosphere of peace and calm.[44] Ostensibly, the clergy were to take the lead in the selection of candidates. These candidates were ideally to be members of the local clergy, and were to be at least thirty years of age and sexually continent, though in practice under-age or 'boy bishops' were far from unknown.[45] The higher clergy and nobility of the region were then to give testimony to a candidate's suitability, and finally the lesser clergy and 'people' were to give their consent. Above all, no candidate was to be forced upon an unwilling clergy and people. Before consecration of a new bishop, the metropolitan bishop was to confirm the suitability of the candidate, with any disputed or contested elections being referred to Rome. This at least was the theory. In reality, however, throughout the earlier middle ages, most bishops, including the bishop of Rome, were nobles with important family connections, who were designated by the emperor or some other important secular power. Not infrequently, these bishops were laymen or monks (who had not necessarily been ordained as priests) at the time of their selection, and thus had to be ordained as priests before promotion to the seat of St Peter.

Despite the reasonable amount of information in canon law and various pontificals (books containing liturgical ceremonies, masses and prayers) for the procedures regulating the election and especially the consecration of new bishops, there is surprisingly little evidence within canon law of rules specifically governing the election of the bishop of Rome himself. While an *ordo* for papal elections was promulgated at the Lateran Council of 769, which stipulated that a cardinal-priest or deacon of the Roman Church should be elected as pope and subsequently be confirmed by the Roman laity, this appears to have been either largely unknown or at least unused. Further Carolingian legislation had emphasized that the election of the pope was the business of the Romans alone, but had made little mention of actual procedures. Indeed, as the eleventh-century author of *On the ordination of the pope* made only too plain, in his effort to present a canonical alternative to what Henry III had done at Sutri, there was no real guidance in canon law apart from the forgotten *ordo* of 769 and stipulations regarding the new pope's consecration, which was a time-honoured prerogative of the cardinal-bishops of Ostia, Porto and Albano.[46] Thus promulgation in 1059 of a decree that laid down clear rules for the election of a pope was not only a decided innovation, but it also constituted a significant attempt by the papacy to regulate its own affairs. How did this come about?

In 1057 when Peter Damian was appointed to the cardinal-bishopric of Ostia, the privileges of the cardinal-bishops were essentially the liturgical ones discussed in Chapter 1. Damian took the opportunity to advance what has been termed his 'Lateran ideology'. In a theologically complicated letter to the other cardinal-bishops, Damian used the unique status of the Lateran basilica – the *ecclesia Salvatoris* – and the universality it conferred, to derive a 'political' role for the cardinal-bishops: the right *to elect* a new pope instead of their strictly liturgical prerogatives inherent in their right to *consecrate* a new pontiff.[47] In the aftermath of the contested election of 1058–59, Damian returned to his earlier ideas and, appealing to what he understood as the constitutive role of the cardinal-bishops in the elevation of a pope, laid the groundwork for the new decree.[48]

The task that faced the reformers, however, was not simply to deny the claims of Benedict X and to promote those of Nicholas II. Rather, their aim was to establish how papal authority and the privileges of St Peter were uniquely conferred on a legitimate pope. This meant dispensing with the idea that election and especially consecration had to take place at Rome to confer papal authority. Damian had addressed this issue in his earlier letter of 1058 to Nicholas and Hildebrand, where he had indicated that a legitimately elected pope was already the head of the Church on earth and fully invested with the powers of St Peter and his office.[49] Behind this lay the concept whose implications had yet to be fully grasped, that a true *electus* was in full jurisdictional possession of his office even before consecration.[50] Damian's earlier Lateran ideology also solved the problem of defining who was empowered to elect the pope and to convey his legitimacy: the primary role would be restricted to the cardinal-bishops whom Benedict X had ignored to his peril.

Nicholas II's legitimacy was ultimately provided by the papal election decree issued at his important reforming synod of 1059, which will be discussed in further detail below. According to the decree's preface, the new legislation had been prompted by the confusion that had followed Stephen IX's death. Thus, in a striking acknowledgement of the ambiguity of the canons previously regulating papal elections, the decree was consciously framed to eliminate all uncertainty for the future. Furthermore, by preparing for various contingencies, the decree of 1059 was clearly designed to re-secure the hold upon the Roman Church that the Roman reforming circle had almost lost during the brief but nonetheless significant schism. The primary role was confined to the cardinal-bishops, whose decision was to be confirmed by the clergy and people of Rome.[51]

It also fell to the cardinal-bishops to ensure the worthiness of candidates. This was justified by the rather strained analogy that as the apostolic see, unlike other bishops, had no superior or metropolitan to undertake the role of oversight, the cardinal-bishops as electors were the only possible custodians of integrity. Following the tradition of the *ordo* of 769, the *gremium* ('bosom') of the Church, meaning the Roman Church itself, was the preferred source of candidates. Most important though, the decree of 1059 sanctioned election by the cardinal-bishops *outside* Rome, even if only in the presence of a small audience of clergy and laymen, when circumstances such as war or other intimidation might hinder a free and canonical election.[52]

The most significant canon for developments in papal authority, however, was the explicit affirmation of the powers of a legitimate papal *electus*.[53] This canon was reiterated at the Roman Council of 1060, where it was emphasized that a papal *electus* had the same status as an enthroned pope. Behind this lay the first clear re-articulations of the important distinction that went back to Leo I between the purely jurisdictional and the purely sacramental powers of papal office. According to the decree of 1059, a legitimate papal *electus* obtained the power of ruling and disposing (*auctoritas regendi et disponendi*). These represented the non-priestly powers of the pope: in other words, jurisdictional and administrative headship over the Church and her members (both clerical and lay), and, even more important, stewardship of the Church's properties and possessions. What is so very striking about this clause is the acknowledgment that before 1059 enthronement had been the decisive element in papal elections.[54] In other words, before 1059, only an enthroned and consecrated pontiff had entered into full jurisdictional possession of his office. Not surprisingly, the implications of this – especially in terms of Nicholas II's exercise of office prior to enthronement – were conveniently set aside.[55] Even more striking, this canon was an exceptional clause, valid only when war or unrest prevented consecration and enthronement at Rome. Otherwise, under normal circumstances, only with enthronement would the pope exercise the full *auctoritas regendi et disponendi*.[56]

71

This is not to suggest that henceforth papal elections followed the stipulations of the decree of 1059. They most assuredly did not. Most papal elections were 'irregular' in one way or another until well into the twelfth century and even beyond, though the decree provided a convenient precedent that could be used to bolster or deny the claims of rival candidates. Others simply ignored the decree. The canonist and cardinal-priest Deusdedit, for instance, never ceased to rail against it, and he included the old papal *ordo* of 769 in his canonical collection, probably with some self-interest on account of the *ordo*'s stipulations that either a cardinal-priest or deacon be elected. Moreover, the decree did not, as some historians have seemed to claim, completely preclude any role for the emperor.

The decree of 1059 in fact conceded to the infant King Henry IV 'due honour and dignity', but made it clear that this was a concession from the Roman Church and *not* an automatic right. At this stage, it is unlikely that Nicholas II's supporters and the framers of the decree intended to exclude the emperor from any part in papal elections. Yet the wording indicated a sharp difference from the days of Henry III. It is this and the exceptional clauses that reveal the decree's political and perhaps ultimately propagandistic quality. It was clearly intended to justify Nicholas II's legitimacy, but also and perhaps especially to fortify the position of the reformers in a world that was changing dramatically. With the young king, Henry IV, destined for a long minority, imperial interests were increasingly recognized by the Roman reforming circle as merely one of the forces – and certainly not the most powerful – to be taken into account. The subsequent papal alliance with the Norman rulers Robert Guiscard and Richard of Capua only reinforced this, as did similar rapprochement with other secular princes at this time. The papacy was beginning to look ever more outwards, and slowly but surely the claims of papal authority were being extended or least made effective.

The election decree of 1059 also had the effect of exposing a degree of disunity among the reformers and hence it exposed the realigning of positions and interests that are often ignored in the accounts of most modern historians. For instance, Peter Damian alienated some of the reformers after Stephen's death, apparently trying to use the occasion to resign from the cardinal-bishopric of Ostia. Though he in no way supported Benedict X, Damian, it seems, was perceived as having some reservations about Nicholas II.[57] The only source is a letter written by Damian to Hildebrand and Nicholas II, in which he sought to make amends and to excuse what appears to have been a sudden resignation of his office. It is unlikely that Damian had any specific complaint against Nicholas. The possible taint of simony on Nicholas, who had been consecrated as bishop of Florence by Gregory VI – a charge that was apparently levelled in an imperial condemnation of 1060 – would not have troubled Damian, who insisted on the validity of those men who were freely ordained even if by simonists.

Whether Damian, along with Humbert and the new Abbot of Monte-cassino, Desiderius, was concerned about the extension of the power of Stephen's brother, Duke Godfrey of Lower Lotharingia, who had been instrumental in enthroning Nicholas II, remains a matter of speculation. It is clear, though, that certain reformers, chiefly Hildebrand, were exploring various political alliances to further reform aims. Duke Godfrey had undeniably figured in his brother's plans to contain the Normans and extend papal influence over the southern Italian Church. Hildebrand's legation to the German court on behalf of Stephen in 1058 had been aimed at least in part in obtaining imperial consent to Godfrey's acquisition of Camerino-Spoleto in southern Italy. As Nicholas II initially tried to support Godfrey's lordship there before making peace with the Normans, it is fair to assume that Godfrey looked to reap the benefit of supporting Nicholas.[58]

What is undeniable is that the status of Archdeacon Hildebrand among the Roman reforming circle was increasingly becoming divisive, and in fact it is likely that he had played a significant role in the election of Nicholas II. Stephen IX had, after all, sworn the Romans, if he died, to refrain from electing a new pope until Hildebrand's return. When Hildebrand returned from the German court with imperial consent to the extension of Duke Godfrey's power, he found that the unwelcome election of Benedict X had already taken place. In order to placate Duke Godfrey, whose support he deemed as crucial as a counterbalance to both the Normans and the minority government in Germany, Hildebrand looked for a candidate who would at least be receptive to the extension of Godfrey's power in Italy. For Hildebrand, Bishop Gerard of Florence was an ideal papal candidate, one who, as a known reformer and a bishop in Tuscany (where Godfrey's wife Beatrice ruled), would serve all interests.

These frictions, or realignments among the reformers, can also be seen in the legislation of Nicholas II's important council at Rome in 1059. In addition to the papal election decree, the council issued strident condemnations of simony and clerical marriage, in an effective summary of the preoccupations that had been at the forefront of reform since the early part of the century. Yet at the same time, there were moves towards extending reform initiatives to regulate the communal or common life of canons, who, unlike monks, were individually permitted under the Rule of Aix to own private property. Perhaps echoing the stipulation enjoined by Leo IX on the canons of Lucca, Hildebrand strongly advocated a stricter life for canons in which property would be held in common. Despite his apparent vehemence, the stipulations were watered down in the final decree, which advised but did not actually insist that canons reject personal property.[59]

Other changes were also afoot, which were beginning to position the papacy further from the co-operation with the emperor advocated by Leo IX. In the first place, there was the highly significant reversal of Leo IX's antagonistic policy towards the Normans late in 1059.[60] Whether this was the initiative of Hildebrand or of Abbot Desiderius of Montecassino remains unclear, but Nicholas was persuaded to seek a rapprochement with the Normans, clearly as a counterpoise to the Germans. At Melfi in August, the pope recognized the Normans' rights to most of southern Italy, which still remained largely in either Byzantine or Muslim hands. Robert Guiscard was invested with Apulia, Calabria and Sicily (which had not yet even been conquered) in return for swearing obedience to the papacy, promising to defend the rights of St Peter, and undertaking to pay an annual tribute in recognition of the papacy's overlordship. With these new allies, who were among the first of the *fideles sancti Petri* (the vassals of St Peter), the papacy – by asserting its claims to control over southern Italy and by securing Norman financial and military assistance – was positioning itself firmly at the forefront of political affairs. As a consequence, the papacy was enhancing its ability to exert control over all the churches of Latin Christendom.

At the same time, other events in northern Italy prompted the first unambiguous articulation of papal authority in centuries. Written by Peter Damian, the text known as *De privilegio Romanae ecclesiae* ('On the privilege of the Roman Church') revealed the extent to which earlier claims had made an impact. Ostensibly, the text was a report of a legation to Milan in 1059, undertaken by Damian and Bishop Anselm I of Lucca (later Pope Alexander II) at the request of Pope Nicholas II. The legates had been charged with investigating the turbulent situation in the city that had resulted from attempts by a group of lower clergy and laymen known as the Pataria to impose reform, even by force, upon a largely unwilling Milanese clergy.[61] The papacy had actively supported the Pataria's initiatives against simony and clerical marriage since 1057, when the movement's leaders Ariald and Landulf Cotta had come to Rome following their excommunication *in absentia* at a synod in Fonteveto. At that time, Pope

Stephen IX had sent a legation to Milan, but this had served only to deepen suspicion towards Rome among the Milanese clergy. In many ways, the embassy to Milan was a test case. The see was regarded as having been saved from the Arian heresy by St Ambrose after his election as bishop in 374 and, as a consequence, it claimed a high degree of autonomy. If the reforming papacy could intervene successfully in Milan, its claims to a universal primacy would have to be taken more seriously.

The *De privilegio* was addressed to Hildebrand, and acknowledged his well-known request for a collection of decrees setting out the privileges and authority of the apostolic see. This itself indicates the extent to which reformers were turning to canon law to bolster their position. At the heart of the treatise, and especially the sermon that Damian apparently preached in Milan, was a powerful statement of Roman primacy, and consequently of Rome's right to determine the norms of clerical life.[62]

Damian had begun his sermon by saying that he had not journeyed to Milan to enhance the honour of Rome but out of concern for the spiritual well-being of his audience.[63] His main purpose, though, was a statement of the universality of jurisdiction of the *ecclesia Romana*, which had been founded by Christ alone, and from which no one was exempt.[64] For Damian, Christ had exclusively given the privilege of jurisdiction (that is, of binding and loosing) to St Peter, and thus to the Roman Church, whose special status had been further enhanced by the martyrdom of the Apostles in that city.[65] In this, he was refining an argument advanced in his letter to Nicholas and Hildebrand in 1058 noted above, where he had drawn the conclusion, echoing Leo I, that the unique privilege –the universality of Rome's jurisdiction – was continued in Peter's true successors.[66]

Damian next considered the repercussions of any failure both to acknowledge and to be obedient to Roman authority. He then vehemently proclaimed that anyone who either denied or disregarded this authority in matters of the correct faith automatically fell into heresy.[67] Hildebrand/ Gregory VII would later take this further, equating the term *hereticus* with any act of disobedience to the papacy.[68] Even so, Damian's sermon was a remarkable definition of the new-found status of the papacy. For him, the failure of the Milanese was less their refusal to obey Rome but rather their implicit denial of the universality of Rome's right to overlordship. The ramifications of such ideas are obvious. Although in the end the legation effected no real amelioration in the situation in Milan, Damian's *De privilegio* – unintentionally perhaps – gave the papacy an extremely potent justification of the absolute primacy of the Roman pontiff. These ideas would be refined by Nicholas' successors and their canon lawyers, effectively giving the pope a mandate to intervene wherever and whenever he deemed the interests of the Church so required.

Following Nicholas' death in 1061, another schism arose that would scar the papacy's relations with the empire for the remainder of the century, and as a consequence would also have important ramifications for co-operation between the two powers in the promotion of reform. In July 1061 after Nicholas's death, the Roman populace sent envoys to the young Henry IV, still a minor, asking for the designation of a new pope. Before any reply was received, on 30 September, the reformers – now led definitively by Hildebrand (Humbert had died on 5 May) – elected Bishop Anselm of Lucca as Pope Alexander II, and installed him the following day with military assistance from the Norman leader and papal vassal, Richard of Capua. At the German court in late October, however, Bishop Cadalus of Parma was selected as Pope Honorius II. This was apparently at the instigation of Wibert, the imperial chancellor in Lombardy, along with the support of the delegation that had arrived from Rome, the Lombard bishops, and probably a significant number of German bishops who had participated in the earlier condemnation of Nicholas II.

When the subsequent struggle to possess Rome by both men proved indecisive, they agreed at the suggestion of Duke Godfrey to return to their respective sees until a council could be convened in the presence of the king. Although support for Cadalus had initially seemed stronger, a variety of circumstances favoured Alexander, chiefly the *coup* through which the reform-minded Archbishop Anno of Cologne brought the young Henry IV under his direct tutelage. In October 1062, the council at Augsburg provisionally recognized Alexander as the legitimate pope, though a final decision was reserved until such time as Bishop Burchard of Halberstadt could further investigate the accusations of simony against Alexander. Yet even when Alexander had been fully restored to the apostolic throne, armed forces supporting Cadalus once again attacked Rome.

While on a legation in France, Peter Damian seems to have again raised the issue of Alexander's legitimacy by appealing in a letter to Anno of Cologne for a new council to deliberate on the schism.[69] Though Damian later insisted to Alexander and Hildebrand that his concern was solely the danger presented to the Christian faith by the schism and not Alexander's worthiness, the letter once more revealed the chronic friction amongst the reformers at Rome.[70] Tension had already been apparent in Damian's *Disceptatio synodalis*, written to promote a favourable decision for Alexander at the synod of Augsburg. With its emphasis on the necessity of conciliar debate, the treatise suggests that Damian may well have been looking to persuade those, like Hildebrand, who (he may have felt) were not prepared to bring the problem to an imperial council and preferred to rely on the military might of their Norman allies to bring the schism to an end.[71]

Although Alexander was allowed to preside at the subsequent synod held at Mantua in 1064, he was humiliatingly forced to respond publicly to the charge of simony with a sacred oath.[72] This surely contributed to Damian's steadily deteriorating relations with Alexander and Hildebrand, which effectively continued until Damian's death in 1072. The schism, however, left its mark not only among the Hildebrandine camp, in a new sense of intransigence and unwillingness to compromise that seems evident in the rift with Damian, but also in the suspicion the schism engendered between the reformers and the German court and episcopate, which would make it increasingly difficult for the Germans to fall into line with reform measures promulgated in Rome.

The pontificate of Alexander II (1061–73) was an extremely important one for the reform movement and papacy alike, far more so than is often recognized. After the resolution of the schism, Alexander pursued the promotion of reform with vigour in the manner of his predecessors, especially Nicholas II, whose programme he largely reiterated. Alexander held numerous councils in Rome, promoted the Pataria in their reform efforts in Milan, and waged a concerted campaign against simony and the misuse of ecclesiastical resources. Unlike his predecessors, he retained the bishopric of Lucca during his pontificate, and his material efforts both in terms of consolidating ecclesiastical property and the rebuilding of the cathedral there are further indications of his work to promote ecclesiastical authority.

There is also evidence that Alexander was increasingly concerned with lay interference in the promotion of abbots and especially bishops. This is not to suggest that there were any specific moves against lay interests at this time, in spite of Humbert of Silva-Candida's treatise *Three Books against the Simoniacs*, where he had warned that lay investiture needed to be suppressed, as it invariably led to simony.[73] Rather, Alexander looked where possible to secure respect for ecclesiastical independence. The Norman conquest of England and the elevation of Lanfranc to the archbishopric of Canterbury in particular offered a welcome opportunity for Alexander to reorganize the English Church in line with the principles of reform. William the Conqueror was seen as a model partner in the work of reform and also the means of securing the removal of the despised former Archbishop of Canterbury, Stigand, who had received his *pallium* from the anti-pope Benedict X. In Germany too, in 1066, the occasion of Henry IV's majority seemed initially to be a cause of celebration. But when the king, perhaps predictably, failed to be the (subservient) 'partner' that Alexander and the Roman reformers desired, several of the king's advisors were excommunicated just prior to the pope's death. The papacy under Alexander II had now come to see itself as a force directing affairs: rulers who co-operated were beloved sons, while those who did not were to be sternly rebuked, and firmly shown their place in the new order of things. The papacy was coming of age.

On 23 August 1073, the day after his predecessor's death, the most passionate of all advocates of reform, Hildebrand, was swept onto the apostolic throne as Gregory VII, in a tumultuous election. Although, as Cowdrey rightly emphasizes, he did not operate with a fixed agenda, but rather responded, even in somewhat *ad hoc* fashion, to events and situations as they unfolded, Gregory VII first and foremost had a sense of mission.[74] He lived and acted with the unshakable conviction of the pope's right and duty to intervene at all levels of Christian society. It was a conviction that was to remain as strong in effective defeat and exile in Salerno after 1084 as it had been at the outset of his papacy.

Though there will be much more to be said about Gregory and his attitude towards reform in following chapters, it is his understanding of papal authority and the position of the pope as the head of the Church that is our chief concern here. Believing that it was imperative for clergy of whatever rank to be thoroughly versed both in the rules of religion and holy scripture, Gregory felt that this was all the more important for the pope, who, as St Peter's representative, was the earthly judge of *iustitia* (justice). This conviction is nowhere more apparent than when, in a letter summoning the bishops and abbots of Brittany to a council in Rome in 1074, Gregory succinctly and with characteristic force expressed his understanding of the pope's role. The burden of office required that he not only oversee the affairs of all churches, but also that he ensure that they maintained both the Christian faith and the dictates of scripture. Insisting that they attend the forthcoming council, he noted that he was aware that they were not as diligent as they ought to be.[75] For Gregory VII, it was the pope's duty to be both the definer of canonical norms as well as the arbiter of faith.

Claiming throughout his pontificate that everything he did or enjoined others to do in his behalf was in accordance with canon law, Gregory, more forcefully than his predecessors, insisted on the pope's right, and indeed duty, to legislate for the needs of the Church. As the decrees from his many reforming councils demonstrate, Gregory saw it as the pope's obligation to correct what needed to be corrected and to confirm what needed to be confirmed.[76] This attitude is perhaps nowhere more apparent than in the *Dictatus papae*, the twenty-seven sentences on the powers of the papacy inserted in his *Register* as 2.55a, that acknowledged the pope's power not only to depose emperors, to accept the judgment of inferiors, and even to be regarded as a saint, but also to make law 'according to necessity'. What is most striking about these sentences, however, is the fact that not only were all the papacy's powers now drawn up in one single document, but also that, with only a few exceptions, these principles were supported by long-standing canonical tradition.[77] Real innovation, and hence a seeming break with canonical tradition, could be seen in only a few of the sentences: that the pope alone was to be called universal (2), that he could depose the absent (5), that he could depose emperors (12), that with his permission inferiors could judge superiors (24), and that he could absolve sworn oaths of fidelity (27).

What is even more intriguing is the fact that many of these principles were rarely exercised in practice. While later detractors characterized Gregory, together with Urban II and the canon lawyers Anselm of Lucca and Desiderius, as effectively using *Dictatus papae* as their agenda, in fact Gregory tended far more often to react to situations as they happened. For instance, in his dealings with the German bishops, in whose eyes he was a 'dangerous man', Gregory had recourse to judging them *in absentia* only when all other measures to force to them to Rome to answer charges proved ineffective. Although he did on occasion accept the accusations of inferiors against their superiors, by and large he acted within canonical norms. Even in his claim of the right to depose emperors, there were precedents in canon law.[78] Gregory's real innovation, and ultimately his significance, lay above all in the uncompromising language in which he set out apostolic prerogatives and demanded adherence to them. It is in this context that his reform legislation needs to be viewed. Apart from the decree against lay investiture, most of his decrees against simony, clerical marriage and lay interference were not new in themselves. It was simply that they were increasingly promulgated in the context of the ecclesiological and political battles being waged between Gregory and his opponents in northern Italy and Germany. As a consequence, these measures and especially any transgression of them effectively became issues of 'right belief', about which Gregory VII could never compromise.

It is impossible here to discuss in any kind of detail the ever-deteriorating relationship between Gregory and King (later emperor)

Henry IV which led to their first rupture in 1076, and the final clash in 1080 that resulted in Henry's promotion of the anti-pope Clement III.[79] What is of relevance here is what the conflict meant for the position of the papacy. At the outset of his pontificate, despite concern over the continued presence of the excommunicate advisers near the king, Gregory clearly looked to Henry IV as a partner in the promotion of reform, frequently addressing him in his letters as 'beloved son'. Indeed, Gregory regarded Henry as the appropriate person to whom he intended to entrust the Church when he thought of embarking on crusade in 1074.[80] But Gregory and Henry's conceptions of their respective roles within Latin Christendom made a clash almost inevitable. This was exacerbated in part by Henry's need to consolidate his kingship after the long years of minority, the revolt of the Saxons in 1073, and the growing resentment felt by many German and northern Italian bishops towards what they regarded as the pope's heavy-handed tactics. Moving, perhaps inescapably, as will be seen below, from preoccupations with simony and clerical marriage to the issue of lay investiture, Gregory, for his part, perhaps inevitably, articulated an interpretation of Gelasian dualism that even more emphatically placed priestly authority above royal power.

Even after the reconciliation of the pope and the king at Canossa in 1077 following the first excommunication of Henry IV, Gregory's conviction about the superiority of priestly authority led him to arrogate to himself the decision as to who was the more suitable ruler: Henry IV or the anti-king Rudolf of Rheinfelden. Meanwhile, he continued his efforts to reach out to rulers and nobles on the periphery of Latin Christendom in order to secure at least some respect for the authority and objectives of the apostolic see.[81] But the withdrawal of allegiance by the German and northern Italian bishops and the election of Wibert of Ravenna as anti-pope Clement III at the synod of Brixen in 1080, together with Henry's long siege of Rome after 1082, meant that such visions could not be realized. Despite the unflagging efforts of his ally Countess Matilda of Tuscany and her supporters, Gregory was forced to take refuge in Salerno among his Norman allies, where he died in May 1085. The battle he had tirelessly waged and seemingly lost would fall to his legate and successor Gerald of Ostia.

In 1088 after the brief pontificate of Desiderius as Victor III (elected 24 May 1086: forced to return to Montecassino before consecration; May–September 1087), Urban II inherited a papacy in exile, kept out of Rome by the presence in the city of Henry's anti-pope Wibert, and spent most of his pontificate in southern Italy, with a year in France, only beginning to gain a foothold in Rome from 1094. His hard-won success was the result of an immensely pragmatic reassertion of papal primacy, but one that was increasingly built on the consensus and support of the cardinals. Though referring to himself as Gregory's disciple in all things, Urban set about a cautious but extraordinarily effective plan of extending reform through his network of associates in the area of Constance, through the support of Matilda of Tuscany in northern and central Italy, and through councils held throughout western Europe.

Careful to offer the possibility of reconciliation by papal dispensation with all the schismatics excepting Henry IV and Wibert, Urban ultimately returned to Rome without having committed himself to subservience to the Normans, and as the leader of the *peregrinatio* or armed pilgrimage to recover the Holy Land. By 1096, the reorganization of the papal administration had begun, and Urban had now set the papacy on its path to becoming the head of a supranational institution whose authority was felt throughout Latin Christendom and beyond. Though the anti-pope Clement was still alive, the real bishop of Rome was increasingly the supreme representative of God on earth in fact as well in as theory.

Papal government

Just as important as the theoretical and practical articulations of papal authority during the eleventh century were the changes in administrative practices, even if it is anachronistic to speak of a 'papal government' before the twelfth century. This is not to suggest that there was no papal administrative apparatus or government during the eleventh century and before; the increasing issue of papal privileges was clearly indicative of an expanding administration. Yet the government that existed was one of limited capabilities, geared chiefly to the administration of the city of Rome along with the dioceses and lands belonging to the patrimony of St Peter. Although many historians use the term 'curia' to describe the papal administration, the word was not used by contemporaries before the pontificate of Urban II, who was responsible for the reorganization of the papal financial institutions, the creation of the apostolic camera, and so in many ways was the true architect of what is now recognized as the *curia Romana*: that is, the camera or financial administrative office, the chancery and the chapel. These offices were intimately connected with the college of cardinals, which itself only emerged in definitive form *circa* 1100.[82] Yet, the more regular administrative practices that developed in the eleventh century were undeniably a major factor in the transformation of the papacy.

The chief administrative centre of the Roman Church was the palace adjoining the Lateran basilica, the *sacrum palatium Lateranense*. The *palatium* had a staff of various officials, some of whose offices had existed for centuries, and whose duties were simultaneously religious and civil.[83] Of especial prominence throughout the earlier middle ages were the papal chancellor and the papal librarian, who were concerned with administration of the Roman Church, Rome itself and its environs. Below these officials were the seven palatine judges (*iudices palatini*), who traditionally had been the pope's special advisers. Their role, however, was increasingly marginalized to a mere ceremonial one with the aggrandizement of the cardinal-bishops, especially after 1059, and with the expansion of the chancellor's functions during and after the pontificate of Urban II. There were many other officials, often men in minor orders with ceremonial as well as civil roles in the palace and also in the papal household, the most important of whom were the *vestararius*, who oversaw the papal vestments and papal treasure, and the *vicedominus*, who was in charge of the household. During the earlier eleventh century, the responsibilities of these officials were increasingly assumed by the archdeacon of the Roman Church. By the 1050s, this office was already a position of some prominence, being held by Hildebrand prior to his election as Pope Gregory VII. Hildebrand's role in reorganizing the administration of ecclesiastical property was clearly important in his rise to prominence within reforming circles.[84]

The eleventh century saw major advances in the workings of the papal administration, especially during the pontificate of Urban II. Of course, the apparent advances may only reflect increasing documentation, and many of the offices or functionaries that seem to suddenly appear in the later eleventh century may have existed previously. Some administrative improvements are indisputable, such as the shift from papyrus to more durable parchment, and the progressive adoption of the minuscule script that could be read all over Latin Christendom. This meant that record-keeping and documents improved in quality and clearly facilitated the improvement of day-to-day governance, and thus the ability of the papacy to extend its authority. Nevertheless, we should not overestimate the organization even in the later eleventh century. The inability to preserve papal correspondence, apart from the *Register* of Gregory VII, itself incomplete, shows that the administration remained a rudimentary one.[85]

It is clear, however, that – from as early as Leo IX's pontificate – the papacy was beginning to make modifications to an administrative system whose rudiments had existed for centuries. Much of the innovation was instigated by Urban II, who inherited a papacy that was effectively without an administration following the papal schism of 1080 and Gregory VII's exile to Salerno in 1085.[86] While this can be most clearly seen in the incipient emergence of the cardinals, who were increasingly drawn from outside Rome and hence beyond the reach of the Roman families, other equally significant extensions of governance can be seen in the developments in three age-old traditions: councils, legates and canon law, all of which were vital in extending papal authority and the papal promotion of reform.

Councils had long been a central feature of the Church, but what is peculiar to the eleventh century is that Rome managed to use these gatherings to her advantage. In the early Church, they had often been rivals to papal authority, with ecumenical councils exercising a universal jurisdiction concerning faith and doctrine which would later become associated more with the papacy itself. In fact, the first ecumenical or universal council at Nicaea in 325 had been convened by the Emperor Constantine; Pope Silvester I (314–25), who was unable to attend on account of age and ill health, merely sent representatives. This set a precedent that continued for the first seven ecumenical councils that were recognized as authoritative by both the Eastern and Western churches up to Nicaea II (787): they were all convened by emperors and the popes sent representatives rather than being personally present. Only from the eleventh century onwards, were matters of faith to be more often decided by the pope with the assistance of councils, such as when Innocent III convoked the Fourth Lateran Council in 1215.

While popes such as Silvester II believed that regional councils were the best places for resolving most local ecclesiastical issues, there was an increasing appreciation by the eleventh-century papacy of the benefit of convening councils, especially in Rome, as a means by which the papacy could promote its reform agenda. That said, most of the councils that took place in the later tenth and early eleventh centuries were still either diocesan or provincial ones, or else were convened by the emperor or king rather than the pope, such as the council of Winchester in c.973 which regularized monastic practice in England, or the councils in Ravenna and Pavia in the 1020s, though these latter were convened jointly with the papacy. It was only with the elevation of Pope Leo IX in 1049, however, that councils began to be significant instruments of the papacy, being convened not only at Rome itself, but also across the Alps, as when Leo presided over councils at Rheims and at Mainz in 1049. Thereafter the papacy increasingly summoned what they termed general councils in

Rome as an effective demonstration of their leadership of the Church, requiring bishops and abbots from across Europe to make the journey *ad limina apostolorum.* By the pontificate of Gregory VII, the papacy was holding councils twice a year, attendance at which was obligatory for all summoned, with papal legates frequently presiding over additional regional councils in France, the empire and elsewhere in western Europe. Later, when Pope Urban II was prevented from returning to Rome by the emperor, Henry IV, he held critically important councils at Melfi (1093), Piacenza (1095) and Clermont (1095) which continued to legislate for reform and were instrumental in promoting both papal authority and his own position.

Side by side with the papacy's use of councils was the growing use of legates or special envoys as instruments of papal power. From the time of the early Church, the bishops of Rome had sent out and maintained envoys to represent their interests at the imperial court in Constantinople and later at the court of the Carolingian emperors, as well as appointing individuals to act in their behalf in specific places or for specific purposes, such as Augustine's mission to England in 596. The use of legates on an unprecedented scale as the pontiff's personal representatives, however, was an innovation of the papacy after the mid-eleventh century, one specially aimed at disseminating new ideas about papal primacy. What Robinson describes as the 'abrupt transformation of the Roman envoy into an instrument of the reform' dates from the 1050s, when Archdeacon Hildebrand began to exercise authority as the pope's special representative in France.[87] In 1056, the future Pope Gregory VII presided over a synod at Châlons, and deposed several bishops who were found guilty of simony.

From that time, the papacy began to rely on legates in earnest, and by the pontificate of Gregory VII, the practice of employing 'standing legates' (men with long-term commissions to act on behalf of the pope) had been adopted: with Bishop Hugh of Die and Amatus of Oloron in France, Anselm of Lucca in central Italy, Altmann of Passau in Saxony, and Cardinal-Deacon Bernard and Abbot Bernard of St Victor in Marseille, who were sent to the anti-king Rudolf of Rheinfelden. Even the future Urban II had, as Gerald of Ostia, been a legate in Germany. The resentment that such individuals engendered among local bishops, whose jurisdiction was undermined by the legates' superior authority, later forced Urban II to abandon, temporarily, the practice of standing legates. Yet by extending the pope's presence and authority, presiding over councils, negotiating with rulers, investigating important cases, some of which were referred back to Rome, collecting money owed and later organizing crusades, the legates became a critical part of papal government and forcefully made the pope's authority felt throughout Latin Christendom.

By far the most significant extension of papal government in the eleventh century came through a new emphasis on canon law and the compilation of innumerable canonical collections. Canon law had, of course, existed since the early Church. On the most basic level, it was what defined the Church as an institution, governing its beliefs, ceremonies, and organization, as well as its interaction with the rest of society. Moreover, even in the early Church, canon law had been inextricably associated with ideas of reform, functioning as it did to bridge the gap between a Church that was simultaneously an otherworldly entity and an institution requiring procedures to operate in this world. As a consequence, from the time of the early Church, there had been a search for better translations and more authoritative canons, as can be seen in Dionysius Exgiuus' collections in the fifth century, in 'national' collections such as the *Vetus Gallica* or the *Collectio Hispana*, or within the collections emanating from the Carolingian reforms such as the *Dionysio-Hadriana*.

It can be argued, though, that the canonical collections of the second half of the eleventh century should particularly be seen as 'reform collections'. While early eleventh-century compilations, such as Bishop Burchard of Worms' *Liber decretorum*, the *Collection in Five Books* and their localized derivatives (which continued to be copied throughout the eleventh century and were never eclipsed), were in some ways aimed at the renewal and regularization of ecclesiastical life, they did not stress the role of the papacy in terms of its leadership of the Church as the later eleventh-century collections would do. New works of canon law compiled in the 1070s and 1080s, such as the *Collection in Seventy-Four Titles*, the collections of Anselm of Lucca and Deusdedit, and the *Polycarpus* of Gregory of San Grisogono, all reflected the new significance of papal prerogatives and jurisdiction. More works of propaganda than practical manuals for use by bishops, the reform collections, especially that of Anselm of Lucca, were books of 'principles'. Using texts such as the Pseudo-Isidorian *Decretals*, but transforming their implicit acknowledgement of the papal role in protecting the episcopate into a declaration of papal supremacy, these collections sought to provide a legal justification for the papacy's role in articulating and effecting change.

Conclusion

Throughout the course of the eleventh century, the papacy underwent nothing short of a phenomenal transformation. From being a revered, but restricted, local centre of power with at best intermittent ability to make its authority felt beyond Rome and the papal patrimony, by the pontificate of Urban II the papacy had acquired something of an unassailable position. By emphasizing and refining (if not, on occasion, inventing) the theoretical justifications of papal authority from the early Church, by capitalizing on the need of local monasteries and churches across the Latin West for privileges confirmed by apostolic authority, which the papacy turned to its own advantage, by forging links with kingdoms and lay rulers on the periphery of the Latin West, and by extending the apparatus of administration (however rudimentary it may have remained), the papacy was increasingly able both to direct its own affairs and to impose its authority more consistently. By the end of the eleventh century, even if it remained unable wholly to impose its will and demand complete obedience to its commands, the Roman papacy had become a power that rulers, churchmen and society at large could disregard only at an extremely high price.

Notes

1 For a more detailed discussion, see J. Canning, *A History of Medieval Political Thought, 300–1450* (London, 1996), 29ff.

2 Leo I, *Sermo*, 3.4 (PL, 154.147). Cf. Canning, *Political Thought*, 30–1.

3 Canning, *Political Thought*, 31–2.

4 Gelasius I, *Epistola* 12, ed. A. Thiel, *Epistolae Romanorum Pontificum* (Braunsberg, 1886), 350–1; partly trans. in B. Tierney, *The Crisis of Church and State 1050–1300* (repr. Toronto, 1988), 13–14.

5 For example, W. Ullmann, *The Growth of the Papal Government in the Middle Ages*, 3rd edn (London, 1970), 36ff; W. Ullmann, *A Short History of the Papacy in the Middle Ages* (London, 1972), 51ff. Cf. C. Straw, *Gregory the Great: Perfection in Imperfection* (Berkeley, CA, 1988).

6 See above, Ch. 1.

7 B. H. Rosenwein, *Negotiating Space: Power, Restraint, and Privileges of Immunity in Early Medieval Europe* (Manchester, 1999).

8 See above, Ch. 1.

9 Rosenwein, *Negotiating Space*, 156ff. For the foundation charter, see *Recueil des chartes de l'abbaye de Cluny*, ed. A. Bernard and A. Bruel, 6 vols (Paris, 1876–1904), 1.126, no. 112. The charter is translated on the Medieval Internet Sourcebook, www.fordham.edu/halsall/sbook.html.

10 See Rosenwein, *Negotiating Space*, 171ff.

11 *Papsturkunden*, 2, no. 558, 1052–4.

12 Gerbert of Aurillac, *The Letters of Gerbert with his Papal Privileges as Sylvester II*, ed./trans. H. P. Lattin (New York, 1961), nos. 256, 257, pp. 350–2, and intro. 17–18.

13 Ibid., e.g. nos. 237 (Quedlinburg), 243 (Fulda) and 250 (St Gervaise), pp. 313–16, 324–6, 337–8.

14 *Ottonis III. Diplomata*, no. 389 (MGH, *Diplomatum regum et imperatorum Germaniae*, 2), 818–20.

15 T. Reuter, *Germany in the early Middle Ages, c.800–1056* (London, 1991), 279.

16 P. Toubert, *Les structures du Latium médiéval: le Latium meridional et la Sabine du IXᵉ siècle à la fin du XIIᵉ siècle*, 2 vols (Bibliothèque des écoles françaises d'Athènes et de Rome, 221; Rome, 1973), 2.968–1037; D. Whitton, 'Papal Policy in Rome, 1012–1124', D. Phil. thesis (Oxford, 1980), 63ff. Also, see above, Ch. 1.

17 Toubert, *Les structures*, 2.1015–22; Whitton, 'Papal Policy', 63ff.

18 The almost simultaneous deaths of both Sergius IV and the *patricius* John Crescentius on 12 and 18 May gave rise to the suspicion that neither man died a natural death.

19 Toubert, *Les structures*, 2.1022–4; Whitton, 'Papal Policy in Rome' 63ff.

20 *Papsturkunden*, 2, no. 478, 906–9; no. 528, 1004–5.

21 *Heinrici II. Constitutiones*, no. 30 (Ravenna), no. 34 (Pavia) (MGH, *Constitutiones et acta publica imperatorum et regum*, 1), 61–2, 71–8.

22 *Papsturkunden*, 2, e.g. nos. 474–5, at 899–902 (immunity for St Bénigne de Dijon); no. 494, 935–6 (papal protection for Montamiata); no. 497, 941–7 (immunity for Subiaco); no. 505, 959–61 (immunity for Fécamp); no. 530, 1007–10 (papal protection for Cluny). The significance of the Tusculan popes' concern for Farfa, Subiaco and especially Grottaferrrata – their *plantatio specialis* – are discussed by Toubert, *Les structures*: 2.1035–6. The Tusculans seem to have been substantial patrons of Montecassino.

23 John was forced to invalidate his privilege to Grado (*Papsturkunden*, 2, no. 561, 1057–61) not only by making it subject to Aquilea, but also by making Aquilea the metropolitan of all of Italy: no. 576, 1090–1. He was also forced to comply with the translation of Zeitz to Naumberg: no. 581, 1097–8. Cf. *Conradi II. Constitutiones* (MGH, *Const.*, 1), no. 38, 82–4.

24 *Papsturkunden*, 2, nos. 558, 570–4, at 1052–4, 1083–9.

25 Ibid., 2, no. 599, at 1128–9 (Simon of Trier); no. 611, at 1151–3 (Montecassino); no. 618, at 1159–64 (Grado). See R. Lane Poole, 'Benedict IX and Gregory VI', *Proceedings of the British Academy*, 8 (1917), 199–235.

26 *Die Briefe des Petrus Damiani*, Letter 13, ed. K. Reindel, 4 vols (MGH, *Briefe der deutschen Kaiserzeit*, 5: 1–4; Munich, 1983–93), 1.142–5; English trans. by O. J. Blum, *The Letters of Peter Damian*, 4 vols (The Fathers of the Church, Medieval Continuation; Washington, DC, 1989–99), 1.130–3. Subsequent references will include both Reindel's edn and the translation by Blum.

27 *Herimanni Augiensis Chronicon a.1046* (MGH, SS, 5), 126; Cf. *Heinrici III. Constitutiones*, no. 46 (MGH, *Const.*, 1), 94–5. The later *Annales Romani* made the state of the Roman Church the impetus of Henry's expedition; it is more probable that his motives were chiefly political.

28 *Herimanni Aug. Chron. a. 1046*, 126.

29 The sentence was either suspended or never enforced, as he continued to function as Bishop of Sabina until at least 1062.

30 *Herimanni Aug. Chron. a. 1046*, 126.

31 Peter Damian, Letter 40 (Reindel, 1.501–2; trans., 2.180–1); for his reaction to Gregory VI: Letter 13 (Reindel, 1.142–5; trans., 1.130–3).

32 *Ex Chronico S. Benigni Divionensis* (MGH, *SS*, 7), 235–7.

33 *Anselmi gesta episcoporum Leodiensium*, c. 53 (MGH, *SS*, 7), 24. Peter Damian, however, praised the deposition: Letter 20 (Reindel, 1.199–202; trans., 1.194–6).

34 *Anselmi gesta*, c. 65, 228–9. Although no specific canonical source was invoked, Wazo probably had in mind the fifth-century text attributed to Silvester I, the *Constitutum Silvestri*, which insisted on the complete immunity of the pontiff from judgment.

35 *Der sogennante Traktat 'De ordinando pontefice': Ein Rechtsgutachten in Zusammenhang mit der Synode von Sutri (1046)*, ed. H. H. Anton (Bonn, 1982), text 75–83.

36 Clement II and Henry III held a council in Rome in Jan. 1047 at which simony was condemned, and a penance of 40 days imposed on those knowingly ordained by simonists: *Heinrici III. Constitutiones*, no. 49, 95.

37 *Vita Leonis IX*, 2.4(2), *La vie du pape Léon IX (Brunon, éveque de Toul)*, ed. M. Parisse (Paris, 1997), 72–4.

38 Ibid., 2.5, 74–5.

39 Ibid., 1.1, 6–8. See also ix–xi.

40 *Herimanni Aug. Chron. a. 1049*, 128; *Vita Leonis*, 2.10(4), 86–8.

41 Peter Damian, Letter 40 (Reindel, 1.498–500; trans., 2.204–5).

42 Peter Damian, Letter 112 (Reindel, 3.280–1; trans., 4.278).

43 Stephen had apparently sworn the Romans, in the event of his death, to refrain from electing a new pope until Hildebrand's return from Germany. See Peter Damian, Letter 58 (Reindel, 2.193–4; trans., 2.392). Cf. Cushing, *Papacy and Law*, 27–31.

44 Leo I, *Epistolae*, 10.6, 14.5 (PL, 54.633–4, 673).

45 This is not to be confused with the later meaning of boy bishops as those carnivalesque mock-bishops at Christmastime.

46 See P. Fabre, *Etude sur le liber censuum de l'église romaine* (Paris, 1892), c. 58.81, p. 312.

47 Peter Damian, Letter 48 (Reindel, 2.52–61, esp. 55–7; trans., 2.263–71, esp. 266–7).

48 Letter 58 (Reindel, 2.191–2; trans., 2.390–1). Cf. K. M. Woody, '*Sagena piscatoris*: Petrus Damiani and the Papal Election Decree of 1059', *Viator*, 1 (1970), 33–54.

49 Letter 57 (Reindel, 2.157; trans., 2.370–1).

50 See R. L. Benson, *The Bishop-Elect: A Study in Medieval Ecclesiastical Office* (Princeton, NJ, 1968), 6–10, 35ff.

51 Council of Rome (1059), *Decretum electionis pontificae*, c. 3, (MGH, *Const.*, 1), 539.

52 Ibid., c. 7, 540.

53 Ibid., c. 8, 540.

54 Benson, *Bishop-Elect*, 42–3.

55 Sources for Nicholas II's activities prior to enthronement are scanty. He consecrated a new abbess for St Hilary, and also confirmed its immunity, sometime in Dec. 1058: *Regesta Pontificum Romanorum*, ed. P. Jaffé, 2nd edn by S. Loewenfeld (JL: an. 882–1198), F. Kaltenbrunner (JK: an. ?–590), P. Ewald (JE: an. 590–882), 2 vols (Berlin, 1885–89), JL 4392. This would have been in accordance with his episcopal powers. According to Bonizo, he was present at a synod in early January where Benedict X was condemned as a perjurer and usurper: *Liber ad amicum*, 5 (MGH, *Libelli de lite*, 1), 593, though he was not described as presiding. Cf. Baronius, *Annales ecclesiastici*, 12 vols (Cologne, 1609), 11 (a. 1059), 324.

56 Council of Rome (1059), *Decr. elect. pont.*, c. 8, 540. Cf. Benson, *Bishop-Elect*, 43.

57 Letter 57 (Reindel, 2.157ff; trans., 2.369ff). Cf. *Chronica monasterii Casinensis*, 2.99 (MGH, *SS*, 7), 695.

58 For Nicholas's support of Godfrey, see Peter Damian, Letter 60 (Reindel, 2.203–5; trans., 2.402–6). On Hildebrand's legation, see G. B. Borino, 'L'archdiaconato di Ildebrando', *Studi Gregoriani*, 3 (1948), 463–515, esp. 491–5.

59 See G. Bardy, 'Saint Grégoire VII et la réforme canoniale au xiᵉ siécle', *Studi Gregoriani*, 1 (1947), 47–64. Cf. C. Dereine, 'Le Probléme de la vie communale chez les canonistes d'Anselme de Lucques à Gratien', *Studi Gregoriani*, 3 (1948), 278–98.

60 On the Normans, see G. Loud, *The Age of Robert Guiscard: Southern Italy and the Norman Conquest* (Harlow, Essex, 2000).

61 On the Pataria, see below, Ch. 5.

62 Peter Damian, Letter 65 (Reindel, 2.230ff; trans., 3.24–39). For further discussion, see Cushing, *Papacy and Law*, 22–7.

63 Although his explicit authorities were scriptural, he clearly had in mind a number of canonical sources, all of which were clearly intended to reinforce the traditional mother–daughter relationship of Rome and Milan that had existed since the time of St Ambrose. See J. J. Ryan, *St Peter Damiani and His Canonical Sources: A Preliminary Study in the Antecedents of the Gregorian Reform* (Toronto, 1956), nos. 106–14, 60–8.

64 Peter Damian, Letter 65 (Reindel, 2.232–3; trans., 3.27). Cf. Ryan, no. 106, 60.

65 Ibid., Letter 65 (Reindel, 2.233–4; trans., 3.28).

66 Ibid., Letter 57 (Reindel, 2.157; trans., 2.370–1).

67 Ibid., Letter 65 (Reindel, 2.233–4; trans., 3.27). Cf. Letter 88 (Reindel, 2.521; trans., 3.315).

68 Ryan, *Peter Damian and His Sources*, no. 109.

69 Peter Damian, Letter 99 (Reindel, 3.97–100; trans., 4.103–6).

70 Ibid., Letter 107 (Reindel, 3.185–8; trans., 4.192–4).

71 Ibid., Letter 89 (Reindel, 2.531–72; trans., 3.326–69).

72 *Annales Altahenses maiores a. 1064* (MGH, *SS*, 20), 814.

73 *Humberti cardinalis libri III. adversus simoniacos* (MGH, *LdL*, 1), 95–253. See below, Ch. 5.

74 Cowdrey, *Pope Gregory VII*, e.g. 158ff, 331–3, 689–90. Cf. U.-R. Blumenthal, *Gregor VII. Papst zwischen Canossa und Kirchenreform* (Darmstadt, 2001).

75 *Registrum Gregorii VII.*, 2.1, ed. E. Caspar (MGH, *Epistolae selectae*, t. 2, 2 vols; Berlin, 1920–3), 124; H. E. J. Cowdrey, *The Register of Pope Gregory VII, 1073–1085: An English Translation* (Oxford, 2002). Subsequent references will include both Caspar's edn and the translation.

76 For example, *Reg.*, 5.14a, 368 (trans., 260). Cf. R. Somerville, 'The councils of Gregory VII', *La riforma gregoriana e 'Europa'* (Studi Gregoriani, 13; Rome, 1989), 33–53.

77 Cushing, *Papacy and Law*, 37–9.

78 Ibid., 39–40, 103ff.

79 For background and detailed discussion, see U.-R. Blumenthal, *The Investiture Controversy: Church and Monarchy from the Ninth to the Twelfth Century* (Philadelphia, 1988), 106–34; Cowdrey, *Pope Gregory VII*, 75–271; and Robinson, *Henry IV*, 105–236.

80 *Reg.*, 2.31, 165–8 (trans. 122–4). See H. E. J. Cowdrey, 'Pope Gregory VII's crusading plans of 1074', repr. in his *Popes, Monks and Crusaders* (London, 1984), art. X.

81 See Cowdrey, *Pope Gregory VII*, 423–80.

82 See I. S. Robinson, *The Papacy, 1073–1198: Continuity and Innovation* (Cambridge, 1990), esp. 33ff, 244ff.

83 For more details, see R. Elze, 'Das *sacrum palatium Laterenense* im 10. und 11. Jahrhundert', *Studi Gregoriani*, 4 (1952), 27–54.

84 See D. B. Zema, 'Economic Reorganization of the Roman See During the Gregorian Reform', *Studi Gregoriani*, 1 (1947), 137–68. Cf. Robinson, *Papacy*, 249–50.

85 The unbroken line of papal registers dates only from the pontificate of Innocent III (1198–1216).

86 Robinson, *Papacy*, 244ff.

87 Ibid., 146.

5

Reform in practice

Material renewal

'**B** EFORE there was a centre, there was reform'. In this striking formulation, John Howe emphasized that while historians have tended to focus their attention on events in Rome and at royal courts, reform actually had its origins as much in localities and centres away from royal courts and Rome as in them.[1] Indeed, initiatives such as those of the Aquitainian bishops in summoning councils to promote peace in the 990s, of the Benedictine reformer John Gualbertus who founded the Vallombrosan order in 1039, or Robert of Molesme's removal to the wilderness of Cîteaux in 1098, were all undertaken without recourse to papal or royal power. At the same time, Howe's work reminds us of the importance of recognizing that the fundamental work of 'reform' also comprised the 'bricks-and-mortar' reality of building monasteries, other convents and churches, like those established by Dominic of Sora (c.960–1032) in San Salvatore at Scandriglia, San Pietro in Lago, and Trisulti, those built by Romuald (c.952–1023/7) at Cuxa, Pareo and Val di Castro, as well as those by numerous other unnamed individuals.

These initiatives, like the massive rebuilding undertaken by abbots Mayeul and Odilo at Cluny in the later tenth and early eleventh centuries, were not simply the fundamental precursors to the promotion of reform but 'real' reform initiatives in themselves. The boast reportedly made by Odilo (echoing Caesar Augustus), that he found Cluny made of wood and left it marble, was a statement of satisfaction that would have been shared by many others whose achievements were on a smaller scale.[2] They contributed to building projects, organized the clearing of land and the construction of embankments, or supervised the building of churches and monasteries, the notice of which repeatedly stands out in the sources for the first half of the eleventh century.

The oft-cited text of the Cluniac chronicler Rodulf Glaber underlines this activity in early eleventh-century Europe and it is still worth quoting:

> Just before the third year after the millennium, throughout the whole world, but most especially in Italy and Gaul, men began to reconstruct churches, although for the most part the existing ones were properly built and not in the least unworthy. But it seemed as though each Christian community was aiming to surpass all others in the splendour of construction. It was as if the whole world were shaking itself free, shrugging off the burden of the past, and cladding itself everywhere in a white mantle of churches. Almost all the episcopal churches and those of monasteries dedicated to various saints, and little village chapels, were rebuilt better than before by the faithful.[3]

Whether or not one accepts Glaber's description as evidence of 'transformation', 'mutation' or of millennial eschatology, he clearly intended to set the reconstruction of the fabric of religious life, like the 'peace of God', in the wider context of reform.[4] For Glaber, spiritual reform and material renewal were the rightful accompaniments to the millennial anniversaries of Christ's birth and passion. The point is worth labouring, for it is all too often disregarded that when a church, chapel or monastery was founded or reformed, those responsible for that process were preoccupied as much with material reconstruction as spiritual reform. This can easily be seen with, to name but a few, Gerald at Aurillac, the Cluniac reformer William of Volpiano at St Bénigne de Dijon, Peter Damian at Fonte Avellana, Desiderius at Montecassino, and perhaps most of all with Lanfranc, first at Bec, then at St Stephen's, Caen, and especially at Canterbury.[5] For all of these men, reform involved not only spiritual but also material renewal.

While the inspiration for much of this material reform in the tenth and eleventh centuries came from Benedictine monks – such as Aethelwold in England, Romuald in northern Italy, Dominic around Sora, John Gualbertus at Vallombrosa, or Robert of Arbrissel at Fontevrault – as part of their desire to establish a more rigorous monastic observance, there is ample evidence that such concerns were shared also by the episcopate. The Aquitainian bishops, in their efforts to promote peace and order, made the protection of church property their chief ambition. Construction projects in the German empire, such as Henry II's new cathedral at Bamberg or Henry III's foundation of the chapter of Saints Simon and Jude when he extended the *palatium* at Goslar, almost invariably entailed some element of spiritual reform as well, or at least involved the bishop attempting some reorganization of his cathedral chapter, as took place in Italy at Lucca from the 1050s onwards. This linkage of building and reform was increasingly common. Henry III's gifts to the bishopric of Speyer, for instance, were made on the condition that the canons pursue their studies and be rigorous with their prayers. In England, moreover, following the Norman Conquest, with the appointment of churchmen from Normandy and further afield at the death of English bishops and abbots, every major cathedral and monastery was reconstructed. These projects were accompanied by attempts to bring the Anglo-Saxon Church into conformity with Roman practice.[6] In the Iberian peninsula, construction accompanied both the promotion of reform and the suppression of the Visigothic liturgical rite, for instance at Compostella in 1056.[7] Similar large-scale cathedral projects took place at Lucca, Rheims, Cologne, Canterbury, Worcester, Durham, Norwich, Merseburg and elsewhere across Europe under the auspices of bishops looking on the one hand to promote their cities, the relics of their saints and their own glory, and at the same time to be more accountable, or at least receptive, to the needs of their flocks.

Jeffery Bowman pointed to one such bishop, Ermengol of Urgell in the Pyrenees, who was actually referred to as an *episcopus athleticus*. Ermengol was an able administrator who undertook numerous building projects in his diocese for the benefit of his flock before falling to his death in 1035 while supervising the construction of a bridge over the River Segre at Bar.[8] Ermengol's activities were by no means unusual. Like many earlier eleventh-century bishops, he was intimately connected with the local comital family and owed his elevation to the bishopric of Urgell (arranged in his predecessor's lifetime) to a financial and land transaction, in other words to simony. Such relationships were, however, taken for granted, and did not imply the appointment of a lax or uncommitted bishop, however much later reformers might complain. What is important is that Ermengol's reputation and ultimately his sanctity derived specifically from his commitment to building. As Bowman noted 'a saintly bishop was one who built bridges both physical and spiritual' – that is, good bishops were those who looked after their flocks when they were travelling on business or pilgrimage, so helping them in both worlds.[9] Other examples are equally illuminating. In England, for instance, Wulfstan provided continuity between the Anglo-Saxon past and the new Norman realities, while overseeing the reconstruction of the cathedral at Worcester.[10]

The changing depiction or characterization of such bishops, at least in the context of their *Lives* and when these were written up, not only underlines this activity, but also points to the ways in which new dispensations about appropriate behaviour were increasingly coming to the fore. It is of course a common place of hagiography that bishops were required to be energetic leaders, what I have elsewhere termed 'men of action'.[11] Yet, as Maureen Miller has shown, it is the progressive accentuation of the individual agency and even isolation of the bishop that begins to sound a new note in eleventh-century hagiography. A bishop travels the diocese, he cares for the poor and the sick, he builds or rebuilds churches, and in the case of Ulrich of Augsburg (923–73) defeats an army of Magyars.[12] What is striking, as Miller's comparison of the late tenth-century *Life* of Ulrich by the provost, Gerhard of Augsburg with the early eleventh-century *Life* by Abbot Berno of Reichenau, is not only that the later *Life* glosses over Ulrich's loyal vassalage to the emperor as well as the family connections that resulted in his elevation, but also the fact that those who assist the bishop in his many missions and duties all but disappear from view in the text. In the eleventh-century *Life*, the saintly bishop Ulrich, albeit with divine aid, acts alone for the benefit of his flock.

We are, of course, far better informed about the bishops, abbots, noble laymen and women who founded monasteries, reformed churches and made donations *ad sepulturam*. That said, what Moore termed the 'little community' – the populace – were clearly also important, providing the pressure for change that was such a critical factor not only in the peace councils, but also in the increasing momentum for reform, even though it must be conceded that documentation on their activities is meagre apart from fleeting appearances in charters and hagiography as the victims of depredations and evil customs. As will be seen below with the Pataria in Milan in the late 1050s and 1060s, the people, even if elusive, were a significant force not just as witnesses or as the labourers and payers of tithes that permitted the extension of religious life. Their influence was also potent in other ways. This can be seen during an outbreak of ergotism or St Antony's fire, in Limoges in 994, when Bishop Alduin was forced by a near-riot to make what is known as a ritual clamour against the relics of the patron saint, Martial (ritually cursing him to show displeasure at his lack of protection and to stir him into action). According to Landes, the outbreak of ergotism firstly awakened 'a mass religious response of terror and guilt', went on to engender communal acts of penitence and fasting, the gathering of saints' relics from the surrounding regions in Limoges and the raising of St Martial from his crypt (presumably to greet the 'visiting' saints), with numerous other miracles, and finally the nobility swearing to maintain the peace.[13] Here the agency of the people was instrumental in putting pressure on both religious and secular authorities. If reform was partly about the material restoration of religious life, it also focused on the spiritual improvement of those who presided over that life: the clergy. The worldliness of bishops such as Ermengol of Urgell, Hildebrand of Florence, Manasses of Rheims, and countless others was nothing unusual, despite the efforts of some popes and emperors. Sustained recognition of the need for reform emerged in the earliest peace councils such as Le Puy, Limoges and Anse in 994, and Poitiers in 1000/14, again probably with some significant pressure from below.

The evolution of reform thus is far from a straightforward narrative beginning with Pope Leo IX, even if it was not pursued in any sort of uniform or consistent manner before his elevation. From the time of the early peace councils as has been seen above, a myriad of measures appeared that were intended to keep the clergy focused on their spiritual duties. What is more, such measures were not simply prescriptive. For instance, at the Council of Limoges in 1031, a simonist and a married cleric were brought up for judgment. This trend of actively pursuing individuals who disregarded reform measures would be intensified, as can be seen at the Council of Rheims in 1049, where Pope Leo IX opened the council by requiring all bishops and abbots to take an oath that they were not simonists in acquiring their offices or in selling offices to others. Much of the remaining three days of the council was then given over to an examination and judgment of those clerics about whom there was suspicion, several of whom were stripped of office.[14]

The Council of Rheims reiterated prohibitions on clerics bearing arms and addressed other issues of clerical deportment, all of which reveal that part and parcel of the aim of reform was not simply the moral improvement of the clergy, but also the effective delineation and separation of their customs and lifestyles from those of the laity. Although these and additional measures would be continually repeated through the eleventh century and beyond, attention quickly came to focus on two very critical issues: simony and clerical marriage (or concubinage), to which the problematic issue of lay investiture would later be added. It is useful here to consider each in turn.

Simony and clerical chastity

Simony had a long history within the Western Church. It derived its name from Acts 8.18 where Simon Magus attempted to purchase from Peter the gift of the Holy Spirit which had descended on the apostles at Pentecost.

Although repeatedly condemned at ecumenical and regional councils from the time of Chalcedon (AD 431) onwards, and identified by Pope Gregory the Great as a heresy whether by promise or payment, the practice of simony was in many ways inevitable in a society where appointment to clerical and monastic positions gave men control over vast wealth and estates.[15] Clerical offices were positions of power and influence that kings and the aristocracy alike aimed to fill with family or their clients. Furthermore, the combination of secular and spiritual office had long provided a secure, often harmonious, basis for local and regional networks of power, and its disruption was for many a revolutionary threat to the established order. Indeed, in his *Life* of Romuald written about 1043, Peter Damian lamented that until Romuald's time (*c*.952–1023/7) 'the custom of simony was so widespread that hardly anyone knew it was a sin' and he was forced to concede that, despite Romuald's efforts, 'it would be easier to convert a Jew to the faith than bring a heretical scoundrel [meaning a simonist bishop] to true repentance'.[16]

The exchange of money for offices or benefices, though occasionally frowned upon and even condemned by various councils after 1000, was not seen in the earlier part of the eleventh century (despite Gregory I's condemnation) as being particularly objectionable from a sacramental point of view. This remained the case until Humbert of Silva-Candida's *Against the simoniacs*, written about 1050, which denied the validity of sacraments or ordinations performed by simonists.[17] By adopting the Donatist position (that a 'bad' priest corrupted the sacraments he dispensed), this flatly contradicted the view expounded by the Father of the Church, St Augustine, thereby prompting a heated debate with Peter Damian, who maintained that those freely ordained by simonists were untainted, as indeed were their sacraments.[18] Although these arguments engendered much publicity and attention, it seems that what truly turned simony into an especially acute issue after 1050 (notwithstanding the condemnations by peace councils and other earlier eleventh-century councils), was that the payment or promise effectively made the recipient – whether a bishop or a rural parish priest – the king's or the local lord's man, at a time when the increasing disputes over property and rights made it imperative for bishops and priests to be seen as free and impartial arbitrators.

The situation in Lucca is a very good example of this. Throughout the eighth and ninth centuries, the bishopric of Lucca had been considerably enriched by extensive lay donations, especially from small- and medium-sized landholders. Yet by the end of the tenth century, large parts of the bishop's landed property had effectively passed out of episcopal control. As Wickham has documented, the local aristocracy had effectively become episcopal tenants, deriving the bulk of their power from ecclesiastical property and lordships held on lease, often at the expense of episcopal authority.[19] Lucca's bishops had in response been driven to leasing their resources in an attempt both to establish their own kin, and to create military and administrative counterweights to the aristocrats who had become independent lords at the expense of episcopal land. By the mid-eleventh century, the episcopal patrimony was in a dire state, and Bishop Anselm I (Pope Alexander II) not only requested that the *census* or tithes be paid in money rather than in cultivated or raw products, but also prohibited further alienation of episcopal property save in cases of extreme need.

The problem here as elsewhere was not only the depletion of the episcopal patrimony but also the competition presented by the cathedral canons, who in Lucca had become a well-defined group with interests of their own, which increasingly were distinct from those of the episcopate. Jurisdiction over property among the canons was ostensibly held in common, but agricultural rents had probably been divided into individual benefices by the early eleventh century, and were increasingly treated as inheritable property that would revert to a canon's family at his death. The desire of such families to extend their landholding and hence position at the expense of church property (which they had come to see as their own) inescapably fostered a climate in which simony would be rife. This probably explains why the protracted efforts of Anselm II of Lucca (1073–85) to enforce a strict communal life on his canons, which ultimately resulted in his expulsion from the city in 1080, were portrayed by his biographer as a struggle against Simon Magus.[20]

Although the issue of simony became especially critical after 1050, the earliest indications of a sustained concern about simony appear, according to Ademar of Chabannes, in approximately 1014, but from a secular rather than ecclesiastical quarter. Duke William V of Aquitaine, who presided over the Council of Poitiers, apparently sought to restore discipline at the monastery of Charroux by ejecting its abbot, Peter, who was reputed to have obtained his office through the heresy of simony.[21] A similar secular initiative is found in January 1014 at Henry II's synod of Ravenna, which prohibited the ordination of clerics through gifts of money.[22] A more encompassing initiative, however, was undertaken at the Council of Bourges in 1031. In addition to the provision for Sunday masses in the churches, as noted above, the council also stipulated that no gift was to be accepted by the bishop or his ministers in return for holy orders, and furthermore that laymen should not place priests in the churches except through the bishop.[23] In this we first see the connection being made between simony and lay investiture, which would later be taken up by Humbert in his *Against the simoniacs*, where he would call for the abolition of the lay investiture of bishops and abbots as it inevitably led to simony.

In the aftermath of the synod of Sutri in 1046, simony quickly became one of the chief preoccupations of the papacy. The condemnation and prohibition of selling office or any of the sacraments was not simply made at papal councils at Rome, Rheims and Mainz, all in 1049. Rather, papal legates were employed to see that this issue was attacked, for instance at Coyaca in 1050, Narbonne in 1054, Lyons in 1055, Toulouse in 1056 and Compostella in 1056, to name but a few. The Lateran council of 1059 issued particularly strong condemnations and, at a council convened by the papal legate Stephen at Tours in 1060 on the orders of Nicholas II, simony at all levels was condemned absolutely and anyone obtaining a position in this manner was to lose it with no possibility of recovery.[24] Similar prohibitions were made by Alexander II and his legates, such as Hugh Candidus at Gerona in 1068, and repeatedly throughout Gregory VII's pontificate.[25]

The reformers' other early preoccupation was with enforcing celibacy, especially among the higher orders of the clergy (deacon, priest and bishop, though increasingly subdeacons were included) and with eradicating clerical marriage and concubinage. The attempts to require clerics to lead celibate lives, like the struggle against simony, had a long history in the Western Church beginning as early as the fourth century at the councils of Elvira (306–14) and Nicaea in 325, which had prohibited the introduction of women into the houses of clergy for sexual purposes. The inclusion of these and other canons in Carolingian penitentials and canon-law books, and ultimately their incorporation into the influential *Liber decretorum* of Burchard of Worms, whence they were widely disseminated, meant that the issue remained a prominent one up to the early eleventh century, but also one whose enforcement was at best half-hearted and sporadic. Furthermore, canon law prohibited the repudiation or abandonment of wives of those taking orders after marriage without the consent of both parties, though it stipulated that henceforth the couple were to live in fraternal charity.[26] This tended to undermine the reformers' early efforts, and the fact that in the Byzantine Church married clergy were the norm (an issue that would contribute to deteriorating relations after the schism of 1054) offered polemicists like Landulf Senior of Milan a precedent with which to counter the reformers.

Sustained preoccupation with clerical chastity began to emerge in peace councils as early as the Council of Anse in 994. Unlike efforts at eradicating simony, the papacy took up the issue at an early stage, in concert with the German emperor. The synod of Pavia, convened in 1022 and jointly presided over by the Tusculan pope, Benedict VIII, and the emperor, Henry II, issued strident condemnations of clerical marriage and concubinage, calling unchastity 'the root of all evils'. Basing itself on a distortion of the canon of Nicaea in 325, it excluded all women from the houses of priests and called for the deposition of married clergy, including bishops.[27] Furthermore, it decreed that the children and perhaps the wives of priests were to become serfs; according to some accounts, this measure was repeated by Leo IX at Rome and at Mainz in 1049.[28]

Although anxiety about the sexual morality of the clergy was increasing, the issue at Pavia probably had more to do with the economic situation and the poverty afflicting the church in Pavia than with disinterested promotion of clerical celibacy.[29] This was a problem increasingly evident elsewhere. Despite rich endowments, the alienation of church property to the sons of the clergy and for the support of their wives or concubines was impoverishing individual churches and the Church as a whole at an alarming rate. Although, as will be seen in Chapter 6, the issue of ritual purity was increasingly coming to the fore with the extension of the peace and the appropriation of monastic models of purity by reforming popes such as Leo IX, Nicholas II and Gregory VII, concerns about safeguarding property were undoubtedly paramount.

This is evident in other councils, such as Anse in 994, Poitiers in 1000/14 and Bourges in 1031, where priests were required to abstain from sexual contact with their wives (if they had them) on penalty of losing the privilege of saying Mass and their benefices, or, as at Poitiers, on penalty of being degraded. The action at Bourges is particularly relevant: priests, deacons, and even subdeacons who were not celibate were immediately to renounce their wives or face loss of rank, and furthermore clerical children were to become serfs.[30] In this there is evidence of concerns similar to those that lay at the heart of fears about simony, where the recipient of clerical office effectively became the king's or lord's man. A married bishop or priest could be seen as bound first to the needs of his own family. It is in this context that similar prohibitions, such as those made at Rome and Mainz in 1049, at Coyaca in 1050, Compostella in 1056, Toulouse in 1056, Rome in 1059 and 1060, Tours in 1063, Gerona in 1068, and repeatedly throughout Gregory VII's pontificate, need to be understood.[31]

Implementing reform

The constant repetition of these measures up to and beyond Gregory VII's pontificate (Gregory himself repeated the condemnations at his Lenten and November synods of 1074, 1075 and 1078, and frequently reiterated them in letters) – to say nothing of the obvious resistance that such repetitions reveal – forced the reformers to adopt different approaches in achieving their ambition of a freely established and celibate clergy. Through what Robinson long ago called his 'friendship network' as well as a sustained campaign of letters and legates, Gregory VII sought to impress upon both his bishops and the local aristocracy the pressing need to eradicate simony and clerical marriage or concubinage, and thereby he widened participation of those exerting pressure on the clergy to reform.[32] Not only were bishops summoned to Rome for his Lenten and November councils to give an account of their progress at promoting reform, including ardent allies such as Archbishop Siegfried of Mainz or Archbishop Anno of Cologne, who – Gregory felt – were sometimes not 'as zealous as they ought to be', but bishops were often also threatened with possible removal.[33]

Indeed, Bishop Liemar of Bremen was suspended from his episcopal functions in December 1074 until he accounted in person at the Lenten synod in 1075 for impeding the work of the papal legates and inhibiting reform.[34] Bishop Otto of Constance was similarly censured, though not finally deposed until 1084 when the irreproachable reformer Gebhard was installed in his place. Examples could easily be multiplied.[35] Gregory also encouraged inferiors to accuse their superiors of such crimes (as had been set out his *Dictatus papae*), in one famous case even instructing Archbishop Udo of Trier in October 1074 to investigate the accusations of simony and unchastity brought against Bishop Pibo of Toul by one of his own cathedral clerks.[36] What was evident was that it was no longer enough simply for men to hold the privilege of clergy; for Gregory VII in particular, all clergy were actively obliged to take part and to make it their business to eradicate existing conditions in order that the new dispensations of the reformers might take hold.

Members of the nobility and aristocracy who showed themselves to be faithful to the papacy also had an important role in church reform. In the German empire, it was these men to whom Gregory VII increasingly turned as a consequence of his inability to persuade Henry IV to undertake the work of reform consistently, even though it is evident that he expected much from the king in the early years of his pontificate.[37] Writing to Duke

Rudolf of Rheinfelden and Berthold of Carinthia in January 1075, for instance, Gregory enjoined with apostolic authority that they 'should in no way accept the ministrations of those whom you know either to have been simoniacally promoted or to lie in the sin of fornication'. He further called upon them to proclaim these injunctions at the king's court and other assemblies, and to debar such clerics from serving at the sacred mysteries 'even by force if it should be called for'.[38]

The increasing significance of the lay aristocracy is nowhere more apparent than with Countess Beatrice and especially Countess Matilda of Tuscany, who were among Gregory's staunchest allies. Their presence was frequently requested in Rome; they were called upon to assist in resolving disputes; and they were praised for their work in promoting reform, though Gregory did censure Matilda's zeal in the matter of Werner of Strassburg, whom she had seized not knowing that he had made a penitential journey to Rome.[39] The importance to Gregory of these lay *fideles sancti Petri* and the reliance he placed in men and women such as Matilda, Robert Guiscard, Rudolf of Rheinfelden, King William of England, Count Albert of Kalw, Erlembald and countless others is underscored by his firm censuring of Abbot Hugh of Cluny over his reception of Duke Hugh of Burgundy as a Cluniac monk in 1079. Gregory condemned Hugh's lack of foresight in that the duke's monastic profession left his subjects without a guardian and protector when 'there is scarcely a good prince to be found'.[40]

More than anything else though, Gregory turned to public indignation as a force for reform, going so far as to call on the people to boycott the ministrations of simoniac or married clergy. This was not because he adopted the rigorist position of Humbert, that their sacraments were invalid, but rather so that 'those not corrected from the love of God and the honour of their office may be brought to their senses by the shame of the world and the reproach of the people.'[41] Following the model of popular agitation used to such effect by the Pataria in Milan and the Vallombrosans against their simonist bishop, Peter Mezzabarba of Florence, both of whom he had already supported before his elevation as pope, Gregory instructed the clergy and people of Constance to show their bishop neither respect nor obedience, and urged the faithful in Germany do the same if their spiritual leaders were in any way compromised.[42] Those who stood up for such principles were, for Gregory, the ultimate *fideles sancti Petri*.

That this conviction of the need for action was shared elsewhere in reform circles is perhaps nowhere more apparent than in the changing nature of sanctity. Sanctity, at least for certain eleventh-century reformers and their hagiographers, no longer derived solely from miracles, or dying for the faith, or simply bearing solitary witness against abuses like simony and nicholaism.[43] What increasingly mattered to eleventh-century reformers like Gregory VII was effective action, the translation of reform ideals into practice, the way that individuals lived their lives, and not how they died. The role of the saints was no longer merely to set an example, but also to provide a focal point, to articulate and even direct aspirations that were becoming more prevalent within the wider Christian community. Moreover, sanctity or holiness no longer applied simply to those in clerical or monastic orders. Thus, Gregory VII added the Roman prefect Cencius and the Milanese Patarene leader Erlembald to the rolls of the 'very special dead' (i.e., the saints), not on account of any personal virtues or miracles, but precisely because they had ranked among the 'very special living'.[44] Their actions as reformers meant that they were worthy of being held up as models for imitation: Cencius's willingness to set aside his desire for monastic profession in order to remain in the world and promote reform, and Erlembald's unrelenting fight, even to death, against simony and married clergy.[45]

Even more instructive is the case of the Patarene priest, Liprand, who was horribly mutilated in Milan in the anti-Patarene reaction following Erlembald's assassination in 1075. In a bull dated late 1075 – in which Liprand was given papal protection and, unusually, the right to appeal directly to the apostolic see – Gregory VII wrote that Liprand was to be praised even more than the ancient saints who suffered death and dismemberment rather than be divided from their faith.[46] This privilege reveals that what mattered to Gregory VII and other reformers was a willingness on the part of the clergy and lay Christians alike to face and suffer persecution, injury, exile and even death for the sake of righteousness. In the eleventh century, therefore, not only were ideas of holiness being transformed; they were also being extended to a widening circle.

Yet including lesser clergy and even laypeople in the work of reform was to open a Pandora's box, as the Milanese chroniclers had long complained with respect to the Pataria, who had used the force of public indignation to the extreme. The Pataria had evolved as a potent force in Milan in the late 1050s, as a consequence chiefly of the charismatic preaching of a well-educated cleric, Ariald, who came from a family of modest landowners at Cucciago near Milan.[47] Ariald began his campaign as a reformer by preaching against married clergy at Varese in early 1057. Meeting with little success there, he went to Milan where, together with the notary Landulf Cotta, he began again to preach against clerical marriage, urging his audience to boycott the ministrations of married priests. Though detractors disparaged both his preaching style and its content, he was able to exploit public antipathy towards the widespread practice of married clergy in the Milanese Church.

To the dismay of the established clergy, Ariald and Landulf soon attracted many adherents from diverse parts of Milanese society including, perhaps surprisingly, sections of the population such as small traders, moneylenders, artisans and notaries, who potentially had more to lose materially from their participation in popular agitation.[48] A violent encounter was not long in coming. On 10 May 1057, during the translation of one of the city's principal saints, Ariald publicly called for the end of concubinage and clerical marriage. Apparently citing a precise but little-known provision of Justinian and perhaps with reference to the council of Pavia in 1022, he formulated an oath of chastity (*phytacium de castitate*) which the clergy were to sign under threat of death. The ensuing struggle disclosed an important change in tactics: no longer would the Pataria simply boycott the services of compromised clerics; they would use force to prevent them from serving at the mass and would even attack the houses of alleged culprits.[49]

After this clash, the Pataria increasingly turned their attention to simony, which was a natural extension of preoccupations with clerical marriage because of its implications for the misuse of ecclesiastical resources. With the support they were able to gather in Milan from various quarters and strong connections at Rome, the Pataria effectively split Milanese society. Following the death of Landulf Cotta, who had been wounded in a scuffle, the appointment of his brother, the *miles* Erlembald, as the pope's lay representative in 1061, deepened the already widening gulf between Archbishop Guido of Milan and the Pataria. Matters came to a head with the excommunication of Guido by Pope Alexander II on 9 March 1066. A violent anti-Patarene reaction ensued, and during an attempt to flee south to Rome, Ariald was captured, assassinated (according to his biographer by unreformed priests, as laymen had refused to touch the holy man), and his body was dumped in a lake. Almost ten months later, the body was rediscovered and brought back to Milan by Erlembald, who now assumed leadership of the movement, keeping it alive at the expense of even more sharply dividing Milanese society.

The account and reaction of the Milanese chronicler Arnulf to these events is especially instructive. Unlike Landulf Senior, whose slightly later *History of Milan* was effectively an extended defence of clerical marriage (though not concubinage) as part of the city's unique Ambrosian tradition, and who depicted the Pataria as the chaos of the countryside opposing the civilization of the city, Arnulf genuinely recognized that there was a pressing need for reform within the church of Milan. What he objected to were the methods of the Pataria, whose remedy he believed was worse than the situation they sought to rectify. Arnulf, however, reserved his vehemence chiefly for Erlembald, whose judgment and coercion of the clergy as a layman was a violation of right order, and whose rootless dictatorship –ignored by Gregory VII and the Roman reformers – led ultimately to his assassination after he attempted to destroy the chrism of the bishop during Holy Week and began baptisms on Easter morning with a chrism he had obtained elsewhere.[50]

Although the Pataria were anti-clerical at this stage rather than heretical, placing themselves outside of the Church only in the sense of creating a purified 'counter-church' in strictly reformed chapels, the encouragement of lay involvement in the censuring or judging of the clergy presented a serious dilemma. Of course, such campaigns underlined the importance attached to clerical office by those clergy and laymen who were deeply troubled by the existence of clerics compromised by simony or unchastity, whose ministrations they increasingly saw as tainted and even contagious. Yet the Pataria's ideals – and to some extent their tactics, which were to be used by the Vallombrosans in Florence against their simonist bishop Peter – were effectively those advocated by Gregory VII in his boycott decrees, but with the potential not just of serious misunderstanding, but indeed misuse. The Pataria, the Vallombrosans and, perhaps especially, Gregory were all expressing and disseminating an ideal of holiness and spirituality that was at a distance from those who possessed secular power or at least who were seen to be intimately connected to secular power. This ideal of holiness clearly commended itself to those who did not possess worldly power, but who were effectively asked to act as God's agents by impeding and even expelling unworthy priests.

The case of the priest Ramihrd is especially instructive in this respect. In 1076, Ramihrd, whose preaching against simonists and sexually active priests had apparently caused popular unrest in Cambrai, was examined for heresy. Ramihrd impeccably answered all the doctrinal questions put to him by the bishop, but refused to confirm his testimony by taking the Eucharist 'from any of the abbots or priests or even the bishop himself, because they were up to the necks in simony and other avarice'.[51] Following the examination, Ramihrd was placed under arrest in a hut which several of the bishop's servants later set afire. Gregory VII reacted vehemently to the news that 'a man was delivered to the flames because he had ventured to say that simoniacs and fornicating priests ought not to celebrate masses and that their ministrations ought in no way to be accepted' and he instructed Bishop Josfred of Paris to investigate the matter thoroughly.[52] Gregory's naïveté or incredulity has long troubled historians, in particular his inability to comprehend the potentially dangerous social and theological repercussions of his call for all Christians – for 'the people' – to stand up for reform and righteousness, even against the existing order. For, how were 'the people' in a position to judge? How were they to know a good priest from a bad one?

As Moore has noted, chastity is almost always a state that is difficult to prove, and hence invariably becomes a matter of reputation; for how else could it be decided, and more important by whom, whether a woman living in a priest's household was a housekeeper, a wife or a concubine?[53] The same was to some extent true with simony: who, apart from the cleric and lord involved, knew whether a promise of fealty or the ritual exchange of gifts at investiture constituted an actual instance of simony? As such, a considerable burden was placed on local communities by the reformers and especially by Gregory VII, when he called upon lay society to make such judgements, whether or not they were qualified to do so. The resentment and open hostility engendered both against and among the clergy is scarcely surprising. The reformers' inability to conceive the repercussions of drawing on lay society, however, is less so. Their revolutionary gamble – of marshalling a popular enthusiasm that could easily slip into heresy – would come back to haunt the Church in the early twelfth century in the form of men such as Manasses of Ghent, Henry of Lausanne, Arnold of Brescia and others. Only in the later twelfth century, with concerted legal measures such as Pope Lucius III's bull *Ad abolendam* of 1184, the application of the Roman principle of legal infamy and the use of unnamed accusers and witnesses, was the Church able to recover the power to influence and direct communities' judgements.

Lay investiture

Given these difficulties, it is perhaps not surprising that the reformers, while still waging the campaign against simony and married clergy, moved to the simple but visible test of clerical independence and morality with the banning of lay investiture. The practice of the lay investiture of bishops and abbots, like simony and clerical marriage, had a long history in the Western Church. As episcopal office around the year 1000 was at once effectively both spiritual and secular, on account of the lands and rights donated by the king, the practice of royal investiture of a new bishop or abbot with those temporal properties that pertained to his bishopric or monastery was an important and visible indicator of the role of the Christian king in the life of the Church. When a man was selected as bishop, he would swear loyalty to the king and receive from his hands the symbols of his office, usually the pastoral staff and ring. Although the bishop-elect would still require consecration by other bishops, it seemed to many that in the ritual of investiture the king made a priest into a bishop, as though the bishopric was in his keeping, and hence his gift (which was indeed often the case in practice). Analogous ceremonies occurred down the ecclesiastical hierarchy with the presentation to newly appointed clerics of symbols such as keys or books by their local lords. These ceremonies were widely practised and cemented bonds in otherwise rudimentary power structures.

The first rumblings against this practice were apparent, as noted above, at the Council of Bourges in 1031. There it had been stipulated that laymen ought not to place priests in office, save through the bishop. It was, however, Humbert of Silva-Candida who in the 1050s fiercely launched an attack on the practice: he called for its abolition on the grounds that it made moral and financial abuses among the clergy inevitable. There is little evidence that his ideas gained much support among the reformers until the second part of Gregory VII's pontificate and there has been much debate among historians as to when and why Gregory undertook to ban lay investiture. After all, when Humbert's treatise was written, Gregory was serving as a papal legate in Germany and had no scruples about attending the episcopal consecration of Bishop Gundechar of Eichstätt, who had already been invested by the Empress Agnes. Furthermore, in the early part of his pontificate, Gregory's objections to Bishop-elect Anselm II of Lucca's investiture seem only to have stemmed from the possible taint on Henry IV – who was still in communion with royal advisers who had been excommunicated by Pope Alexander II – and not from an objection to lay investiture *per se.*[54]

Much seems to depend on the question of whether or not a prohibition against lay investiture was issued by Gregory at the Lenten synod of 1075. While no such decree is extant, many historians, citing Arnulf of Milan's *Book of Recent Deeds*, have subscribed to the view that investiture was in some way banned in 1075.[55] If such legislation was enacted, however, it seems not to have been a universal prohibition but one aimed especially at Milan and the northern Italian bishoprics, though as Cowdrey argues, Gregory's position on the issue was clearly hardening from 1075.[56] As his letters after that time show, Gregory increasingly began to see lay investiture as an unwarranted intrusion of laymen into ecclesiastical affairs. In November 1078 he promulgated legislation from the point of view of the clergy, and in March 1080, he condemned the practice from the side of laity.[57] Although the issue would not finally be resolved until the Concordat of Worms in 1122, lay investiture became the contentious topic around which the reformers framed and waged their campaign for a freely established clergy especially after Gregory's death.[58] It was only then that the reform movement truly became the 'Investiture Controversy'.

Conclusion

While it has often been thought in the past that reform measures in the eleventh century were disseminated from Rome and that the issues expanded in almost a linear fashion from clerical deportment to attempts to separate the clergy completely from other power structures, it is clear that the evolution of reform objectives and especially their implementation was by no means this straightforward. Reform also encompassed material renewal, and relied as much on the mustering of popular indignation as on the work of legates and the promulgation of canons promoting free election and clerical chastity. Campaigns against simony and clerical marriage began as early as the late tenth century and were prompted as much by the underlying agendas of peace councils as by the desire of secular princes, kings, bishops and popes to impose better standards in religious life. Following the elevation of Leo IX in 1049, however, these issues increasingly took on a new urgency as the reformed papacy struggled to impose its agenda. As a consequence, the reformers were increasingly led to insert their particular objectives of a free and chaste clergy in a wider vision of Christian society in which the spiritual would be irrevocably divorced from the secular.

Notes

1 J. Howe, *Church Reform and Social Change in Eleventh-century Italy: Dominic of Sora and His Patrons* (Philadelphia, PA, 1997).

2 Jotsald, *Vita sancti Odilonis* (PL, 142), 906. The construction of a larger church at Cluny, however, was the work of Abbot Hugh.

3 Rodulf Glaber, *Hist. Libri V.*, 3.iv.13, 114–16.

4 See ibid., lxiii–lxx, introduction by J. France. For 'Mosaic jubilee', see *Hist. Libri V.*, 4.v.16, 197. Cf. R. Landes, 'The Fear of an Apocalyptic Year 1000', 97–145.

5 See M. T. Gibson, *Lanfranc of Bec* (Oxford, 1978); and J. Rubenstein, 'Liturgy

Against History: The Competing Visions of Lanfranc and Eadmer of Canterbury', *Speculum*, 74/2 (1999), 279–309.

6 For good overviews, see B. Golding, *Conquest and Colonisation: The Normans in Britain 1066–1100*, rev. edn (Basingstoke, Hants., 2001), 57–74; and R. Bartlett, *England under the Norman and Angevin Kings* (Oxford, 2000), 46–72. Several dioceses (such as Dorchester) were reorganized, with episcopal centres re-seated in cities in accordance with canon law.

7 *Sacrorum conciliorum nova et amplissima collectio*, ed. G. D. Mansi, 57 vols. (Paris and Arnhem, 1901–27), 19.856–7. The council also issued elaborate stipulations regarding vestments.

8 J. A. Bowman, 'The Bishop Builds a Bridge: Sanctity and Power in the Medieval Pyrenees', *Catholic Historical Review*, 88 (2002), 1–16.

9 Ibid., 10.

10 M. Otter, '1066: The Moment of Transition in two narratives of the Norman Conquest', *Speculum*, 74 (1999), 565–86; cf. E. Mason, *St. Wulfstan of Worcester* (Oxford, 1990); and S. Ridyard, '*Condigna veneratio*: Post-Conquest Attitudes to the English Saints', *Anglo-Norman Studies*, 9 (1987), 197–206.

11 K. G. Cushing, 'Events that Led to Sainthood: Sanctity and the Reformers in the Eleventh Century', in R. Gameson and H. Leyser, eds, *Belief and Culture in the Middle Ages: Essays Presented to Henry Mayr-Harting* (Oxford, 2001), 187–96.

12 M. Miller, 'Masculinity, Reform, and Clerical Culture: Narratives of Episcopal Holiness in the Gregorian Era', *Church History*, 72/1 (2003), 25–52. I am grateful to Maureen Miller for allowing me to see earlier versions and an advance copy of the published article.

13 R. Landes, 'Between Aristocracy and Heresy: Popular Participation in the Limousin Peace of God, 994–1033', in *Peace of God*, 184–218, at 189.

14 Anselm of St Remy, *Historia dedicationis sancti Remigii apud Remos*, in J. Hourlier, ed., 'Anselme de Saint-Remy: histoire de la dédicace de Saint-Remy', in *La Champagne bénédictine* (Rheims, 1981), 179–297, text 200–60; for other edns, see above, Ch. 3, n.29.

15 J. T. Gilchrist, '*Simoniaca haeresis* and the Problem of Orders from Leo IX to Gratian', in *Canon Law in the Age of Reform, Eleventh and Twelfth Centuries* (Aldershot, Hants., 1993), no. iv, 209–35.

16 Peter Damian, *Vita beati Romualdi*, c. 35, ed. G. Tabacco (Fonti per la storia d'Italia, 94; Rome, 1957), 74–6; partial English trans. by H. Leyser in T. Head, ed., *Medieval Hagiography: An Anthology* (New York, 2000), 297–315.

17 Humbert, *Adversus simoniacos*, 95–253.

18 Peter Damian, Letter 40 (Reindel, 1.384–509; trans., 2.111–14). Cf. Gilchrist, '*Simoniaca haeresis*', 212ff.

19 C. Wickham, *The Mountains and the City: The Tuscan Apennines in the Early Middle Ages* (Oxford, 1988), 39ff.

20 Cushing, *Papacy and Law*, 57–63 and literature cited there. Also see above, Ch. 4.

21 See Remensynder, 'Pollution, Purity and Peace', 289.

22 *Heinrici II. Constitutiones*, 30 (MGH, *Const.*, I), 61–2.

23 Mansi, 19.2, 3, 5, 22; here as quoted by Moore, *First European Revolution*, 10.

24 Mansi, 19.926-8, c. 1.

25 Ibid., 19.1069-72.

26 See D. Elliott, *Spiritual Marriage: Sexual Abstinence in Medieval Wedlock* (Princeton, NJ, 1993).

27 *Henrici II. Constitutiones*, no. 34, 77-8. See also U.-R. Blumenthal, 'Pope Gregory VII and the Prohibition of Nicolaitism', in *Medieval Purity and Piety*, 239-67, at 240.

28 On Rome, see Peter Damian, Letter 112 (Reindel, 3.280-1; trans., 4.275); for Mainz: Adam of Bremen, *Gesta Hammaburgensis ecclesiae* (MGH, *SS*, 7), 346-7.

29 Blumenthal, 'Gregory VII and the Prohibition of Nicholaitism', 241.

30 As in Remensynder, 'Pollution, Purity and Peace', 288. See also R. E. Reynolds, 'The Subdiaconate as a Sacred and Superior Order', in his *Clerics in the Early Middle Ages: Hierarchy and Image* (Aldershot, Hants., 1999), 1-39.

31 Mansi, 19.749ff. Cf. Blumenthal, 'Gregory VII and the Prohibition of Nicolaitism', and H. E. J. Cowdrey, 'Pope Gregory VII and the Chastity of the Clergy', in Blumenthal, *Medieval Purity and Piety*, 269-302.

32 I. S. Robinson, 'The Friendship Network of Pope Gregory VII', *History*, 63 (1978), 1-23.

33 For example, *Reg.*, 2.29, 161-2 (trans. 119-20); 2.67, 223-5 (trans. 160-1); Gregory VII, *Ep. vag.* 6, 15. Cf. *Ep. vag.*, 4, 8-10.

34 *Reg.*, 2.28, 160-1 (trans. 118-20).

35 For example, *Reg.*, 1.1, 15, 29; 2.4; 3.2; 4.23; 5.12; 6.26; 9.29, 33. *Ep. vag.*, 2, 6-10, 13, 24, 31.

36 *Reg.*, 2.10, 140-2 (trans. 104-5).

37 For example, *Reg.*, 2.30, 163-5 (trans. 120-1); 2.31, 165-8 (trans. 122-4); 3.3, 246-7 (trans. 176-7).

38 *Reg.* 2.45, 182-5 (trans. 136). Cf. 2.47, 186-7 (trans., 137-8).

39 For example, *Reg.*, 1.40, 47, 50, 77.

40 Ibid., 6.17, 423-4 (trans. 298-9).

41 *Ep. vag.*, 6, 15.

42 Ibid., 10, 23-5; 11, 27. On the Vallombrosans, see below, Ch. 6.

43 Cushing, 'Events that Led to Sainthood', 187-96.

44 Berthold of Reichenau, *Annales a. 1077* (MGH, *SS*, 5), 304-6, esp. 305 for Gregory VII's public commendation at the Lenten synod of 1078. Although there is nothing in the synod protocol, see Bonizo of Sutri, *Liber ad amicum* (MGH, *LdL*, 1), 8, 674. Cf. *Reg.*, 3.21, 287-8 (trans. 204-5).

45 Berthold, *Annales a. 1077*, 304.

46 *Quellen und Forschungen zum Urkunden- und Kanzleiwesen Papst Gregors VII.*, no. 106, ed. L. Santifaller (Studi e Testi, 190; Vatican City, 1957), 94-5: 'Si sanctorum memoriam veneramur, de quorum legimus morte et abscissione membrorum, si patientiam laudamus eorum, quos a fide Christi gladius nec ulla pena divisit: tu quoque, absciso naso et auribus pro Christi nomine laudabilior es, qui ad eam gratiam pertingere meruisti, que ab omnibus desideranda est, qua a sanctis, si perseveraveris in finem, non discrepas. Integras quidem corporis tui diminuta est, set interior homo, qui renovatur de die in diem, magnum sanctitatis suscepit incrementum.'

47 See C. Violante, *La pataria milanese e la riforma ecclesiastica* (Rome, 1955). For more details on the following, see Cushing, 'Events that Led to Sainthood', 187–96.

48 See Moore, 'Family, Community and Cult', 50.

49 Cushing, 'Events that Led to Sainthood', 188–91.

50 H. E. J. Cowdrey, 'The Papacy, the Patarenes and the Church of Milan', *TRHS*, 5th series, 18 (1968), 25–48.

51 *Chronicle of St André de Castres*, excerpt trans. in R. I. Moore, *The Birth of Popular Heresy* (repr. Toronto, 1995), 24–5.

52 *Reg.*, 4.20, 328–9 (trans. 230–2). He also instructed Josfred to prevent unchaste clergy from serving at mass throughout France.

53 Moore, *First European Revolution*, 15.

54 On Anselm, see Cushing, *Papacy and Law*, 48–55; cf. Cowdrey, *Pope Gregory VII*, 546–50.

55 Arnulf, *Liber recentiorum*, 4.7, ed. C. Zey (MGH, *SSRG*, 7; Hanover, 1994), 211–12. For a survey of the debate, see R. Schieffer, *Die Entstehung des päpstlichen Investitursverbot für den deutschen König* (Stuttgart, 1981). Though Schieffer argues against the decree, Gregory's letter to Henry in Dec. 1075 (*Reg.*, 3.10) challenges his argument.

56 Cowdrey, *Pope Gregory VII*, 847.

57 *Reg.*, 6.5b, no. 3, 403 (trans. 283); 7.14a, nos. 1–2, 480–1 (trans. 340).

58 See S. Chodorow, 'Ecclesiastical Politics and the Ending of the Investiture Contest', *Speculum*, 46 (1971), 613–40; Blumenthal, *Investiture Controversy*, 135–74; and I. S. Robinson, *Authority and Resistance in the Investiture Contest* (Manchester, 1978); and Robinson, *Henry IV*, 304–44.

6

The rhetoric of reform

THE work of reform in the eleventh century, as has been seen, was not just many-sided but also was inextricably linked with wider social transformations. At its core, though, reform was about persuasion. If initially reform was about inculcating an acceptance of, or at least outward conformity with, new codes of behaviour, then ultimately it was about persuading individuals to accept a line of demarcation between the previously overlapping spiritual and secular spheres. Among a previous generation of historians, there has been a tendency to conceive of reform as being concerned solely with the morality and conduct of the clergy; in other words, it was viewed as an exercise chiefly in clerical and monastic discipline.

Yet, as has already been suggested above, there was another group – the laity and especially the aristocracy – who also had to be persuaded to change both their conduct and their attitudes if reform was to succeed. Thus, while contemporary sources and modern historiography frequently point to confrontation, opposition and even violent conflict between the secular and ecclesiastical realms, notably the clash of Gregory VII and Henry IV, in fact over the course of the eleventh century the interests of both groups increasingly began to coalesce. This had important ramifications, chiefly in terms of cementing the beginnings of a new social order. This chapter and the next will explore how this was effected, beginning here with how the clergy were rhetorically persuaded to embrace reform.

Purity and pollution

The battle for hearts and minds to win acceptance for this new order was fought on various levels, by means of general and regional councils, by the promulgation of canons, and through the tireless activities of papal legates often in concert with the local aristocracy (see Chapter 5). Its most persuasive expression, however, was in polemic and propaganda, whether in the forms of letters, treatises or, especially, hagiography. The significance of these polemical writings – in drawing attention to the unacceptability of much contemporary clerical behaviour – cannot be underestimated. The reformers had to marshal public opinion so that actions that had previously failed to provoke a general moral indignation within society would come to be regarded as serious moral offences with untold consequences. It is evident that this tactic underlay much of the reformers' propaganda. By increasingly emphasizing the potential for contagion, and by reiterating the paramount need to cleanse the sacred from contamination by the secular, the reformers used the language of purity and pollution, in particular the rhetoric of sexual separation, both to delineate and more sharply enforce what they deemed to be the appropriate spheres of activity both for themselves and for lay society.[1]

Reliance on this type of rhetoric, of course, was scarcely an innovation in the late tenth and eleventh centuries, although, as will be seen, both its prevalence and vehemence was revolutionary. As any historian of the late antique and medieval Church can testify, ecclesiastical sources are full of references to concerns about ritual purity and fears of contamination from an early date. For instance, Irish texts such as the mid-sixth-century Vinnian and mid-seventh-century Cummean penitentials repeatedly display anxiety about the purity of the sacraments and those who handled them. Great was their fear that the altar dishes be defiled or in some way compromised, that the host might fall on the floor, or even worse that a mouse might eat it. Substantial penance was stipulated for these and other infractions, including notably 120 days of fasting for an individual who vomited the host, which was subsequently eaten by a dog.[2] Even an unintentional sin could be defiling and was an occasion for penance.

Unease in the early Church, however, was not solely restricted to objects and individuals associated with the sacraments, but also involved safeguarding certain times and places. For instance, sexual relations during prohibited times or with menstruating women might result, according to Caesarius of Arles, in leprous, epileptic and even demoniac children.[3] Similar fears were by no means unknown in the eleventh century or beyond. In his *Book of the Miracles of St Foy*, Bernard of Angers warned that if anyone passed beyond the first set of iron grilles into the saint's sanctuary without having washed himself after sexual intercourse, even if it was legitimate, he would never complete the day unpunished. Bernard's comment that St Foy 'loved those whom she saw persevering in the virtue of chastity' and how vexed she 'became at anyone who thoughtlessly dared to frequent her sanctuary while in a defiled condition' is one of many indications of how the saints could be polemically mustered in the struggle to promote morality.[4] This clearly echoed the long-standing fear about sexual relations in sacred places, especially churches, which could involve not only re-consecration of the church in question but also a ceremony of reconciliation (though canonical authorities disagreed on this issue).[5] Once more, underlying such anxieties was a fear of contamination though – as the 'peace', the Truce of God, the sacred ban established by Urban II around Cluny in 1095, and the consecration of churches and graveyards in general all show – such practices can also be seen as attempts to secure borders that might be open to potential transgression.[6]

Most often, especially in the earlier middle ages though continuing into the eleventh century, fears such as these largely concentrated on the activities of those members of the spiritual elite, that is, monks, who by virtue of their position as the *agni immaculati* ('pure lambs') needed especially to be insulated from contamination, lest the salvation of the Christian people in general be compromised. Despite cloistering, they were nonetheless seen as being particularly susceptible to corruption, a susceptibility no doubt exacerbated by the exclusion of women and the availability of young boys. That the potential for corruption was under-stood as very real can be seen in the mid-tenth-century *Life* of Abbot Odo of Cluny when it notes the custom at Baume – where Odo had been an oblate – that when a boy (*puer*) needed to relieve himself at night, he needed to be accompanied by not one but two monks and a lighted candle.[7]

Although it was generally accepted that temptation and potential corruption came chiefly from the devil, continual vigilance was required, as well as the establishment of careful, often propitiatory, boundaries. For instance, the pseudo-Ambrosian prayer used at compline petitioned that the dreams and fantasies inspired by the devil be held back and that the supplicants' bodies be kept free from pollution. Evening prayers attri-buted to Alcuin were if anything more explicit, requesting that on retiring to bed the supplicants' 'chaste members' be permitted to rise in the morning as clean temples of the Holy Spirit, ready for God's work.[8] It needs to be underlined here though that, by the late tenth century, virginity was not simply desirable from a moral perspective, but also that it had changed into a critical component of monastic power, one used to bolster claims for privileges and rights to property. Thus Abbo of Fleury's tripartite division of society in terms of a sexual hierarchy of the virgins, the continent and the married made the moral claims of monks to property contingent upon their wholly pure condition.[9]

Yet concerns about purity were by no means limited to the monastic world. Although there had been many attempts in the past to extend monastic ideals beyond the cloister, the later tenth and especially the eleventh century increasingly saw not just the appropriation, but also the recasting, of monastic ideals of purity by the reformers. It has long been accepted that there was a significant resurrection of the ideals of cultic purity in the eleventh century, with attention increasingly falling on the status and disposition of those priests and bishops who dispensed the sacraments or who participated in the ritual of the mass. Effectively, the eleventh-century reformers recast monastic ideals to contend with contemporary vices, particularly those that could be seen as impacting on the performance of sacramental duties. Moreover, to a greater extent perhaps even than in monastic rhetoric, the reformers expressed their anxieties about bishops and priests in terms referring to the body. Especially disturbing was the question of whether sexual relations, or 'occurrences of pollution' as they were often described (that is, seminal emission in contexts other than masturbation or intercourse, which in themselves were problematic enough), even just impure thoughts, were somehow 'spiritually polluting' and therefore ought to prevent participation in sacramental activities.

These concerns too had had a long history, and had found cogent expression in the works of John Cassian, Augustine and Gregory I, all of whom indelibly influenced later writers. Alarmed that the Christian community might be divided by competition for the moral high ground, Augustine had adopted a pessimistic view of human sexuality, perhaps in an effort to disabuse the claims to purity being advanced by the ascetic movement. John Cassian, however, who advocated the rigorous control of the mind – because mental *fluxus* might issue in surplus bodily *fluxus* – saw the occasion of a seminal emission as the opportunity for concerted self-examination. Like Gregory I, however, Cassian also saw voluntary abstaining from ritual as advisable.[10] Yet, as Le Goff has discussed, with the term *caro* ('flesh') increasingly coming by the eleventh century to denote bodily corruptibility rather than the positive image of the flesh assumed by Christ, it is scarcely surprising that virtue was more than ever seen to be mediated through the body, a body that – because of sexual relations, or contact with blood, money and weapons – might compromise the integrity of the sacraments.[11]

Peter Brown has argued that the renunciation of sexual activity by the early Christian clergy – and their distance from menstruation, childbirth and seminal emission – underscored their position as 'creatures perched between nature and the city', with bishops in particular – as men of cities – acting as 'a barrier against the formless, purely biological products of the body that reminded the faithful of their indissoluble connection with the natural world.'[12] In other words, bishops were men set apart, who bridged on any number of levels the distance between sacred and worldly spaces, though chiefly by virtue of their sacramental activities. As a consequence, bishops and by extension the clergy in general were effectively anomalous creatures. Through their sacramental roles and their ideal (at least) of sexual renunciation, they made certain that the Church's connection with all the sources of worldly power was carefully concealed: as Brown noted, they could live with wives as if they had no wives; they could administer the wealth of the Church as if they were men of no possessions.[13]

Yet by the eleventh century, this tacit veiling was no longer acceptable. The priesthood, now claiming for itself the role both of guardian and critic of social and religious morality, increasingly found itself in an ambivalent position; what had previously been acceptable was no longer tolerated. Celibacy and virginity were no longer just the special property of monks, but were now also to be the defining characteristics – as required by their sacramental roles – of the secular clergy, who were increasingly required to distance themselves from worldly contact. Moreover, with the progressive extension of the sacred orders in the eleventh century to include the subdeacons among the higher clergy, outward form was no longer acceptable and increasingly explicit language was deployed to remind the recalcitrant.[14] Peter Damian, for one, insisted on complete celibacy, chastity and the avoidance of all sexual thoughts as essential for the individual who had any sacramental role. This was to be achieved, according to Damian, through ascetic self-denial, fasting and even the 'blessed discipline' of self-flagellation, all of which promoted a pure spirit. We will return to Damian below.

It would be easy to dismiss this language of bodily purity and pollution as nothing more than a convenient rhetorical strategy on the part of ecclesiastical and especially monastic writers. Yet, as Mary Douglas suggested in her classic work, *Purity and Danger*, what societies term as polluting or unclean does not depend on cleanliness *per se* – or, to use the terminology of the eleventh century, on *munditia* – but rather derives from wider cultural norms and their inconsistencies. Her by-now-classic definition of dirt as 'matter out of place' locates un-cleanliness in that which is marginal or liminal, or which otherwise transgresses a society's cultural boundaries and categories. Douglas' analysis revealed that the body was the most frequent symbol on which these anxieties were mapped, as the edges of the body, which are liminal in more ways than one, often stood in for any boundaries that were precarious or threatened.[15]

Our understanding of the expression and meaning of particular anxieties, however, must remain sensitive not only to cultural patterns but also to historical contexts. Eleventh-century society – in the wake of a number of social and intellectual transformations (whether gradual or radical) and exemplifying, as Moore put it, all the characteristics of 'a society at war with itself' – seems to have been especially susceptible to pollution fears, or at least reached for such terminology in order to come to terms with what was, or at least seemed to be, chaotic.[16] Moreover, it is in the eleventh century that we begin to witness the concerted effort of the reformers to infuse their society with the ideal of purity that had been set out in canon law since the fourth century. The priesthood was to be a separate caste, whose special status came from their service at the altar and their contact with the sacraments. Clerics, as we have seen, were to be unmarried, celibate and ideally chaste. Clerics were prohibited from bearing weapons and sporting other secular trappings. Clerics were not to sell or purchase church offices or benefices, or to be in any way influenced by worldly considerations.

Though 'clean hands' had of course mattered to Carolingian kings,[17] it can be argued that the revived emphasis on purity in the eleventh century developed as much from clerical initiatives as from lay pressure, and was perhaps chiefly prompted by the increasing desire of such men to distinguish and privilege themselves over against the rest of society, both monks and laymen, whose activities they would then direct. Purity was to be found in that which was whole, unmixed and separate, whilst impurity remained in that which scandalously mixed what should remain distinct. But these old ideals were now to be turned into reality, and the clergy, both secular and regular, as well as the laity, who did not respect the more sharply drawn boundaries of their categories, became 'matter out of place' who were excoriated in increasingly vehement rhetoric in an effort once more to locate them 'in place'.

On a very important level, the history of reform needs to be understood in terms of a powerful ideal of differentiation. As Moore has noted, a pure priest could be a powerful mediator.[18] Defining the separateness of those who mediated between God and mankind, however, required strategies of demarcation that often took the form of accusations, whether real or rhetorical, centring on the potential for contamination from compromised or tainted priests. This was the case both with simony and clerical marriage, where various reformers and commentators underlined the consequences of tolerating the status quo. They did this not simply to shame individuals or to undermine the status of compromised clerics but also, as with the Pataria and in Gregory VII's boycott decrees, to elicit moral indignation among the people with potentially the most to fear from contamination. The reformers, however, ultimately needed to develop a consistent language of purity.

The rhetoric against simony

Early condemnations of simony drew upon fears of corruption, infection and the propensity to further sin engendered (chiefly, but not exclusively) by avarice and theft. Hence, the Cluniac chronicler Rodulf Glaber noted in his *Histories* that:

> The leaders of the clerical and temporal orders fell into avarice, and they resorted, even more than had formerly been their wont, to robbery to satisfy their lusts. Middling and lesser people followed their example and plunged into monstrous sin. Who ever before heard of so many incests, so many adulteries, illicit marriages between those of the same blood, shameless concubinage, and so much competition in evil? Moreover, to crown this peak of evil, there was none or very few amongst the people admonishing them and correcting these offences, so that the warning of the prophet was fulfilled: 'And it shall be, as with the people, so with the priest' (Isa. 24.2).[19]

Though elsewhere in his *Histories* Glaber played down the moral consequences implicit in the expansion of the Church, meaning that the mobilization of material resources and the assertion of political power inevitably involved the clergy engaging inappropriately in commercial activities and worldly affairs, here he was adamant that avarice underlay the evils of his present day. Earlier in his *Histories*, he had censured the prevalence in the Church of simony and corruption, which for him were directly the product of avarice.[20]

Peter Damian also saw avarice as the root of all evil, noting on one occasion that 'hardly any festering wound causes a more intolerable stench for the nose of God than the excrement that is avarice', and he lamented that 'the avaricious man is guilty of all evil things, for having the roots in the field of his heart, he cannot avoid their poisonous growth.'[21] However, when discussing simony, Damian generally tended towards more overt pestilential imagery. Thus writing in praise of Archbishop Gebhard of Ravenna in 1043, he noted that 'While the dragon of simony after binding the arms of those trafficking wretches in its intricate coil of avarice, is spewing forth its venom, you were almost the exception ... in keeping your church free from its foul contagion.'[22] For Damian, simony was chiefly a 'pestilence', a 'poison ... [that] spread its deadly influence through the kingdoms of the west'. As he wrote in his important treatise on the validity of sacraments even of simonists and heretics, the *Liber gratissimus*, the simonist, like Simon Magus, 'overturn[ed] his pestilential stall' and was a 'thief [who] creeps through the postern gate defiled'.[23] He even recounted a tale of a simoniacal priest who contracted leprosy.[24]

Both Humbert and Gregory VII also resorted to the language of contagion in their condemnations of simony, though in Humbert's case with devastating implications for the efficacy of the sacraments and ordinations of simonists, whom he accused of inflicting corporeal damage to the mystical body of Christ.[25] Although, apart from Humbert, the reformers continued to insist on the integrity of the sacraments of clerics compromised by simony, their rhetoric often blurred fine theological lines. This was apparent even with Damian, who praised his ascetic disciple Dominic Loricatus for voluntarily abstaining from ministering at the altar after learning that his parents had presented a soft goatskin to the bishop before his ordination. This was also the case with Gregory, whose boycott decrees were open to misinterpretation as seen above in the case of Ramihrd.[26]

Yet overall, Gregory's preoccupation with potential contamination clearly derived more from moral considerations than from those of cultic purity. In a letter to Archbishop Siegfried of Mainz in September 1075, Gregory urged him to investigate reports about Bishop Werner of Strassburg and the 'contagion of simony ... so that ... the church may be cleansed from great pollutions'.[27] Gregory employed similar language in a letter to the faithful in the German kingdom in September 1076, urging them to receive Henry IV back if he proved his penitence. Gregory referred here to the king's wicked counsellors 'who, having been excommunicated for the simoniac heresy, have not shrunk from infecting their lord with their own leprosy'.[28] These examples can easily be multiplied. Gregory frequently referred to the 'pestilential trafficking of the simoniac heresy', although he increasingly expressed these sentiments in the context of obedience to the papacy and the proper social ordering, for instance in his letters to Siegfried of Mainz, Werner of Madgeburg and Otto of Constance in 1075, and in his subsequent deposition of Otto from office.[29]

Yet the rhetoric against simony was not couched solely in the language of infection and contagion. It was also expressed in terms of the theft of churches, and even the prostitution or rape of the bride of Christ. Although it is not surprising that diatribes against clerical marriage and concubinage were full of sexual implications, as will be seen below, it is significant that this imagery was directed equally if not more so against simony. Much hinged on the notion of a bishop's or priest's marriage to his church. This of course was an idea that went back to the early Church, and one that derived most of its force from the idea of Christ as the Church's bridegroom. It had been expounded by Christian writers such as Cyprian who used marital imagery to describe a bishop's relationship with the religious community over which he presided. Supported by biblical dicta on the indissolubility of marriage, such arguments were refined and employed by Athanasius of Alexandria against the early Church practice of transferring bishops from one see to another.[30] These ideas found especial prominence in the ninth-century forgery, the Pseudo-Isidorian *Decretals*, where they were used to stipulate not only that a bishop could not be transferred, but also that a lawful one could not be replaced.[31]

That eleventh-century writers were not only returning to these notions but also extending them to different spheres can be seen in the anonymous treatise *On the Ordination of the Pope*, written in the aftermath of the synod of Sutri in 1046. Pointedly referring to the Church as the bride of Christ and noting that a bishop fills the place of Christ with respect to the bride, the anonymous author condemned Pope Gregory VI, whose illicit intrusion into the apostolic see by simony was described not merely as theft, but also as the rape of the bride of Christ.[32] Humbert of Silva-Candida also condemned simony with sexual and marital imagery, warning as well that the practice of lay investiture intruded in this sacred union. For Humbert, a bishop's consecration meant his effective marriage with his church, and his episcopal ring signified that 'like betrothed lovers, they [bishops] should unceasingly show forth and praise the pledge of faith of their own bride, which is the church.'[33] Humbert also censured the selling of ecclesiastical office as the abduction and prostitution of the Church, even using the analogy of how serious such an offence would be against an ordinary woman.[34]

Although Damian clearly preferred to use sexual and marital images in his censures of married clergy, he did resort to this imagery in his condemnations in 1058 of the anti-pope Benedict X, a simonist who in Damian's words 'delighted to carry on in this adultery'.[35] Moreover, in his *Liber gratissimus*, Damian not only characterized simonists as 'even worse than adulterers', but went on to note that they 'exceed murderers, ... surpass plunderers, the sacrilegious and incestuous parricides, and the infamy of nearly all criminals', concluding that 'the very perfidy of the Jews and all heretical depravity are in no wise equal to your excesses.'[36]

Although like Damian, Gregory VII also tended to reserve marital imagery for lambasting married clergy, in a letter to the faithful in Lombardy in 1073, warning against the simoniacal and excommunicated Guido of Milan, Gregory castigated the archbishop, noting that he 'presumed to buy, like a base slave-girl, the church ... [of Milan, and] now, in an attempt to prostitute the bride of Christ to the devil, he has striven to besmirch her with the offence of heresy.'[37] However, this imagery could also be employed in a more positive way. For instance, in a letter to the newly-elected Archbishop Alfanus of Salerno in 1058 discussing the sublime dignity and responsibility of episcopal office, Damian noted that: 'We can properly understand a bishop's wife to be his life and manner of living which indeed should be virginal, kept immune and untouched by the defiling pleasures of an unclean spirit that violates the temple of the soul. ... Therefore, a bishop must beware of marrying a soiled or meretricious wife, but should always display the integrity of a chaste and pure manner of living.'[38]

The rhetoric against clerical marriage

Clerical marriage and concubinage likewise unleashed a torrent of polemic, chiefly focusing on the perceived contamination and confusion engendered by a cleric's sexual activities. It has already been noted above that an early condemnation of clerical marriage and concubinage was made at the joint papal and imperial Council of Pavia in 1022 where unchastity was labeled 'the root of all evils'. The reformers, however, increasingly expressed their condemnations of married clergy by devoting particular attention to the consequences of this sin for the people over whom the tainted bishop or priest presided. Many of these condemnations were contained in moralizing tales of the shameful and even damning consequences of clergy engaging in sexual activity.

In a letter to Pope Nicholas II and Hildebrand in 1058, Damian recounted the story of a hitherto irreproachable priest who was attended by angels at his daily offering of the mass. One day, however, when the priest was saying mass in the presence of the count and was beginning the consecration of the eucharist, an angel appeared and began to scrub the priest's entire body. After the consecration, the angel reappeared and poured the grimy water over him to the amazement of all present, at which point the now thoroughly defiled priest confessed that he had slept with one of the count's maids the previous night.[39] There are many other similar moralizing tales of punishment and public shame, like the miracle of St Foy noted above. Moreover, it often fell to religious women to identify and accuse incontinent clergy through divine illumination. In his *Life of the Blessed Herluca*, Paul of Bernried – the biographer of Gregory VII – after detailing the crimes of a certain priest Richard of Eppach, described how Herluca, having been cautioned by Christ to avoid this priest on account of his sexual incontinence, shamed him into confession and penance. Herluca's vision of the soul of another bad priest, Adalbert, being carried off to hell (a topos frequently reiterated elsewhere) – in one version on account of his married status – vividly underscored the consequences for married priests.[40]

Damian, however, was not in the least hesitant about tackling the topic of sexually-active clergy directly and in far more graphic language than other writers generally elected to use. One of his most vehement condemnations of married and unchaste clergy is found in his letter to Nicholas II, written between January and July 1059, probably as a consequence of the important Roman council of that year, where clerical marriage had been condemned and it had been stipulated that no one should hear the mass of a priest who kept a concubine. Deploring the situation of bishops living in public concubinage, who (unlike priests) had not explicitly been censured in the council's decrees, Damian stated the situation in unequivocal terms: 'But what a criminal situation! Shamelessly this epidemic has been so audaciously revealed that everyone knows the houses of prostitution, the fathers-in-law ... and other close relatives ... and lastly to remove all doubt, you have the obvious pregnancies and the squalling babies.'[41] He implored the pope to depose those 'who had no fear of soiling the purity of ecclesiastical chastity' and who thus 'so expelled [would] deter others'.[42]

In this letter, he also resorted to his customary rhetorical practice of directly addressing the fornicating bishops, asking what business they had to handle the body of Christ while wallowing in the allurements of the flesh. Reminding them that the 'Son of God was so dedicated to purity of the flesh that he was born not of conjugal chastity but rather from the womb of virgin' and that as an infant he had been tended by pure hands, Damian stipulated that Christ wanted to be served in the mass and at all other times by 'unstained hands'. Damian would return to this theme later in a letter to the archpriest Peter, insisting that the consecration of Christ's body in the Eucharist ought in no way to be performed by a priest who had just risen from his bed and from fondling the genitals of what Damian referred to as 'his whore'.[43] Later, Damian went so far as to equate incontinent clerics with heretics, and lamented to Pope Alexander II that the whole world was full of 'sex, avarice and gluttony.'[44]

At the heart of Damian's rhetoric against married or sexually active clergy clearly lay fears of pollution. In the letter of 1059 to Nicholas II, rather forgetting his earlier vehement insistence on the validity of the sacraments of simonists or even unchaste clergy in the *Liber gratissimus*, Damian warned of the 'unholy confusion' engendered in the body of Christ by the sexual activities of a bishop, who potentially contaminated all orders within the ecclesiastical hierarchy by virtue of his position at its apex and of his role as the ordainer of priests, the consecrator of churches and of the chrism: 'And since all ecclesiastical orders are accumulated in one awesome structure in you, you surely defile them by associating with prostitutes.' Moreover, he was explicitly graphic: 'As you lay your hand on someone the Holy Spirit descends upon him; and you use your hand to touch the private parts of harlots'.[45]

At the same time, Damian worried about the contamination of what he called the 'spiritual incest' perpetrated by sexual relations with the women for whom a priest was trusted to act as a pastor and confessor, and who were effectively his 'children'.[46] His *Book of Gomorrah* (written in 1049) had added yet another dimension to these fears of contamination, that of sodomy. Damian lamented that a bishop's or abbot's unnatural relations with the priests and monks with whom he was entrusted was not only the gravest possible sin, but all the more defiling because of the spiritual incest with his 'sons'.[47] It is well worth noting that concerns about incest in general were promoting the shift from the Roman method of calculating degrees of consanguinity to the much more restrictive Germanic method, led largely it seems by Damian.[48] Again fear of contamination seems to have been a chief concern.

Inevitably, much of Damian's rhetoric centred on women. In a letter to Bishop Cunibert of Turin in 1064 (originally intended for Countess Adelaide of Turin), he recounted the story of a priest who, ignoring the counsels of a venerable abbot, decided to marry again after the death of his mistress. Proceeding with a lavish wedding celebration and taking on 'a new playmate like one who consults the register of a brothel', Damian grimly noted that at 'the very moment he poured out his semen, he also breathed out his soul', concluding that 'thus will one be rewarded who decides to abandon the sanctuary of the Lord to enter a filthy brothel and the wallowing place for swine'.[49]

Elsewhere in this letter, Damian resorted once more to the rhetorical device of direct address, when he said to the women who corrupted priests:

> And now, let me speak to you, you charmers of clerics, nasty tidbits of the devil, expulsion from paradise, venom of the mind, sword that kills souls, poison in the drink, toxin in the food, source of sinning and occasion of damnation. I am talking to you, you female branch of the ancient enemy, hoopoes, screech owls, nighthawks, she-wolves, leeches, calling without ceasing 'Give, give'. So come and listen to me, you strumpets, prostitutes waiting to be kissed, you wallow for fat pigs, den of unclean spirits ... you are harpies flying about the sacrifice of the lord to snatch up those who are offered to God and cruelly devour them. ... You furious vipers, by the ardour of your impatient lust you dismember your lovers by cutting them off from Christ who is the head of the clergy.[50]

This and similar invective has understandably led to Damian being classified as the most misogynistic of the reformers at the forefront of the movement to bring about what has been termed the 'erasure' of the priest's wife.[51] His general opinion of women is nowhere more evident than in a letter to his widowed sisters Rodelinda and Sufficia, where he advised them to persevere in both bodily and spiritual chastity, contrasting their lives with certain women 'who live according to the flesh'.[52]

Although, as McNamara and others have argued, one of the chief results of a newly celibate clerical hierarchy in the eleventh century was the reshaping of the gender system to reinforce male domination, it has increasingly been suggested that the real struggle was not that of men against women but rather of clerical men against lay men.[53] Thus, overtly misogynistic language such as the above, in which women were effectively rhetorical devices, can be seen as having been directed chiefly at priests. Furthermore, such language was rooted in the reformers' construction of an alternative masculinity: one that was not only more powerful but also more deserving of power, precisely because it was not undermined by association with the weaker sex or the other trappings of lay males.

Elliott has argued that the harsh criticism of women by men like Damian was in fact particularly a warning against the way that women, with their devouring lust, actually emasculated men.[54] Peter Damian's exhortation in his *Book of Gomorrah* that bishops should *viriliter execute* ('act in a manly fashion') can be understood similarly: all sexual activity (the kind of that activity may have been less important) had an inherently emasculating effect.[55] For Damian then, celibacy and especially chastity were not just marks of difference, but signs of superiority, ones that reinforced clerical masculinity precisely in terms of self-control over all aspects of physical desire.

That this was the case can be seen in the fact that, when women received lavish praise, it was chiefly in the context of being 'unwomanly' or 'manly'. Adelaide of Turin is a prime example. Likened to the Old Testament heroine Deborah, she was commended 'since as a woman you are as strong as a man'.[56] Like Matilda of Tuscany, Adelaide was encouraged essentially to act *viriliter*, and was requested not only to enforce episcopal discipline on the bishops living on the lands she administered, but also to 'apply the vigour of your worldly power to the women', for as Damian noted, 'there were only three kinds of women God knew': virgins, widows and wives. For Damian, women who lived with clerics 'were not deserving of recognition by God'.[57]

In contrast to this position of contamination stood Gregory VII who, as with simony, tended to treat clerical marriage or concubinage as an issue of obedience. Like Damian, though, he did emphasize in a letter reprimanding Bishop Otto of Constance in 1075 that 'the whole company of the catholic church are either virgins or chaste or married. Whoever stands outside these three orders is not numbered amongst the sons of the church or within the bounds of the Christian religion.'[58] For Gregory, though, any use of sexual imagery or pollution rhetoric was inextricably bound up with his desire to enforce adherence to canonical norms. Hence, in a letter to Archbishop Anno of Cologne in 1075, Gregory urged him to inculcate the chastity of the clergy 'according to the decrees of the fathers and the authority of the canons'.[59] Here as elsewhere, Gregory stressed how needful chastity was 'for the chamberlains of a virgin bridegroom and a virgin bride', that fornicating priests ought not to 'foist upon their Saviour an unclean ... service' and that 'the pollutions of filthy lust' be eradicated, and constantly reminded his addressees of the 'madness ... and crime it is at one and the same time to touch the body of a harlot and the body of Christ', yet his message was invariably one of conformity to canon law.[60]

In letters to Siegfried of Mainz, Werner of Magdeburg and Otto of Constance, Gregory explicitly linked the promotion and enforcement of chastity to the paramount need for adherence to the decrees of the fathers and obedience to apostolic authority.[61] Indeed, Otto's failure to act was condemned as the 'unparalleled insolence that a bishop should despise the decrees of the apostolic see, should set at naught the precepts of the holy fathers'. This letter was, unusually for Gregory, supported by direct canonical references.[62] Moreover, in letters to the faithful in Constance, Germany and Italy, the failure of bishops to eradicate the practice of married and unchaste clergy, for which Gregory urged the people in no way to obey these bishops or follow their precepts, was presented as an issue not simply of obedience but also of right faith.[63] As he stipulated in his *Dictatus papae* and elsewhere, no one could be considered a catholic who was not in concordance with the Roman Church. In other words, for Gregory, issues of personal behaviour had become matters of correct faith.[64]

The 'pollution complex'

While the impression has perhaps been given by the above that reform issues were addressed in isolation from each other, most often they were handled together, especially simony and clerical unchastity. Pope Leo IX's council at Rheims in 1049 is an important example of the way in which anxieties over individual issues of clerical purity coalesced to form what Remensnyder called a 'pollution complex',[65] and this council is worth considering in some detail. Although it is evident from the decrees promulgated at the conclusion of the council that a large number of matters had been deliberated, the canons themselves, which inevitably present something of a seamless *fait accompli*, do not do justice to the complicated nature of the proceedings as reflected in other sources, especially the *Historia dedicationis sancti Remigii apud Remos* ('History of the Dedication of St Remigius at Rheims') and thus have often escaped the notice of historians. Though ostensibly an account of the re-dedication of the church of St Remy written *circa* 1055 by the monk Anselm, the *Historia* juxtaposes the dedication with a quite detailed account of the three-day council in 1049, and it is an important corrective to the canons for the way it reveals that specific infractions were increasingly being treated as inter-related pollutions.[66]

At Rheims, although simony was the chief issue, it is evident that a wide variety of topics was addressed, dealing both with clerical and lay behaviour. Among the issues were ecclesiastical goods held by laymen and the 'evil customs' introduced into the churches as a consequence, as well as incestuous marriages among laymen and adulterous second unions of those who had repudiated their first wives. The council furthermore deliberated on the apostasy of clerics and monks, clergy who occupied themselves with military matters or bore arms, unjust seizures and captures of the poor, sodomy and certain other unspecified heresies which were said to be polluting northern France.[67]

Somewhat surprisingly, there was no specific mention of clerical concubinage or marriage at Rheims, in either the canons, the *Historia* or in the *Life of Leo IX* whose account bears strong similarities to the *Historia*. This stands in contrast to the ever well-informed, if later, Orderic Vitalis who noted that at Rheims Leo prohibited clerics from bearing arms and having wives.[68] Although clerical marriage was not formally prohibited, at least in Normandy, until 1064 at the Council of Lisieux (though it had little impact),[69] it is unlikely that no action whatsoever was taken against married clerics at Rheims, as it was an issue that preoccupied Leo from the start of his pontificate. While simony had been the main issue at the first of his councils at Rome in April 1049, there is also evidence that the pope attacked clerical concubinage, decreeing that all wives and concubines of priests in Rome were to be declared unfree and were to become the property of the Lateran palace.[70] The same was true at the council held at Mainz in later October 1049. There, according to Adam of Bremen, alongside condemnations of simony, Leo ordered that the wives of priests be expelled from the city.[71] Moreover, subsequent councils held by papal legates – at Coyaca in 1050, and at Toulouse and Compostella in 1056, to mention but a few – all treated the three abuses of simony, arms and clerical unchastity as being inter-related pollutions.[72]

Nevertheless, it is clear from the *Historia*'s account that simony was the principal issue with regard to the clergy at Rheims. On the first day, all the bishops and abbots present were required publicly to vow that they were not simonists, either in acquiring their own offices or by selling orders to others.[73] Although the archbishops of Trier, Lyons and Besançon, along with most other assembled bishops and abbots, purged themselves from suspicion, Archbishop Wido of Rheims requested a delay so that he might speak privately with the pope. The bishops of Langres, Nevers, Countances and Nantes – along with some unnamed abbots – also equivocated and were given until the following day to clear themselves. According to the *Historia*, Leo closed the first day's proceedings by reminding the suspect clerics that they were to remain until the end of the council on pain of immediate excommunication.

When the council reconvened on the second day, the cases of the suspected clerics were again taken up. After private discussions with the pope, the Archbishop of Rheims was granted further time to prove his innocence, in fact until the council of Rome held the following year. Others, however, were less fortunate in their efforts to thwart the proceedings, none more thoroughly than Bishop Hugh of Langres, who was accused not only of having obtained his bishopric by simony, but also of a whole complex of crimes including the sale of offices, bearing arms, murder, adultery, extortion, genital torture and sodomy.[74]

The case of Hugh of Langres is significant for a number of reasons. According to the *Historia*, whose account is mirrored by the *Life of Leo*, as the accusations were made, Hugh tried valiantly to defend himself, appealing to the archbishops of Besançon and Lyons to speak on his behalf. When Hugh of Besançon – according to both narratives a man of great piety and verbal eloquence – rose to speak, he was suddenly struck mute.[75] Halinard of Lyons then rose to say that Hugh of Langres was guilty of simony and extortion, but not the other crimes. Recognizing that there was not enough time to debate the issue satisfactorily, Leo ordered that the canon regarding those who sell offices be recited and the council was adjourned until the following day.[76] When it reconvened, and it was discovered that Hugh of Langres had fled, he was excommunicated by the order of the pope, not for the crimes alleged against him, but according to the decrees of the fathers that had been read out at the start, namely that no one under suspicion was to leave the council.

The story, however, does not end there. After the sentence was passed, Hugh of Besançon, who had speedily recovered, rose and confessed that what had condemned him to silence on the previous day had been the power of St Remy. Moved to tears both by Hugh's devotion and shame at having been prepared to speak on behalf of so unworthy a priest as Hugh of Langres, Leo ordered all the participants to prostrate themselves at the saint's tomb and recite his antiphon with devotion.[77] The council then resumed with the cases of the remaining suspect bishops, who not surprisingly were humiliated into confessing their guilt. The bishops of Countances and Nevers were permitted to remain in office as the simony had been effected by family members without their knowledge.[78] The bishop of Nantes, however, who was more implicated in the act of simony, was stripped of episcopal office.

This account is an important one, and it would be wrong to dismiss the story of the miraculous muting of Hugh of Besançon as nothing more than Anselm's proof of the power of St Remy. In the logic of the text, the council had become disordered with the disturbing case of Hugh of Langres, who had been accused of a whole gamut of particularly unpleasant crimes, the muting of Hugh of Besançon and the uncertainty of the status of the remaining suspect bishops. It required legal judgment according to the canons as well as the purifying power of the saint to restore order. The difference between the account here and that in the *Life of Leo* – where events follow on immediately (that is, the miracle was venerated instantly)

– is significant. In the *Life of Leo,* sacred space (at least textually) had not been corrupted or made unclean: God would simply not permit a man as good and eloquent as Hugh of Besançon to 'pollute himself' in speech.[79] But there were clearly other issues at stake, as Leo's ultimate handling of the case reveals. Hugh of Langres travelled to Rome the following year, and with mortifying fasts, tears and bare feet, made public confession to Leo at the Lenten council of 1050.[80] It is unclear to what Hugh confessed: simony, sodomy or simply leaving the council. In any event, Leo restored him to the episcopal office, though Hugh (perhaps conveniently, given the nature of his supposed crimes) died on the return journey.

What the various accounts of the council of Rheims reveal, however, is that at least by 1049 the reformers had not yet found anything like a consistent language of purity or even a single image of pollution that could delineate, at least discursively, appropriate and inappropriate behaviour.[81] Leo's rather lukewarm reaction to Peter Damian's *Book of Gomorrah,* written around this time, with its demand that the pope take action to eradicate sodomy, offers further evidence that rhetorically charged invective had not yet coalesced into any sort of deliberate strategy of separation. Making Hugh of Langres as wicked, as sexually deviant, as soiled and compromised as possible, much like Guibert of Nogent's later characterization of Thomas of Marle would do, underscored both the increasingly restricted and restrictive sphere in which the reformers competed for the moral high ground, where 'otherness' would be the ultimate penalty.

The problem of lay investiture

In many ways, it was the issue of lay investiture that made the reformers' efforts to find a clear rhetoric of purity far simpler. This is in no way to suggest that concerns about simony, clerical chastity or other issues of conduct disappeared from the reformers' agenda. Yet it is evident – especially after 1078 and 1080, with Gregory VII's decrees first against clergy receiving office from laymen and later against laymen presuming to give office – that the reformers were moving from money and sex as measures of clerical purity towards the simpler test in which clerical separateness was most visibly contaminated through the act of homage to laymen and their bestowal of the insignia of church office.[82] As discussed above in Chapter 5, lay investiture had occasionally appeared as an issue of concern, first at Bourges in 1031 and especially with Humbert in the 1050s: he saw simony and other abuses as the inevitable results of lay intrusion, though his views had not been widely persuasive at the time.

After the second excommunication of Henry IV in 1080 and the election of the anti-pope Clement III, however, lay investiture increasingly became (in the words of Gregory VII) the paramount crime both of 'ambition and disobedience', 'through which the Christian religion is trampled underfoot'.[83] As is perhaps to be expected, the issue was often explicitly a matter of obedience. At the same time though, it was also one of perception in that the sacred – the sacramental powers of consecration and ordination – could be seen to be transmitted through laymen (albeit kings) in the public ritual of investiture, worryingly placing the recipient under their power. Such perceptions without doubt gave rise to fears that, as with simony, clerics would be led to 'prostituting themselves to laymen'.[84]

The idea that clerics were potentially restricted by the authority of laymen had long been a concern to the reformers on account of both potential contamination and the impression it promoted for the rest of society. Early in his career, Damian had warned that any gifts from laymen were 'polluting' and 'infected the soul'. He expressed the opinion they should be rejected, lest they inhibit a cleric's freedom of action to intervene and especially his frank speech in rebuking and correcting laymen.[85] Similar worries were evident in the thinking of Gregory VII, whose frequent invocations of Jeremiah 48.10 ('Cursed is the man who withholds his sword from blood') and Isaiah 58.1 ('Cry, do not cease; lift up your voice as a trumpet and announce to my people their offences') underlined both the right and moral duty of the pope (and all clergy) to denounce error.[86]

But it is clear that the matter was principally one of perception. This is revealed notably in Gregory's extraordinary defence of his policy to Bishop Herman of Metz in 1081, where he noted that 'kings and dukes have their origins from those who, being ignorant of God, [rise] by pride, rapines, treachery and murder'.[87] In the letter to Herman, Gregory was unabashed in his exaltation of the priestly order as superior to royal authority in view of its indispensable pastoral duties of admonition, chastisement and judgment, and contrasted the sublime powers even of the exorcist (the lowest clerical order) with the nefarious origins of kings whose salvation depended upon the clergy. Such rhetoric was not merely an attempt to reduce the stature of such kings as Henry IV or Philip I of France, but also revealed the fear that in public perception royal or princely power was on a par with episcopal authority in terms of consecration. This may well account for the almost complete absence of any discussion of lay investiture in Gregory's voluminous correspondence, apart from the decrees of 1078 and 1080. Lay investiture only became a prominent issue in the polemical literature circulated after his death during the pontificates of Urban II and Paschal II, who were forced to contend with the daunting ramifications of its being banned.[88]

The subsequent compromise in 1122 between the papacy and the German emperor, Henry V – similar to that agreed for England in 1107 – is in itself revealing. Bishops were to be canonically elected, and the emperor agreed to give up investing them with the ring and staff. He was, however, permitted to be present at the election and also to receive homage from the newly-elected prelate for the temporal possessions of his church. As a king could, in theory, refuse to accept homage from unacceptable nominees, he maintained in effect a veto over episcopal installation. In practice then, secular rulers continued to exert a large influence over the appointment of bishops, but the pope could also find satisfaction in the fact that the perception of the ruler conferring divine office had been thoroughly eradicated.

Blurring the lines

Although the reformers would ultimately find in the practice of lay investiture the defining test of clerical purity, it is important to remember that censuring and invective were directed not simply at the slackers among the clergy, but also ironically at those individuals who lived the most blameless or pure lives, and who often were deemed the most holy. While other telling examples could be attested, again it is Peter Damian who offers the most cogent illustration. In the early part of 1067 in a letter to the people of Florence following a visit there, Damian sharply criticized the activities of certain monks against their bishop, Peter Mezzabarba, who (as Damian knew full well) was strongly suspected of simony. According to Damian, these unnamed monks – it is clear he meant the Vallombrosans – were dangerously using their reputation for sanctity, which he labelled odious, to intrude 'like locusts' in matters of reform that were not their concern.[89]

The earliest independent evidence for a campaign against Mezzabarba is a letter written *circa* 1064 by Pope Alexander II. With reference to the Council of Chalcedon, which prohibited monks from wandering in cities, the pope ordered an unnamed group of monks in Florence to return to their cloister – without doubt the Vallombrosans.[90] Not only did they refuse, but they appear to have intensified their preaching activities, and openly denounced Mezzabarba as a simonist and heretic. At the same time, and potentially far more damaging, the Vallombrosans urged the Florentines to reject the ministrations of any priest ordained by Mezzabarba because their sacraments would be invalid.[91] The city remained openly divided until sometime in 1066 or 1067 when, in an effort to silence the protests, Mezzabarba sent armed men to the Vallombrosan house of St Salvi to burn the monastery to the ground.[92] Entering while the monks were saying the office of nocturns, the bishop's men apparently attacked the monks they found, then pillaged and set fire to the monastery. This attack not only attracted wide attention to the issue of simony in Florence and beyond, but garnered invaluable support for the Vallombrosans. With the status of quasi-martyrs and with considerable lay support, the monks redoubled efforts to oust Mezzabarba, ultimately proving his guilt by means of an unauthorized ordeal by fire performed by a Vallombrosan monk at Settimo in Florence. It was an act that made further inaction by the pope untenable, and Alexander II removed the bishop from office.

The conflict in Florence was but one of many problematic, violent clashes that took place in the second half of the eleventh century as a result of attempts to translate reform ideals into practice. Like similar incidents in Milan or Lucca, it is important for what it reveals not simply of the progress of reform but also (and especially) of concerns about the proper roles for various individuals in the promotion of reform. At the same time, it draws attention to the evidently more problematic issues of how, and by whom, these roles were to be defined. Phyllis Jestice has recently seen these developments as part of a broader change in monasticism during the eleventh century, and her work draws much-needed attention to the new emphasis on a more active role for monks in the life of Church, dating that change far earlier than is often thought.[93] That said, if it is accepted that an exercise in persuasion was at the centre of efforts to implement reform, we need to be equally sensitive to how the changing character of reform, and especially that of reform rhetoric, increasingly brought forth a certain rivalry between the secular clergy and ascetics, who used their reputation for holiness in order to intervene in the affairs of the secular Church. The Vallombrosan example is informative, and Damian's letter reveals the tension amongst the reformers as they grappled to balance the ideals they hoped to achieve and the means of so doing.

It is evident that by the 1050s the monastery at Vallombrosa, founded in 1039 by John Gualbertus, was not only esteemed for its rigorous Bene-dictine observance but had become something of a centre for the promotion of ecclesiastical reform.[94] Moreover, the reformist activities of the Vallombrosans, at least initially, met with more than just tacit papal approval. Indeed, according to Bonizo of Sutri, at the Roman council of 1050, Pope Leo IX called upon monks, especially in Tuscany, to aid the secular clergy in preaching against married clergy and other abuses.[95] An established Benedictine house whose high reputation had attracted recruits and received requests to help reform other monasteries clearly seemed to be an ideal partner for the papacy in the promotion of reform.[96] Papal support, however, would become increasingly strained with the election in 1062 as bishop of Florence of Peter Mezzabarba, whom the Vallombrosans accused of simony.

In his *Liber gratissimus* written *c.*1049, Damian had made the distinction between a person who was called holy on the merits of a ministerial position and a person who was said to be holy on the merits of his or her life; in other words, he drew a distinction between institutional and personal holiness.[97] It is a theme prominent throughout his writings, though perhaps nowhere more so than in the letter to the Florentines, where he condemned the Vallombrosan monks who presumed on the basis of their 'holy lives' to be holier than St Paul, and who believed that through the arrogance of their sanctity they could reject the judgment of the apostolic see.[98] Damian himself was no stranger to the vagaries of irregular monks. Indeed, his own career and the models he promoted are of particular relevance. However much he may have crossed the boundary into the secular church as cardinal-bishop of Ostia, a position he repeatedly tried to abandon before finally being given permission by Alexander II, he remained at heart a hermit and a monk, styling himself to the end *Petrus peccator monachus* ('Peter the monk, a sinner'). The ambivalence of his position is apparent in his own desire as a hermit to avoid the 'pollution of the world'. Indeed, it could be argued that – given the vast extent of his correspondence – he used letters as a means of avoiding direct contact, even if a number were probably never sent to their supposed recipients. This ambivalence is especially clear in his *Life of Romuald*, where he tried to reconcile Romuald's monastic humility with what was an unmistakably irregular existence, as well as his active participation in clerical reform.[99] According to Damian, Romuald not only rigorously promoted the communal life for canons and clerics in the world, but also openly and publicly denounced as heretics those secular clerics and bishops who obtained their offices through simony.[100] What is striking is the fact that the action and example of holy life that was commendable in Romuald and others was utterly rejected with the Vallombrosans.[101] In that case though, it was not simply a matter of monks acting in the world (which Damian believed to be inappropriate in almost every instance), but rather that the Vallombrosans were misguidedly and even dangerously using both their holiness and their separation from the world to act within it. For, as he stressed in the letter to the Florentines, he who wanted to be holy should not display his spiritual arrogance in the face of his weaker brother.[102] The duty of a monk, as he insisted elsewhere, was to weep for sins, not to denounce them.[103]

Damian's opinion, however, was seemingly no longer as persuasive with the changing trajectory both of reform objectives and the means of realizing them, and, at least for the time being, the active model of the Vallombrosans found considerable support. Hildebrand staunchly defended them in 1067, and his letter to the Vallombrosan congregation after the death of their leader John Gualbertus in 1073 makes it clear that he looked to promote their continued active role.[104] Others also saw nothing anomalous in the Vallombrosans' actions. In his *Miracles of St Benedict*, Desiderius – who would also briefly 'cross over' from the monastic to the secular Church as Pope Victor III – matter-of-factly depicted their activities, even thoughtfully providing their leader, John Gualbertus, with a speech denouncing the bishop.[105]

In the second half of the eleventh century, the objectives of reform were shifting, as were the means of persuading individuals to accept those expanding goals. Just as, in episcopal hagiography, bishops increasingly had to be seen not only as practical men of action but also true 'religious' successfully negotiating the tension between the spiritual and the secular, so too ascetics were being called back into the world for active roles. Persuading the clergy to accept new codes of behaviour meant not simply delineating what the reformers deemed to be appropriate and inappropriate activities with an ever more vehement and consistent language of purity, but also (and perhaps especially) more sharply enforcing them. For the reformers, this increasingly meant walking a very thin line between customary social assumptions and their ever-changing vision of Christian society.

Notes

1   I need to acknowledge my debt here to R. I. Moore, whose work on the connection between pollution fears and reformist ideas has fundamentally shaped and guided my thinking on these issues, especially his 'Family, Community and Cult', his *The Formation of a Persecuting Society* (Oxford, 1987), and more recently his *First European Revolution*.

2   L. Bieler, ed., *The Irish Penitentials* (Scriptores Latina Hiberniae, 5; Dublin, 1963), e.g. *Pen. Cummeani*, c. 11.1–22, 130–2; *Pen. Vinniani*, cc. 10, 15–16, 21, 76, 78, 80.

3   *Sancti Caesarii Arlatensis sermones*, 44.7, ed. G. Morin (Corpus scriptorum ecclesiasticorum latinorum, 103), 199.

4   Bernard of Angers, 1.27, *The Book of St Foy*, 97.

5   For example, 'Reconciliatio violatae ecclesiae' from *Le Pontifical Romano-Germanique du 10e siècle*, ed. C. Vogel and R. Elze, 2 vols (Studi e Testi, 226–7; Vatican City, 1963), 1.182–4. Cf. D. Elliott, 'Sex in Holy Places: An Exploration of Medieval Anxiety' in her *Fallen Bodies: Pollution, Sexuality and Demonology in the Middle Ages* (Philadelphia, PA, 1999), 61–80.

6   See Rosenwein, *Negotiating Space*, 1–3, 156–83.

7   *Vita Odonis*, 1.30 (PL, 133.43–76), 56. Cf. I. Cochelin, 'Besides the Book: Using the Body to mould the Mind – Cluny in the Eleventh and Twelfth Centuries', in C. Muessig and G. Ferzoco, eds, *Medieval Monastic Education* (London, 2000), 21–34. Such traditions would leave traces in later monastic customaries deriving from Cluny, including the eleventh-century *Liber tramitis aevi Odilonis abbatis*, ed. P. Dinter (Siegberg, 1980), e.g. 21, 219ff.

8   See J. Le Goff, *The Medieval Imagination* (Chicago, 1988), 225, and D. Elliott, 'Pollution, Illusion and Masculine Disarray: Nocturnal Emissions and the Sexuality of the Clergy', in Elliott, *Fallen Bodies*, 14–34, at 20.

9   E. Dachowski, '*Tertius est optimus*: Marriage, Continence and Virginity in the Politics of Late Tenth- and Early Eleventh-Century Francia', in *Medieval Purity and Piety*, 117–29.

10 Augustine, *Civitate Dei*, XIV.13–15 (CCSL, 48), 434–8; Cassian, *Institutiones*, ed. J.-C. Guy (Sources Chrétiennes, 109; Paris 1961), VI.20; *Conlationes*, ed. E. Pichery, 3 vols (Sources Chrétiennes, 42, 54, 64; Paris, 1955–9), XII.15; Gregory I so advised Augustine of Canterbury: see Bede, *A History of the English Church and People*, 1.27, trans. L. Sherley-Price (Harmondsworth, 1955), 81–2. For other sources and literature, see P. J. Payer, *Sex and the Penitentials: The Development of a Sexual Code, 550–1150* (Toronto, 1984), esp. 49–52. For a more detailed discussion, see C. Leyser, 'Masculinity in Flux: Nocturnal Emission and the Limits of Celibacy in the Early Middle Ages', in D. M. Hadley, ed., *Masculinity in the Middle Ages* (London, 1999), 103–20, and C. Leyser, *Authority and Asceticism from Augustine to Gregory I* (Oxford, 2000), 13–19 *et passim*. For a different perspective, see Elliot, 'Pollution, Illusion', 20.

11 Le Goff, *The Medieval Imagination*, 96.

12 P. Brown, *The Body and Society: Men, Women and Sexual Renunciation in Early Christianity* (London, 1988), 434.

13 Ibid., 443.

14 R. E. Reynolds, 'The Subdiaconate as a Sacred and Superior Order', in his *Clerics in the Early Middle Ages*, 1–39.

15 M. Douglas, *Purity and Danger: An Analysis of the Concepts of Pollution and Taboo* (London, 1966), 36ff.

16 See Moore, 'Family, Community and Cult', 49–69.

17 M. de Jong, '*Imitatio morum:* The Cloister and Clerical Purity in the Carolingian World', in *Medieval Purity and Piety*, 49–80.

18 See Moore, 'Family, Community and Cult', 51.

19 Rodulf Glaber, *Hist. Libri V.*, 4.v.17, 199.

20 Ibid., 2.vi.10–12, 68–74.

21 Peter Damian, Letter 97 (Reindel, 3.67, 70–1; trans. 4.71, 74). Cf. Letter 96 (Reindel, 3.46–64; trans. 4.51–67).

22 Letter 3 (Reindel, 1.107; trans. 1.88).

23 Letter 40 (Reindel, 2.388–9; trans. 2.180, 112).

24 Letter 14 (Reindel, 1.147; trans. 1.136). On leprosy, see R. I. Moore, *The Formation of a Persecuting Society*, 45–65.

25 Humbert, *Adversus simoniacos*, 1.19, 132–3. Cf. 2.26, 2.28, 3.4, 165–72, 174, 179, 201.

26 Peter Damian, *Vita venerabilis viri Dominici Loricati*, c. 6 (PL, 144.1013). Damian did not mention simony explicitly, but noted that Dominic had been *malae promotus*. See also Cowdrey, 'Pope Gregory VII and the chastity of the clergy', 269–302.

27 *Reg.*, 3.4, 249 (trans. 178).

28 Ibid., 4.3, 298 (trans. 212).

29 For example, *Ep. vag.*, 6, 7, 9, 10, pp. 15ff.

30 See M. McLaughlin, 'The Bishop as Bridegroom: Marital Imagery and Clerical Celibacy in the Eleventh and Early Twelfth Centuries', in *Medieval Purity and Piety*, 209–38, though her concern was chiefly with the application of this imagery to clerical celibacy.

31 Ibid., 210. It is worth noting here that Gregory VII ascribed the power to translate bishops to the apostolic see according to necessity: *Reg.*, 2.55a, n.13, 204 (trans. 149).

32 *Der sogennante Traktat 'De ordinando pontifice'*, ed. H. H. Anton (Bonn, 1982), 11. Cf. McLaughlin, 'Bishop as Bridegroom', 210–11.

33 Humbert, *Adversus simoniacos*, 3.6, 205.

34 Ibid., 3.5, 203. Cf. McLaughlin, 'Bishop as Bridegroom', 216, to whom I owe this reference.

35 Peter Damian, Letter 58 (Reindel, 2.193; trans. 2.391).

36 Peter Damian, Letter 40 (Reindel, 1.505; trans. 2.210).

37 *Reg.*, 1.15, 24 (trans. 16).

38 Peter Damian, Letter 59 (Reindel, 2.197, 199; trans. 2.397, 398).

39 Peter Damian, Letter 57 (Reindel, 2.183–4; trans. 2.384).

40 *Vita beatae Herlucae, Acta Sanctorum quotquot toto orbe coluntur*, ed. J. Bollandus et al., 67 vols (Antwerp, 1643–1940), Apr. II, 549–57.

41 Peter Damian, Letter 61 (Reindel, 2.208; trans. 3.4).

42 Peter Damian, Letter 61 (Reindel, 2.217; trans. 3.12)

43 Peter Damian, Letter 61 (Reindel, 2.215–16; trans. 3.10–11); and Letter 162 (Reindel, 4.145–62, at 146; trans. not yet appeared). Damian noted that this applied to the three grades after the bishop, which might imply the subdeacon.

44 Peter Damian, Letter 114 (Reindel, 3.300–1; trans. 4.299); letter 96 (Reindel, 3.57; trans. 4.61).

45 Peter Damian, Letter 61 (Reindel, 2.215–16; trans. 3.11).

46 Ibid. (Reindel, 2.214; trans. 3.10).

47 Peter Damian, Letter 31 (Reindel, 1.284–330, at 296; trans. 2. 3–53, at 15).

48 Peter Damian, Letter 19 (Reindel, 1.179–99, trans. 1.171–93); cf. Letter 36 (Reindel 1.339–45, trans. 2.64–70). See below, Ch. 7.

49 Peter Damian, Letter 112 (Reindel, 3.275–6; trans. 4.274–5); cf. Letter 114 (Reindel, 3.296; trans. 4.294–5).

50 Ibid. (Reindel, 3.277; trans. 4.276–7).

51 For example, D. Elliott, 'The Priest's Wife: Female Erasure and the Gregorian Reform'; and 'Avatars of the Priest's Wife: The Return of the Repressed', in her *Fallen Bodies*, 81–106, 107–26. Cf. C. Leyser, 'Custom, Truth and Gender in Eleventh-Century Reform', *Studies in Church History*, 34 (1998), 75–91.

52 Peter Damian, Letter 94 (Reindel, 3.31–41; trans. 4.33–45).

53 J. McNamara, 'The *Herrenfrage:* The Restructuring of the Gender System, 1050–1150', in C. Lees, ed., *Medieval Masculinities: Regarding Men in the Middle Ages* (Minneapolis, 1994), 3–29.

54 Elliott, 'The Priest's Wife', esp. 82.

55 Peter Damian, Letter 31 (Reindel, 1.322; trans. 2.42). Cf. Elliott, 'The Priest's Wife', 82–3.

56 Peter Damian, Letter 114 (Reindel, 3.297; trans. 4.295).

57 Ibid. (Reindal, 3.299; 4.297).

58 *Ep. vag.*, 9, 21.

59 *Reg.*, 2.67, 223 (trans. 161).

60 Ibid., 2.68, 225–6 (trans. 162); and 4.11, 310 (trans. 220).

61 *Ep. vag.*, 6–8, 14ff.

62 Ibid., 9, 20.

63 Ibid., 10–11, 32, pp. 22–7, 86–6.

64 *Reg.*, 2.55a, no. 26, 207 (trans. 150).

65 Remensynder, 'Pollution, Purity and Peace', 280–307.

66 *Historia dedicationis sancti Remigii apud Remos*, in J. Hourlier, ed., 'Anselme de Saint-Remy' in *La Champagne bénédictine*, 179–297, text 200–60. As before, subsequent citations will be from Hourlier with reference to PL (in parentheses).

67 Ibid., c. 16, 238 (c. 14, 1431); cf. c. 34, 250–2 (c. 16, 1436–7).

68 Orderic Vitalis, *Hist. eccles.*, 5.12, vol. 3.120.

69 As the case of Archbishop John of Rouen, stoned in 1072 at the Council of Rouen when trying to enforce the decrees of Lisieux, makes quite clear: see Orderic Vitalis, *Hist. eccles.*, 4 (2.200). On the Council of Lisieux, see ibid., p. 290, n.1.

70 Peter Damian, Letter 112 (Reindel, 3.280–1; trans. 4.278). See above (Ch. 4, nn.41–2).

71 Adam of Bremen, *Gesta Hammaburgensis ecclesiae* (MGH, *SS*, 7), 346–7.

72 Mansi, 19.787–90 (Coyaca), 847–54 (Toulouse), 856–7 (Compostella). This would also be the case at the Council of Gerona in 1068: see 19.1069–72. It is worth emphasizing that this combined attack had a much longer pedigree than the uncompromising statements voiced by Hildebrand and others at the Roman council of 1059. Interestingly, the two Spanish councils also mingled ritual and liturgical concerns with their reforming canons. Cf. Remensynder, 'Pollution, Purity and Peace', 280–307.

73 For the following, see *Hist. ded. sancti Remigii*, c. 26, 238 (c. 14, 1431–2).

74 Ibid., cc. 29–30, 242–4 (c. 15, 1434). Cf. *Vita Leonis*, 2.11 (4), 90.

75 *Hist ded. sancti Remigii*, c. 30, 244 (c. 15, 1434).

76 Ibid., c. 30, 246 (c. 15, 1435).

77 Ibid., c. 32, 248 (c. 16, 1436).

78 In an act of perfect ritual humiliation that preceded the sentence against Hugh of Langres, the Bishop of Nevers laid the symbol of his office at Leo's feet and offered to resign.

79 *Vita Leonis*, 2.11 (4), 90: 'ut profecto patesceret Deum noluisse falsis excusationibus verorum criminum tanti pontificis *inquinari linguam* (my italics)'. Cf. *Hist. ded. sancti Remigii*, c. 32, 248 (c. 16, 1436).

80 *Vita Leonis*, 2.11 (4), 90.

81 See C. Leyser, 'Cities of the Plain: The Rhetoric of Sodomy in Peter Damian's *Book of Gomorrah*', *Romanic Review*, 86 (1995), 191–211.

82 *Reg.*, 6.5b, 400–6 (trans. 281–5); 7.14a, 479–87 (trans. 340–4). Cf. Leyser, 'Cities of the Plain', 210.

83 *Reg.*, 7.14a, 480 (trans. 340); 6.5b, 403 (trans. 283).

84 Peter Damian, Letter 69 (Reindel, 2.301; trans. 3.90–1).

85 Letter 14 (Reindel, 1.150; trans. 1.139).

86 For example, *Reg.*, 1.9, 1.15, 1.17, 2.66, 4.1, 7.14a, pp. 15, 23, 28, 221, 291, 483 (trans. 10, 16, 19, 159, 207, 342); *Ep. vag.*, 54, 130–1.

87 *Reg.*, 8.21, 552 (trans. 390).

88 See Robinson, *Authority and Resistance*, esp. 179–83.

89 Peter Damian, Letter 146 (Reindel, 3.541–2; trans. not appeared). See P. Golinelli, *'Indiscreta sanctitas': Studi sui rapporti tra culti, poteri e società nel pieno medioevo* (Istituto Storico italiano per il medio evo, studi storici, fasc. 197–8; Rome, 1988).

90 *Regesta Pontificum Romanorum*, ed. P. Jaffe, 2nd edn, 2 vols (Berlin, 1885–9), JL 4552.

91 See Peter Damian, Letter 146 (Reindel, 3.533ff; trans. not appeared). The Vallombrosans made provision for ordinations to be performed by the irreproachable Bishop Rudolf of Todi.

92 It is difficult to be precise about the chronology of these events, especially as to whether the burning of St Salvi took place before or after Damian's visit and letter. See Reindel, 3.332, on the dating of the letter.

93 P. Jestice, *Wayward Monks and the Religious Revolution of the Eleventh Century* (Leiden, New York and Cologne, 1997), 210–47.

94 See S. Boesch-Gajano, 'Storia e tradizione vallombrosane', *Bullettino dell'Istituto Storico Italiano per il medio evo e Archivio Muratoriano*, 76 (1964), 99–215, at 171–73; and Jestice, *Wayward Monks*, 210–47.

95 Bonizo of Sutri, *Liber ad amicum* (MGH, LdL, 1), 5, 589. Like Alexander II, in 1091 Urban II would curtly order them back into the cloister: see P. Kehr, ed., *Italia Pontificia sive Repertorium privilegiorum et litterarum a Romanis pontificibus ante annum 1197* (Berlin, 1908), 3.1, 35, and G. Vedovato, *Camaldoli e la sua congregazione delle origini al'1184: Storia e documentazione* (Italia Benedettina, 13; Cesena, 1998), 3.3, 178–80. Cf. Boesch-Gajano, 'Storia', 115ff. See also Jestice, *Wayward Monks*, 210–47, though she may be overly dismissive of the Vallombrosans' actions as 'hagiography written twenty years later'.

96 Cf. Y. Milo, 'Dissonance Between Papal and Local Reform Interests in Pre-Gregorian Tuscany', *Studi Medievali*, ser. 3, 20 (1979), 69–86.

97 Peter Damian, Letter 40 (Reindel, 1.417–18; trans. 2.136): 'Aliud namque ex vitae meritis sanctum esse, aliud ex ministerio conditionis dici.'

98 Peter Damian, Letter 146 (Reindel, 3.540; trans. not appeared): 'quis est monachus qui pro suae sanctitatis arrogantia sedis apostolicae debeat iudicium reprobare, ubi scilicet non hominis meritum, sed aecclesiasticae dignitatis attenditur institutum?'

99 Peter Damian, *Vita beati Romualdi*, e.g. 35, 75. See H. Leyser, *Hermits and the New Monasticism* (London, 1984); D. Baker, '"The Whole World a Hermitage": Ascetic Renewal and the Crisis of Western Monasticism', in M. A. Meyer, ed., *The Culture of Christendom: Essays in Medieval History in Commemoration of Denis L. T. Bethell* (London and Rio Grande, 1993), 207–23; C. Phipps, 'Romuald – Model Hermit: Eremitical Theory in St Peter Damian's "Vita beati Romualdi", cc. 16–27', *Studies in Church History*, 22 (1985), 65–77; and J. Howe, 'The Awesome Hermit: The Symbolic Significance of the Hermit as a Possible Research Perspective', *Numen*, 30 (1983), 106–19.

100 Peter Damian, *Vita beati Romualdi*, 35, 75.

101 For example, Peter Damian, Letter 129 (Reindel, 3.129; trans. not appeared), c.1065/66 to Rodulf, Vital, Ariald and Erlembald in Milan, encouraging action.

102 Peter Damian, Letter 146 (Reindel, 3.542; trans. not appeared).

103 For example, Letter 165 (Reindel, 4.223; trans. not appeared).

104 *Ep. vag.*, 2, 6.

105 *Dialogi de miraculis s. Benedicti*, 3.4 (MGH, *SS*, 30/2), 1146–7.

7

Hierarchy and social control

PERSUADING the clergy was one thing, though this, as has been seen, was by no means an easy or even assured task. Yet the success of reform depended upon more than ensuring that the clergy accepted – or at the least conformed to – the new dispensations set out by the reformers. For there was another group, the laity and especially the aristocracy, whose behaviour and cultural traditions needed to be fundamentally modified if reform was not only to take root but also to have any truly lasting effect. In the eyes of the reformers, the aristocracy had to do more than cede their all-too-obvious control of churches and appointment to church office. Not only were they required to subscribe to fundamental changes in patterns of inheritance and marriage, but they also needed among other things to redirect their militaristic inclinations towards approved outlets. The fact that the reformers were ultimately able to persuade the aristocracy to accept what was essentially a redefinition of their position within society was, as Moore has noted, nothing short of revolutionary.[1]

The alterations in behaviour, thought-world and cultural outlook that helped transform the aristocracy over the course of the eleventh and twelfth centuries cannot, of course, be ascribed solely to the implementation and working out of ecclesiastical reform. It will already be evident from previous chapters that reform itself was a very complicated process. Moreover, it would be foolish in the extreme to identify any single factor as the sole catalyst for the far-ranging changes in the realignment of aristocratic familial structures, the shift in inheritance and marriage arrangements, or the promotion of courtly culture amongst the aristocracy that helped to shape, or at least regularize, conduct in terms of fighting, feuding and private wars. To argue that the reform movement alone effected these changes would be ludicrous, even though it, like the *mutationniste* argument, may be useful as a framework for understanding change.

It is clear, however, that various social and religious factors underlay the transformation of the aristocracy. At least with respect to fighting and the conduct of warfare, the various networks of affiliation and association that monasteries made with nobles probably had considerable influence in ameliorating and regularizing aristocratic conduct in war. That said, Gregory VII's promotion of the *militia* or *fideles sancti Petri* had an equally important role in reshaping notions of appropriate activities for the lay aristocracy.[2] Yet, as will be argued in this chapter, the movement for reform, to say nothing of individual reformers, clearly promoted a community of mutual interest between them and the lay aristocracy. Even if it cannot be denied that changes in aristocratic life were prompted as much from within the aristocracy as from without, the reformers undeniably reinforced the pursuit of their own objectives by appealing to, cajoling and censuring the aristocracy as well as setting boundaries for its future roles. It is important, therefore, first to consider in some detail these 'independent' developments emerging within aristocratic society in order then to assess the role of the reform movement in promoting or at least justifying such changes.

The starting point for understanding how the reformers extended their work of persuasion to the lay aristocracy lies inevitably in the work of Georges Duby, whose legacy continues to influence, if no longer to dominate, interpretations of the development of the aristocracy in eleventh- and twelfth-century Europe in the wake of the collapse of the Carolingian world.[3] Challenging the previously received orthodoxy that in the early part of the eleventh century a 'new' aristocracy replaced an 'old' one, Duby argued that the period actually witnessed the replacement of one form of family structure with another.[4] Even though the antecedents of the castellans and knights whose dynasties would coalesce to form the aristo-cracy of the high middle ages and beyond often cannot be traced back beyond a generation or two, it is now more than evident that these 'new men' were not *arriviste* opportunists, but mostly the direct descendants of those who had held power since the eighth century.[5]

For Duby, the most important issue was the way that the aristocracy effectively recreated itself during the course of the eleventh century – a re-creation, as will be seen, that the reformers also encouraged and extended. At the heart of this reformulation was what Duby termed the 'patrimon-ialization of the fief' or, in other words, the restriction of inheritance through the paternal line to one designated heir. This, he argued, arose as a direct result of the disintegration of the Carolingian empire.[6] By at least the mid-tenth century (if not earlier), many great families of the Carolingian empire had been brought to effective ruin by the combined practices of partible inheritance – that is, dividing inheritances among all the children of a generation (including females in some cases) – and extensive monastic endowments that were often a means of protecting inheritances for multiple heirs as well as being the prevailing cultural custom.[7]

As a consequence, or so Duby believed, from about 970 the knightly class –itself socially rising to the extent that *miles* (originally meaning foot-soldier but quickly coming to denote mounted warrior) was soon equated with *nobilis* – turned towards exploiting the peasantry and the Church in order to compensate for the loss of plunder and tribute provided through conquest. Often known as the castellan revolution, this exploitation took the form of mounted knights (*milites*) effectively terrorizing local communities by usurping the ban (traditionally the imperial power to command and constrain) and exacting justice from the peasantry and the Church at the expense of the king.[8] Furthermore, by constructing motte-and-bailey castles (initially wooden but later stone), these castellans increasingly imposed, especially from *c.*970–1030, what are known as 'evil customs' (*malae consuetudines*), which included among other things tolls, oven and milling rights, and other exactions stipulating labour services such as *corvées* (usually forced labour).

Yet the private appropriation of what had previously been royal power in terms of the ban and other revenues derived from justice also meant that the aristocracy could not continue to live as they formerly had done. The loss of the land, plunder and tribute on the frontiers, and the rewards formerly engendered by royal service, meant that the aristocracy increasingly needed to obtain more from their own lands. At the same time, in order to maintain its position, a family's possessions could no longer be divided among all the children who previously might have expected to inherit. It was here that the interests of reform came to overlap with the needs of aristocratic families. For the Church, this meant an increasingly stringent definition of marriage, the extension of the degrees of consanguinity that limited marriage between relatives, and also the enforcement of clerical celibacy.[9] Moreover, it is evident that the Church and the aristocracy quickly came to realize that it was in both their interests to do away with the multiple expectations of inheritance that had characterized the Carolingian world. Thus, at the heart of their mutually reinforcing alliance lay the issue of property.

The increased emphasis on territory or landed property, which now more than ever was seen as the key to power in eleventh-century Europe can perhaps be seen most clearly in its impact on the composition and structure of aristocratic families. Although it is clear that lordship based on land ownership rather than one derived simply from commanding men meant that income could be both regularized and maximized, it also, perhaps inevitably, brought about animosity and conflict that could mean the effective destruction of a family. There is often a tendency to see aristocratic families as inherently stable, with their status more securely fixed than those of lower classes, who were more exposed to the exactions or whims of their social superiors. In reality, however, there was as much if not more pressure on aristocratic families. Not only could alliances suddenly and inexplicably shift, but political conflict could result in their effective dispossession and reduction to poverty.

The example of the noble widow Beatrice, sister of Bishop Udo of Hildesheim, reveals the extent to which such sudden changes could imperil an entire family. We know about Beatrice's predicament chiefly from a letter she wrote to Udo c.1079.[10] Not only had her elder sons been exiled for their siding with the Saxon and south German princes in the rebellion against Henry IV of Germany, but the family's estates had also reverted to the king for distribution among his faithful *ministeriales* – the 'unfree knights' to whom the king had turned because of the disaffection of his great nobles as he sought to regain the control and dignity he had lost during his minority.[11] As if this were not trouble enough, the ultimate blow for Beatrice was the fact that her daughter Sophia was now exposed to the exceedingly unwelcome prospect of an ignoble marriage with one of these *ministeriales*. Beatrice's pleas to her brother 'that just as an increase in her honour reflects the shared honour of her family, so her dishonour is our common shame' reveal the extent not only to which class identities had coalesced, but also how fragile they were in practice.[12]

The aspirations and stability of an aristocratic family were threatened by other factors. Marriage without offspring could seriously jeopardize an aristocratic family, and many women were forced to take the veil on account of their husbands' need to produce healthy male offspring to assure dynastic succession. Moreover, it is evident that families could and did die out within a generation or two, as the case of the eleventh-century Giroie family underlines. William Giroie was able to continue to direct his family's affairs and its continued aggrandizement from within the monastery of Bec, where he had been forced to retire following his blinding and castration at the hands of William Talvas, the son of his rival William of Bellême. He did this first by marrying off his four sisters to local and more distant lords and later through the foundation of the monastery of St Evroul with two of his nephews. His immediate family, however, quickly fell into poverty and was unable to perpetuate itself much beyond a second generation. The bad luck, quite as much as anything else (if not William's personal fate of blinding and castration), that afflicted the family was probably a much repeated reality.[13]

At the same time, the pressures both to maintain and extend status and power were particularly demanding. For example, the long battle of Hugh of Lusignan in the early eleventh century to obtain what he expected as his hereditary right, the *honor* of Parthenay (the castle and the rights pertaining to it) held formerly by his uncle Joscelin from his lord Duke William IV of Aquitaine, underlines the extremes of violence and intrigue to which aristocratic men often needed to go to ensure their positions.[14] Their extraordinary final agreement details Hugh's prolonged and violent struggle to establish an unassailable hereditary right to his *honor* from William, whose heavy-handed tactics contrasted sharply with the idealized duties of mutual aid and co-operation between a lord and his vassals, a statement of which he had in fact commissioned from Bishop Fulbert of Chartres. The agreement reveals that a lord effectively had authority over all of his vassals' activities. Not only could he claim the right to control their marriage plans, but he could also dispose of their widows in second marriages. In other words, a lord could arbitrarily demand all sorts of varied services and even punish his men as he saw fit.

The Church faced similar problems. It also needed to secure, maintain and extend its material base and its prestige, for its own extended *familia* ('family'), as it was often known. As has already been seen, the Church (meaning here individual monasteries, bishops and as a whole) was itself, especially from the later tenth century, in the process of becoming a significant seigniorial power with as much at stake as secular lords. Although the Church's interests could be seen to be in opposition to those of secular lords (as in one reading of the 'peace of God' discussed above), their ambitions on a number of levels were fundamentally the same. There was, however, one important difference. The Church's wealth derived chiefly from benefactions from the aristocracy and the king. Moreover, these gifts, chiefly of property, had been presented in exchange for the spiritual services of prayer and *memoria*. It was clearly in the Church's interest to continue this reciprocal gift exchange, while at the same time maintaining their autonomy over earlier donations. The intersection of ecclesiastical and aristocratic objectives, as well as their not-infrequent clashes, had a profound impact not simply on the constitution of aristocratic families but also on patterns of inheritance and the transmission of land or power.

With the fragmentation of the empire, the inability of the post-Carolingian aristocracy to support themselves and reward their own followers by no means implied the end of the aristocracy. Rather, it forced them to take advantage of new avenues for wealth and for the foundation of their lordships, which a number clearly realized. It is evident that success was achieved principally by those castellans, counts and (importantly, also) churchmen, chiefly abbots, who were able to extend both their holdings and profits through the reclamation of marsh and woodland, the construction of embankments, and other improvements that led to greater productivity and further colonization.[15] Those individuals able to dominate the land, and exact tolls and other customs and services associated with its possession or use, were able to flourish.

It is perhaps also here that we ought to see most clearly the root of the so-called anarchy that is so prevalent in the written sources of the late tenth and early eleventh centuries. The disputes and conflicts were primarily between those individuals trying to tap into these sources of power. Although many were able to increase their holdings and correspondingly their power, this was often accompanied by fierce and even violent competition. Moreover, as Moore notes, the ability to exact more from one's lands could mean that less extensive lands were necessary to support a community, whether it be monks or knights, and that this enabled the size and number of such communities to increase.[16] It is more than evident that the early eleventh century witnessed a tremendous proliferation in the numbers both of monasteries and castles.[17] Yet this transformation of the landscape throughout western Europe – notably in Italy, France and eastern Saxony, and in England after the Norman Conquest – inevitably multiplied the opportunities for conflicts and clashes regarding rights. This tension was inevitably exacerbated by the ever-more-dense settlement, to say nothing of the visible demonstration of power made apparent by the construction of castle fortresses.

Moore suggests that it was at this point that it became increasingly essential for the aristocracy (and by extension the Church) to do more than simply maintain a general dominion over territory.[18] Moreover, in order to sustain the higher levels of productivity, it was increasingly in the lords' interest that the responsibility for the obligations or services associated with a property or office be entrusted to a single individual.[19] This effectively meant a fundamental change in the structure of the aristocratic family. Whereas, in the earlier middle ages, power and land were often shared among a much more extended family network, from around the mid-tenth century smaller family units appear to have started claiming specific lands that would later be passed on to children. Moore cautions that we must not assume that the significance of the extended kin group had become negligible.[20] Yet it is clear that the trend towards establishing individual patrimonies was becoming more pervasive.

These concerns clearly led to the increasing practice of primogeniture, that is, the property passing wholly to the eldest son, in eleventh-century Europe, especially in northern Europe. It is important to stress, though, that this was neither immediate nor uniform. A variety of inheritance patterns persisted into the twelfth century, and it is evident as well that a strong sense of broader kin solidarity, to which Beatrice clearly appealed in her letter to Udo of Hildesheim, also persisted. In Normandy, for instance, a system of what is known as *parage* was followed. In principle this meant that, although an inheritance was divided equally, the eldest son became the head of the family and his siblings might be required to perform homage to him. In Provence, the custom of *frerèche* proved durable. This had more in common with the older practice of a broadly based kin-group inheriting and holding land in common. It is worth pointing out here that different customs prevailed amongst lower classes where, more often than not, the youngest son was the chief inheritor.

What all these arrangements had in common was the increasing significance of determining descent through the father. Although this entailed the progressive exclusion of the maternal line, and ultimately a deterioration in the position of women at least as inheritors, it would be a mistake to assume that maternal lineage had no significance whatsoever. As Duby and others have shown, the *nobilitas* of a prospective bride was of the highest importance in terms of contemporary medical belief that women provided the material substance of a child whilst the father accounted for the soul.[21] Hence bloodlines, and the aristocratic or knightly *virtu* carried by women, were crucial. As inheritors, however, aristocratic women, much like younger sons, were chiefly the losers in these new arrangements, no longer sharing in the family's wealth. At the same time, throughout western Europe, the level of marriage settlements, bride gifts and dowries also diminished, though in varying ways. In England, for instance, there was a shift away from settlements that would be permanently alienated towards dowries, which would revert to the bride's family in the event that the marriage was childless.[22] Women were even occasionally prevented from entering second and third marriages so as to stop the division, and loss, of land.

These changes, however, carried other important social ramifications. For the practice of primogeniture fundamentally altered relationships within a single family, chiefly between the *seniores* – those who inherited the titles and/or estates – and the *iuniores* – the younger sons or brothers, whose position now depended on their fathers or elder brothers, to whom, as indicated above, they might have to perform homage. As Leyser has characterized it, the choice for these younger sons was effectively *le rouge* or *le noir*: to become a knight in search of secure patronage, or else to enter a monastery or the priesthood.[23] This meant either a vow of celibacy or delaying marriage indefinitely, and perhaps even permanently. As wandering knights in search of patronage, however, the opportunities for dramatic social or financial improvement were few and far between.

The rare exceptions were those *iuvenes* or youths who were able to improve their lot by marrying the daughter of a man without sons, or the adventurers like Robert Guiscard and his brother Roger, two of the supposed twelve sons of the knight Tancred of Hauteville, who established for themselves conquest lordships in southern Italy and Sicily in the mid- and later eleventh century. These were the fortunate ones, though even Guiscard's eldest son Bohemond was forced to seek his fortune in Asia Minor and Palestine after his uncle Roger extended his own power at Guiscard's death in 1085.[24] Moreover, as the case of William the Conqueror's son Robert Curthose makes all too clear, even the eldest sons of kings could not expect immediately to enter into their rights and were kept as 'youths' despite having achieved the physical age of adulthood.[25]

It is useful now to turn to the role that the Church played in all these developments, and in particular to the question of whether they reinforced or opposed the new secular arrangements. As was seen above in Chapter 3, it was clearly in the Church's interest to promote greater stability, peace and order in western European society from the late tenth century onwards. It is important, however, not to envisage this as some sort of deliberate policy on the part of the Church and especially the reformers to effect some new social order, however much it may be argued that pursuing their agenda necessitated a move in that direction. As we have seen, while individuals were being increasingly categorized in terms of their functions as the *oratores*, the *bellatores* and the *laboratores* during the course of the eleventh century, they were equally being classified in terms of sexual order as the *virgines*, the *continentes* and the *coniugati*.[26]

Moreover, and clearly not without coincidence, such elaborations invariably included a depreciation of the *coniugati* as the lowest state in the sexual–moral hierarchy, well behind the continent and the virgins. The reformers' rhetoric, as has been discussed, was accompanied by increasing accusations of sexual misconduct, more frequent allegations of both spiritual and genealogical incest, and at the same time an increasing exaltation of chastity, continence, asceticism and even spiritual marriage. The reformers undoubtedly believed that these new values were in the best interests of Christian society. Yet, as Moore notes, what they essentially persuaded many people to accept was a reconstruction of the customs and values of social life that was largely detrimental to the interests of most of them.[27]

Like the aristocracy, the Church also needed to safeguard its properties and rights, to pass them on intact and to continue to augment them when and where possible. This, as has already been explored, had ramifications for the Church also to clean up its own house, so to speak – for instance, to prohibit clerical marriage, as the children of the clergy could be a serious drain on ecclesiastical resources. But it was clearly a case of doing more than ensuring that its own personnel were brought into line and its own wealth protected. The Church also needed to ensure that the flow of donations and revenue would continue. It was thus inevitable that the reformers would seek to influence aristocratic morals, family structures and inheritance patterns. They thus needed to persuade the aristocracy that it was in their best interests to adhere to the Church's new views on marriage and sexual behaviour in general.

Given that the new practice of inheritance meant that those who were now to be excluded from a share in a family's wealth also had to be kept from marriage and having children, it was crucial to establish what actually constituted legitimate Christian marriage, as well as to underline who was, and who was not, permitted to marry. The Church, however, had never defined this precisely. Indeed throughout the earlier middle ages and well into the eleventh century, marriage was not considered to be a sacrament, and in fact was something over which the Church had little if any control.[28] This remained the case up to the ninth century when Carolingian bishops attempted both to define marriage and to set rules for the laity. For the ninth-century Carolingian reformers, marriage was monogamous. It was to be entered into voluntarily by means of harmonious betrothals and never by the abduction of an unwilling bride. Moreover, marriages were only to take place between people beyond seven degrees of kinship. The Carolingian reformers also attempted to regulate the married state more closely by reminding married men that adultery was a grievous sin, even though they regarded fornication by unmarried men as less serious. Furthermore, the repudiation of wives was prohibited, as was the practise of forcing women into making a religious profession to secure those ends.

If it was absolutely necessary that a marriage be ended, this was to be done solely with the consent of the diocesan bishop.[29] At this time, moreover, the clergy had little role in any rituals of marriage apart from perhaps occasionally blessing the marriage bed.[30]

This, at least, was the ideal. In reality, however, such requirements inevitably clashed with the practical needs of aristocratic families. This, after all, was a society where marriage linked families rather than individuals. Aristocratic families needed, on the one hand, to produce as many children as possible, and on the other, to make as many alliances as possible through marriage among their extended kin. The ecclesiastical rules, therefore, were effectively ignored. Indeed in the tenth and early eleventh centuries, the marriages of aristocratic warriors and even of kings were technically incestuous, that is within the prohibited degrees of kinship, and many were probably made under duress if not by abduction. The practise of concubinage existed openly, as in fact did clerical marriage as seen above in the famous example of Bishop Hildebrand of Florence. Husbands easily and frequently put aside their wives, took new ones and also maintained concubines. This was clearly not prompted, as Duby and Brooke have stressed, from any deliberate rejection of the ecclesiastical stipulations, but rather from the interests to make and extend alliances between families, as well as for the children who would carry knightly virtue in their blood.[31]

Duby saw the increasing provisions for marriage as being intrinsically related to the changing economics of feudal property.[32] When, in the earlier middle ages, a lord's wealth had derived chiefly from conquest and plunder, it had been in his interest to have as many children as possible: sons to fight against his enemies and daughters to give in marriage to create alliances, secure treaties and make the peace.[33] Multiple marriages and widespread concubinage, however much the Church might protest, were essential requirements that established and maintained social order. When the transmission of an undivided inheritance, however, became the aristocracy's primary concern, all this had to change. The eldest son and heir needed to be firmly established and the claims of any potential rivals lessened and even eradicated where possible through entrance (forced or otherwise) to religious life. Moreover, while previously a lord's sons had stood as effective equals at least in status regardless of whether they were the children of a legitimate wife, a second, a third or even a concubine, children of legitimate marriages now took pride of place and bastards were increasingly marginalized as unfit holders or transmitters of lineage and power. A famous example will prove the point. Although bastardy had proved no impediment to William of Normandy's successful claim to the duchy or his later kingship of England, his bastard grandson Robert of Gloucester was seemingly never thought of in the tangled struggle for succession to Henry I.[34]

A further change towards what Duby called the 'sacralization of marriage' is especially evident from the early eleventh century, but particularly from mid-century, with the tightening of incest prohibitions.[35] Since the time of the early Church, there had always been opposition to marriage between individuals who were too closely related. The precise nature of this, however, had never been uniformly agreed. Gregory I's stipulation that there should be no union between children of full brothers and sisters had largely provided the standard such as it existed. This was expanded in the eighth century to prevent marriage between individuals with common ancestors within four generations. During the ninth century, in accordance with their customary policies of *correctio* and uniformity, Carolingian bishops undertook to resolve the issue once and for all by adopting a demarcation of seven degrees of consanguinity, calculated according to what was known as the Roman method, which meant that a sister would be a relative in the second degree, a niece in the third, a (first) cousin in the fourth degree, and so on.

Widespread divergences, however, clearly remained the rule as can be seen in the legislation from the Council of Elne-Toulouges in 1027, which prohibited marriage within six degrees.[36] It is evident from this point, though, that the issue had attracted the interest of the eleventh-century reformers. At the Council of Rheims in 1049, though no precise degree of affinity was stipulated, incestuous unions were condemned, and laymen were warned not to abandon a legitimate wife in order to take another.[37] The Council of Coyaca in 1050 called upon priests to compel to penance a whole raft of thieves, murderers, those polluting themselves with animals, adulterers, those of 'mixed blood' (*sanguine mixtos*) and the incestuous, though again they did not stipulate the precise degree of consanguinity.[38] In 1056, the Council of Compostella demanded that incestuous unions be separated under penalty of excommunication.[39] At the Roman Council of 1059, Pope Nicholas II sought to impress this throughout Western Christendom and prohibited marriage within the seventh degree under penalty of excommunication.[40] At Tours in 1060, this was reiterated.[41]

Around this time, however, there was an important shift in the way the Church calculated degrees of affinity. Although it is unclear whether this took place before or after the council of 1059, the Church turned to the much more restrictive Germanic method of calculating kinship, perhaps influenced by Peter Damian and his treatise, *De parentelae gradibus*.[42] This method defined degrees of kinship much more broadly; hence a sister would be a relative in the first degree, a niece and a cousin would be relatives in the second degree, and so on. The shift to the Germanic method is difficult to understand, for it had the effect of making most marriages impossible within the non-prohibited affinities of seven degrees. The fact that bishops were repeatedly obliged to promulgate the new dispensations underscores the widespread opposition to this change. However much the aristocracy vigorously opposed the new strictures, they quickly came to recognize and exploit the potential of such 'incest' when it was expedient, either to discard unpleasing or unpromising partners, as in the case of Philip II and Ingeborg of Denmark, and even to prevent unions from happening in the first place. In the end, however, the need to establish alliances within kin, and especially the all-important transmission of honour and virtue required by the aristocracy meant that the Church's position was reversed at the Fourth Lateran Council of 1215, which restored the measure of four degrees of affinity.

The example of King Philip I of France is often used to underline the Church's lack of immediate success in promoting such sweeping changes in marriage regulations. Although the king was repeatedly excommunicated for abandoning his own wife, Bertha of Frisia, and stealing Bertrada (the wife of his vassal the Count of Anjou), whom he finally married in 1093, it is worth emphasizing that he was the first anointed king to be excommunicated for sexual behaviour.[43] Yet throughout the later eleventh and especially twelfth century, the Church was slowly gaining the upper hand. However much clerical marriage continued to be a problem, marriage was now to be reserved solely for the laity, and concubinage increasingly lost its legitimacy, if not its frequency. Ecclesiastical sanctions and even secular laws sought to reinforce these new realities as early as the mid-eleventh century. For instance, Emperor Henry III prohibited illicit marriages in 1052; at the Council of Compostella in 1056, the prohibition of bigamy was reiterated; and at the Council at Rome in 1063, Alexander II noted that a layman who had both a wife and a concubine was unable to communicate.[44] By 1215 and the Fourth Lateran Council, marriage had been effectively 'sacralized'. It was essentially established as a sacrament supported by a theology of consent, and priests presided over the pledges and gift exchanges at betrothals and also made nuptial blessings. Monogamy had prevailed, and aristocrats and rulers alike were prepared to accept the Church as the appropriate forum if a marriage needed to be dissolved, chiefly in the hope that an unwanted spouse would be discovered to be too close a relation. It is worth noting that the Church was aware of this eventuality as early as 1060, when, at the Council of Tours, it was stressed that wives could not be put aside without episcopal permission under the 'guise of a consanguineous union'.[45] Yet, as Duby, Brooke, Moore and others emphasize, the acceptance of a new model of Christian marriage was not the product of the aristocracy placing a higher value on complying with ecclesiastical regulations rather than pursuing their own familial ambitions; it was simply that their interests had fundamentally coalesced with those of the Church and also that they had to pay too high a price for not complying.[46]

Duby argued that at the heart of changes in marriage – from the looser arrangements of the earlier middle ages to the monogamous tradition increasingly supervised by the Church – there was an important new emphasis on hierarchy.[47] The new patterns of inheritance reinforced this development. Not only did they tend to increase the authority of the older generation, especially a father's control over all his children, but also the authority of older males over their younger siblings, whose disinheritance under primogeniture made them dependent on their elder brothers. But the increase of authority often had other, perhaps unforeseen, consequences, including stronger control over women in general, however much a theory of consent (rather than consummation), as the principle that established a legitimate union afforded both women and their families some protection. Yet in the new order of things, a father/husband maintained authority over the property and sexuality of his daughter/wife. While the father henceforth stood firmly as the hierarchical head of his household, he also had increasingly to be seen as the master both of the private life and sexuality of his family, thereby demonstrating to society that he was a fitting holder of power.

This development was paralleled by an increasingly 'paternalistic' (if we can use the expression) Church, which claimed authority over the laity in regard not just to marriage but spiritual matters at large. At the same time, the Church also needed to ensure that its personnel, whose celibacy and even virginity had been used to establish them as the appropriate custodians both of property and power, lived up to the ideal of Christian perfection by removing themselves from all the trappings of male lifestyles. Perhaps, as has been suggested by Leyser, this was in some ways a sort of compensation for the disinherited: their possibly unwilling vows of chastity and poverty allowed them – at least potentially – to exercise extensive power and oversee tremendous wealth.[48]

This inevitably draws attention to what many historians have more recently referred to as a 'crisis of masculinity' in eleventh-century Europe.[49] It will already have been evident from the preceding pages that the socio-religious and political changes in the eleventh century were chiefly about men. As has also been revealed through the examination of various texts and legislation in previous chapters, at the centre of reform preoccupations in the eleventh century lay the issue of the behaviour and the customs of men, whether clergy or laymen. This preoccupation, as we have seen, most often found its expression in the condemnation of specific activities for both groups, for instance in the prohibitions of incest or those barring the clergy from bearing weapons. Moreover, it has already been argued that what underlay both these preoccupations and the legislation was the issue of what kind of man was the appropriate one to exercise power in and over society.

For the clergy, however, this issue had important ramifications for their identity as men. Indeed, as Miller has discussed, the legislation promoting the separateness (and superiority) of the clergy effectively denied them the cultural symbols of lay masculinity within eleventh-century society, whether it was the right to bear arms, have hunting dogs, visit taverns or enjoy women.[50] But a crisis of identity can equally be applied to laymen in the eleventh century. Ecclesiastical censures, with their reference to 'typical' (in other words, 'bad') lay behaviour, clearly underscored not only the lower status of laymen as compared with the clergy, but also implicitly emphasized the inferior quality of their claim to exercise power. It can scarcely be denied that part and parcel of the reformers' claim to direct society included a concerted undermining (at least in rhetorical terms) of lay authority as a whole. For the younger sons, however, who had been denied the right to become fully gendered adult males because of familial pressures and the need to transmit estates intact in a system of primogeniture, the outlook was not just bleak in 'real' terms but also in terms of their function or identity within society. In fact, with so many ecclesiastical writers both censuring men and prescribing appropriate male behaviour – chiefly to distance and privilege certain groups or types of men (e.g., clergy) from their competitors – can it be any wonder that male identities as a whole were threatened?[51]

Swanson has recently suggested using the analytic category of a 'third gender' in order to explain the identity of the reforming clergy in the eleventh century and beyond. By taking into account the ambiguous status of the clergy's position simultaneously as men, but also as 'brides of Christ' vowed to celibacy, he argued that the reform period essentially witnessed the construction of what he termed 'emasculinity'.[52] Yet, as Miller has shown, such a category may not be the best model for understanding the social and cultural context that shaped the reformers' definition of their own masculinity and also that of laymen. Indeed, as she, Elliott and others have compellingly shown, the reform clergy unambiguously described and thought of themselves as men.[53] The implicit and explicit encouragements to 'act in manly fashion', which, as we have seen, were frequently used by Peter Damian, suggest that the reformers actually constructed a new and stronger identity for themselves as men over against laymen, as an essential part of defining their separateness and superiority.

For the reformers, clerical masculinity was much more powerful than lay masculinity because it was not compromised by connection with secular interests or familial bonds, and was removed from all sources of contamination: female impurity, blood, money and weapons. Moreover, the clergy stressed their masculinity in terms of the self-control that they, as individuals and collectively, exerted over all aspects of physical desire. Unlike lay masculinity, true manliness for the Church derived from self-denial to the extreme. Their ability, or at least their claim of the right to censure all manner of laymen, even kings, made this position even more unassailable. On one important level, therefore, we have come full circle from Peter Brown's description of the clergy as 'creatures perched between nature and the city', bridging the distance between sacred and worldly spaces but concealing the Church's connection with the sources of worldly power because of their clerical status, but also beyond Damian's concern about monks using their reputations of holiness to act as they saw fit within the world.[54] Clerics' separateness and even their anomalous position had given them by the second half of the eleventh century not only a newly enhanced status as 'men', but also unlimited freedom of action.

The foregoing will inevitably seem rather deterministic. There can be no question either that lay aristocratic behaviour or clerical ideas of masculinity were transformed over night. Equally it cannot be suggested that all nobles became fine and morally upright members of Christian society, who made no unjust exactions, did not oppress the poor, and fell in with the carefully regulated familial arrangements according with ecclesiastical dictates. But the fact that change did occur cannot be denied, as seen from the above. Yet there was one very serious problem that emerged as a consequence of the exaltation of the clerical estate over the lay. This was the question of what then was left to differentiate or privilege the aristocratic fighting man? In other words, what role, if any, did the lay aristocracy have left in the reformers' new social order?

On the one hand, it is clear that aristocratic laymen such as William of

Aquitaine, Albert of Kalw, Alfonso of Castile and countless others established monasteries on their own lands or made gifts and benefactions in an effort to secure both religious and social objectives. These included salvation through the prayers of chaste monks, memory for their families, suitable places for widows and younger children, and a secure burial site in a holy place, as well as the acquisition of prestige in this world. On the other hand, it is clear that a number of lay aristocrats contributed to or founded religious houses with the express intention of joining the monastery during their lifetime, usually nearer the end, in order to make compensation for evil deeds or wicked lives. It is more than evident that monasteries and the Church as whole encouraged this practice. Aristocratic entry to religious life was a valuable source of income and a significant means of recruitment, especially in terms of the social prestige garnered by the entrance of important men. At the same time, the entry of influential men into monasteries set a powerful example of penitential atonement as well as recognition of the need to prepare one's soul, both of which indicated that the Church's fundamental mission of the salvation of the Christian people was being taken to heart.

Although the practice of monastic conversion in later life continued to prevail – after all, removal from the world had always been seen as the highest spiritual calling – its prevalence underwent modifications during the eleventh century in large part, it seems, as a result of some of the changes discussed above. A shift in attitude can be seen first of all in the 'peace of God', where, as has been discussed, the Church sought not simply to eradicate fighting and violent behaviour but also to regulate and redirect militaristic inclinations into new, approved outlets such as fighting for peace or for a just cause. An important change, however, can be seen clearly in Gregory VII's letter of January 1079, rebuking Abbot Hugh of Cluny for receiving Duke Hugh of Burgundy as a monk. Not only had the Abbot of Cluny effectively robbed the duke's people of their guardian but, more important, he had also allowed the self-interest of one to endanger the many. As Gregory wrote, 'Where are they who willingly for the love of God may range themselves against dangers, resist the ungodly, and may not fear to suffer death for righteousness and truth? Behold! Those who seem to fear or to love God flee from the battle of Christ, disregard the salvation of their brothers, and as though loving only themselves seek quiet.'[55]

It is clear from this that for Gregory – and, by extension, for the reform papacy – aristocratic lords had an essential role in the world, and ought not necessarily to be admitted to the quiet of the cloister. This attitude is further apparent when, near the end of his pontificate, Gregory compared those who fight for righteousness with those ordinary knights who fight for their lords, money or ambition:

> If there are some, however pitifully few, who fear God, they have a ready will to contend only for themselves, not for the salvation of their fellows. Who are the men, or how many are they, who exert themselves and toil to the death for the fear or love of Almighty God, in whom we live and move and have our being, as secular knights for their lords or even for their friends and clients? Lo! Many thousands of secular men go daily to their death for their lords; but for the God of heaven and our Redeemer they not only do not go to their death but they also refuse to face the hostility of certain men.[56]

This is not to suggest that Gregory, or the reformers in general, disapproved of the monastic profession of the aristocracy. Indeed, as Cowdrey has shown, Gregory did encourage such profession, notably in the case of Simon of Crépy, although in that instance Gregory believed that there had been adequate preparation.[57] Gregory, however, did refuse to allow other aristocrats like the Roman prefect Cencius to leave the world, because their talents as fighting men, but men fighting for the salvation of their fellow Christians or for righteousness, were indispensable. Gregory also actively discouraged others, such as his important ally, Matilda of Tuscany, from entering religious life.[58] For Gregory, an aristocratic warrior or ruler was instead to be a *fideles* or *miles sancti Petri*, and indeed a soldier of Christ. He was to be a fighter, who, like the original *milites Christi* – the monks – had a role in the divine plan for the salvation of the world. As Gregory's famous *milites* metaphor shows, aristocratic men ought not to waste themselves in the service of a secular lord, but should instead devote themselves to the service of the papacy, to the Church and to Christ himself.

For the reformers, therefore, the lay aristocracy – like clergy and monks, albeit on a lesser level – had come to have a moral and salvific duty in the unfolding of God's plan for humanity. Yet, how could the Church reconcile such a view when the aristocrats' principal profession of fighting was, at least in the eyes of the Church, so distasteful? From its inception, the Church had maintained a decided antipathy towards war, the shedding of blood or the taking of human life, and had required penance for killing even in a just or righteous war. Although the transformation of the Church's position on warfare cannot be discussed here in detail, it is useful briefly to consider the significance and impact of Gregory VII's position on penance in the definition of an appropriate role for the lay aristocracy.[59]

Between 1078 and 1080, as Cowdrey has discussed, Gregory VII turned his attention to a distinction between true and false penances.[60] In this, he clearly had in mind the so-called tariffed or formulaic penances that prescribed specific amounts of fasting and other reparations for specific infractions. From 1078, Gregory seems to have been especially concerned with those such as knights, merchants and officials – whom he specifically mentioned – whose professions in life could not be followed without sin. As a consequence, such individuals could not really exhibit or merit true penance without completely laying aside these occupations. Although his position underwent several modifications, as Cowdrey has shown, Gregory still left just enough room for the righteous knight to continue with his profession insofar as the advice of religious men permitted.[61]

Gregory's distinction between truly penitent individuals and those people whose ritual formalities met the need for public compensation for sin had important ramifications for the development of personal and private confession in the early part of the twelfth century. His views on penance afford, at the same time, important insights into the progressive movement of the Church as a whole towards recognizing the utility not just of kings, but also of other Christian lords and princes. In the opinion of Gregory and other reformers, as long as secular lords were needed in the world to uphold justice, to defend widows and orphans, to protect the poor, and to promote the peace of Christian society, they were obliged to lay aside all thoughts of seeking the welfare of their own souls in monasteries. Their role as defenders of Christian society required nothing less. What this meant was that the lay aristocracy had now more than ever been classified according to their utility for the objectives of the Church. The Church, moreover, had clearly positioned itself as the definer of that utility. That this view prevailed is more than clear from the reaction to Urban II's preaching of the first crusade at Clermont in 1095, where the aristocracy eagerly took up the cross.

For our present purposes, what is more important is the way that the reformers had persuaded the aristocracy not only to accept these new roles, but also the superiority of those who defined them. The way in which the aristocracy had come to acknowledge, if not entirely to subscribe to, and fall in with, the ideal characterization of those who exercised power appropriately, who fought for correct ends and who led Christian society towards the ultimate salvation, is nowhere more disarmingly apparent than in the report of King Harold's scouts before the Battle of Hastings in 1066, in the account of the twelfth-century chronicler William of Malmesbury on the night before fighting began:

> On their return, Harold asked what tidings they brought with them. After enlarging at great length on the leader's superb self-confidence, they added in all seriousness that almost every man in William's army seemed to be a *priest*, all their faces including both lips clean shaven. … The king smiled at the folly of his informants, adding with a merry laugh, that they were not priests, but knights as valiant in battle as they were invincible in spirit.[62]

Although it is scarcely surprising that a monastic writer such as William of Malmesbury would seek to equate men whom he knew to be the 'winning side' with priests, the idea that the clergy set the standards not only in terms of invincible spirit and behaviour, but also that they provided the best model of manliness reveal the extent to which the reformers' reconfiguration of Latin Christian society was in the process of being realized.

Notes

1 Moore, *First European Revolution*, 88–9.

2 See M. Bull, *Knightly Piety and the Lay Response to the First Crusade* (Oxford, 1993).

3 G. Duby, *La société aux XIe et XIIe siècles dans la région mâconnaise* (Paris, 1953); G. Duby, *Hommes et structures du Moyen Age* (Paris, 1973), in English as *The Chivalrous Society*, trans. C. Postan (London and Berkeley, CA, 1977), though omitting 11 articles; G. Duby, *The Knight, the Lady and the Priest*, trans. B. Bray (Chicago and London, 1983). Cf. R. I. Moore, 'Duby's Eleventh Century', *History* 69 (1984), 36–49, and more recently D. Barthélemy, *La société dans le comté de Vendôme de l'an mil au XIVe siècle* (Paris, 1993).

4 For example, Duby, 'Lineage, Nobility and Knighthood', in *Chivalrous Society*, 65–6.

5 For example, Moore, *First European Revolution*, 5.

6 For the argument outlined here, see Duby, 'Lineage, Nobility and Knighthood' and 'The Transformation of the Aristocracy', in *Chivalrous Society*, 59–80, 178–85; cf. Moore, 'Duby's Eleventh Century', 33–4; and R. Bartlett, *The Making of Europe: Conquest, Colonisation and Cultural Change, 950–1350* (Harmondsworth, Middx, 1993), 5–23.

7 K. J. Leyser, *Rule and Conflict* (London, 1975), 63–70.

8 For a useful survey, see A. Debord, 'The Castellan Revolution and the Peace of God in Aquitaine', in *Peace of God*, 135–64.

9 Duby, *The Knight, the Lady and the Priest*, 23–53; C. Leyser, 'Custom, Truth and Gender', *Studies in Church History*, 34 (1998), 75–91; Moore, *First European Revolution*, 88–97.

10 Trans. in E. van Houts, *Memory and Gender in Medieval Europe* (Basingstoke, Hants., 1999), 154–5.

11 See I. S. Robinson, *Henry IV of Germany* (Cambridge, 1999), 4–5, 357–60.

12 van Houts, *Memory and Gender*, 155.

13 Orderic Vitalis, *Ecclesiastical History* (Oxford, 1969–80), 3.2.18: 2.15–17, 31–32. For more details and context, see Moore, *First European Revolution*, 71–5.

14 'Agreement between Count William V of Aquitaine and Hugh IV of Lusignan', ed. J. Martindale, *English Historical Review*, 84 (1969), 541–8; English trans. at Medieval Internet Sourcebook (www.fordham.edu/halsall/sbook.html).

15 See Bartlett, *Making of Europe*, 133ff.

16 Moore, *First European Revolution*, 65; cf. Bartlett, *Making of Europe*, 5–23.

17 Good overviews can be found in A. Debord, 'The Castellan Revolution', 135–64; and C. Lawrence, *Medieval Monasticism*, 3rd edn (London, 2002), 83–106.

18 Moore, *First European Revolution*, 65.

19 Ibid., 65–6.

20 Ibid., 75–6.

21 Duby, *The Knight, the Lady and the Priest*, 46ff; cf. T. Laqueur, *Making Sex: Body and Gender from the Greeks to Freud* (Cambridge, 1990).

22 See P. Stafford, *Unification and Conquest: A Political and Social History of England in the Early Middle Ages* (London, 1989), 166–7, 175–6. Cf. H. Leyser, *Medieval Women: A Social History of Women in England, 450–1500* (London, 1995), 88–90.

23 C. Leyser, 'Custom, Truth and Gender', 77–8.

24 On the Normans, see G. Loud, *The Age of Robert Guiscard: Southern Italy and the Norman Conquest* (Harlow, Essex, 2000).

25 W. Aird, 'Frustrated Masculinity: The Relationship between William the Conqueror and his Eldest Son', in D. M. Hadley, ed., *Masculinity in Medieval Europe* (London, 1999), 39–55. Cf. Duby, 'Youth in Aristocratic Society', in *Chivalrous Society*, 112–22, where he notes the example of William Marshall, who effectively remained a 'youth' until about the age of forty-five.

26 See above, Ch. 2.

27 Moore, *First European Revolution*, 89.

28 Duby, *The Knight, the Lady and the Priest*, 29–35; cf. C. Brooke, *The Medieval Idea of Marriage* (Oxford, 1989).

29 See P. Payer, *Sex and the Penitentials* (Toronto, 1984) for sources and literature.

30 Duby, *The Knight, the Lady and the Priest*, 33–4; cf. Brooke, *Medieval Marriage*, 126ff.

31 Duby, *The Knight, the Lady and the Priest*, 35–7; Brooke, *Medieval Marriage*, 119ff.

32 Duby, *The Knight, the Lady and the Priest*, 87ff.

33 Ibid., esp. 118–20. Cf. Moore, *First European Revolution*, 90–1.

34 See K. Leyser, 'The Anglo-Norman Succession, 1120–25', in *Communications and Power and Medieval Europe: The Gregorian Revolution and Beyond* (London, 1992), 97–114.

35 Duby, *The Knight, the Lady and the Priest*, 35.

36 *Peace of God,* 335.
37 Council of Rheims, cc. 11–12, 252 (PL, 142.1437).
38 Council of Coyaca, c. 4 (Mansi, 19.787–90).
39 Council of Compostella, c. 6 (ibid., 19. 856–7).
40 Council of Rome a. 1059 (MGH, *Const.*, 1), no. 384, c. 11, 548.
41 Council of Tours, c. 9 (Mansi, 19.926–8).
42 Peter Damian, Letter 19 (Reindel, 1.179–99; trans. 1.171–93). Cf. Letter 36, where he somewhat modified his views (Reindel, 1.339–45; trans. 2.64–72).
43 Moore, *First European Revolution*, 89–90.
44 *Heinrici III. Constitutiones*, no. 53 (MGH, *Const.*, 1), 101; Council of Compostella, c. 3; Council of Rome, c. 10 (Mansi, 19.856–7; 1023–6).
45 Council of Tours, c. 9 (Mansi, 19.928). Cf. Council of Gerona (1068), c. 4 (ibid., 19.1071).
46 Duby, *The Knight, the Lady and the Priest*, 87–106; Brooke, *Medieval Marriage*, 121ff. Cf. Moore, *First European Revolution*, 90; R. I. Moore, 'Medieval Marriage: A Case for Early Medieval Communism', in *Medieval Purity and Piety*, 179–208.
47 Duby, *The Knight, the Lady and the Priest*, 99–106.
48 C. Leyser, 'Custom, Truth and Gender', 77.
49 D. Elliott, 'The Priest's Wife', 81–106; M. Miller, 'Masculinity, Reform, and Clerical Culture: Narratives of Episcopal Holiness in the Gregorian Era', *Church History*, 72 (2003), 25–52; C. Leyser, 'Custom, Truth and Gender', 75–91; R. N. Swanson, 'Angels Incarnate: Clergy and Masculinity from Gregorian Reform to the Reformation', in *Masculinity in Medieval Europe*, 160–77.
50 Miller, 'Masculinity, Reform, and Clerical Culture', 27.
51 J. McNamara, 'The *Herrenfrage*', in C. Lees, ed., *Medieval Masculinities* (Minneapolis, 1994) 3–29.
52 Swanson, 'Angels Incarnate', 160–77.
53 Miller, 'Masculinity, Reform, and Clerical Culture', 27–28; Elliott, 'The Priest's Wife', 100–6; McNamara, 'The *Herrenfrage*', 3–29.
54 P. Brown, *The Body and Society* (London, 1988), 434. See above, Ch. 6.
55 *Reg.*, 6.17 (423, trans. 299).
56 *Ep. vag.*, 54, 132.
57 Cowdrey, *Pope Gregory VII*, 674–5.
58 Ibid., 675–6.
59 See Erdmann, *Origin of the Idea of Crusade*, 57–94; cf. Cushing, *Papacy and Law*, 122–41.
60 *Reg.*, 6.5a, 14 (404; trans. 284), 7.14a, 5 (481–2; trans. 341). See Cowdrey, *Pope Gregory VII*, 512–13.
61 Cowdrey, *Pope Gregory VII*, 512–13.
62 William of Malmesbury, *Gesta regum Anglorum* ('The History of the English Kings'), 3.239, ed. R. A. B. Mynors, R. M. Thomson and M. Winterbottom, 2 vols (Oxford, 1998), 1.451 (my italics).

CONCLUSION

This book has explored ecclesiastical reform as a religious idea and a movement against the backdrop of social and religious change in later tenth- and eleventh-century Europe. In so doing, it has sought, on the one hand, to place the relationship between reform and the papacy in the context of the debate about 'transformation' in its many and varied forms. At the same time, although recognizing that the reform movement had its origins as much in individuals and events far away from Rome and royal courts, it has looked to act as something of a corrective to the recent tendency among historians of emphasizing reform developments in other localities at the expense of those being undertaken in Rome.

Inevitably, there has been considerable emphasis on how the papacy took an increasingly active part in shaping the direction of reform as well as shaping society. The reform of society became an essential part of realizing the papacy's overt objectives of a free and independent Church. This top-down focus, however, has been balanced by consideration of social, political and economic issues that underlay the 'peace' of God, as well as the wide-ranging transformation of the aristocracy itself, all of which has hopefully served to make both the complexities and the varied nature of reform more apparent than it might have been in the past.

The reformers' rhetoric often suggests that the battle to persuade both the clergy and the laity to accept the new definitions of their respective positions, along with codes of conduct appropriate to each sphere, was one that had been won decisively. It needs to be conceded that the argument for the papacy's role in the transformation of Latin Europe rests largely on polemic and indeed rhetoric that was aspirational in nature. The necessity of continually reiterating the prohibitions against simony, clerical marriage and lay investiture throughout the eleventh century and beyond, and even the increasingly strident rhetoric itself, may imply a less-than-decisive victory. It thus may provide evidence of the strong desire to promote change, rather than real change itself. It therefore needs to be acknowledged that, on one very important level, the reform of the Church and Christian society in the eleventh century tells us more about the image of a perfected society that a small elite minority of high church officials thought was in the best interests of their world. Inevitably, the full reform and reconstruction of the Church and Christian society was an ideal that could never be fully realized. This is not to suggest that there was no real change. The reform movement left an indelible mark on western European society, and its repercussions would be felt for centuries. The development of the Roman papacy as an institution with the capacity to make its authority felt more consistently beyond Rome increasingly enabled eleventh-century popes to take a decisive role not only in impressing reform measures but also in demanding adherence to them. Although there can be no denying that simony, clerical marriage and concubinage, as well as lay control over churches and ecclesiastical appointments, continued after the end of the eleventh century, these would no longer be seen as acceptable or justifiable practices, even if they were often inevitably tolerated in reality, especially at lower levels. Moreover, it is evident that the privileging of the status of the clergy on account of their celibacy and service at the altar, over both the 'fighters' and the 'workers', had contributed to an increasing recognition that their identities lay first and foremost in the ecclesiastical sphere.

The redefining of the behaviour and cultural traditions of the lay aristocracy, though clearly this was not solely the product of the reform movement, nonetheless do give an unambiguous indication of changes in the rules and conventions by which eleventh-century society functioned. Roles within Christian society, even those of anointed kings and emperors, were increasingly being classified according to their utility for the objectives of the Church and especially the papacy – a Church, and again especially a papacy, moreover, that clearly had positioned itself both as the definer and enforcer of that *utilitas*. Furthermore, the elevation of the *populus* – their participation in the 'peace' of God and in the boycott of unworthy clergy – both as witnesses and as tangible forces that made the reforms of Nicholas II and especially Gregory VII so potent and even revolutionary, reveals the extent to which the religious and cultural assumptions of the 'unreformed' Church were being tested and found wanting.

The second and decisive rupture in 1080 between Gregory VII and Henry IV in many ways merely hastened what was always perhaps an inevitable outcome of reform: the irrevocable separation of the secular and the divine. Thus the challenge that faced the reformers of the eleventh century – to renew the Church and Christian life – was ultimately, perhaps inevitably, the wholesale reinvention of Latin European society.

SELECT BIBLIOGRAPHY

Primary sources

This is by no means exhaustive, and includes chiefly those sources for which, as indicated, there is an English translation, or other indispensable sources that have been used extensively in the book.

Adhemar of Chabannes, *Chronique de Ademar de Chabannes,* ed. J. Chavanon (Paris, 1897).

'Agreement between Count William V of Aquitaine and Hugh IV of Lusignan', ed. J. Martindale, *English Historical Review,* 84 (1969), 541–8.

Bernard of Angers, *The Book of Saint Foy,* ed. and trans. P. Sheingorn (Philadelphia, 1995).

Gerbert of Aurillac, *The Letters of Gerbert with his Papal Privileges as Sylvester II,* ed. and trans. H. P. Lattin (New York, 1961).

Gesta episcoporum Cameracensium (MGH, *SS,* 7).

Gregory VII, *Registrum Gregorii VII.,* ed. E. Caspar (MGH, *Epistolae selectae,* t. 2, 2 vols; Berlin, 1920–23); English transl. by H. E. J. Cowdrey, *The Register of Pope Gregory VII, 1073–1085: An English Translation* (Oxford, 2002).

——, *The Epistolae Vagantes of Pope Gregory VII,* ed. H. E. J. Cowdrey (Oxford, 1972).

Historia dedicationis sancti Remigii apud Remos, in J. Hourlier, eds, 'Anselme de Saint-Remy: histoire de la dédicace de Saint-Remy' in *La Champagne bénédictine* (Rheims, 1981), 179–297.

Humbert of Silva-Candida, *Humberti cardinalis libri III. adversus simoniacos* (MGH, *LdL,* 1), 95–253.

Lamperti monachi Hersfeldensis opera, ed. O. Holder-Egger (MGH, *SSRG*; Hanover, 1894).

Orderic Vitalis, *The Ecclesiastical History of Orderic Vitalis,* ed. and trans. M. Chibnall, 6 vols (Oxford, 1969–80).

Papsturkunden, 896–1046, ed. H. Zimmerman, 3 vols (Veröffentlichungen der Historischen Kommission, 3: Denskschriften, 174, 177, 198; Vienna, 1984–9).

Peter Damian, *Die Briefe des Petrus Damiani,* ed. K. Reindel, 4 vols (MGH, *Briefe der deutschen Kaiserzeit,* 5: 1–4; Munich, 1983–93), English trans. by O. J. Blum, *The Letters of Peter Damian,* 4 vols (The Fathers of the Church, Medieval Continuation; Washington, DC, 1989–99).

——, *Vita beati Romualdi,* ed. G. Tabacco (Fonti per la storia d'Italia, 94; Rome, 1957); partial English trans. H. Leyser in T. Head, ed., *Medieval Hagiography: An Anthology* (New York, 2000), 297–315.

Quellen und Forschungen zum Urkunden- und Kanzleiwesen Papst Gregors VII., ed. L. Santifaller (Studi e Testi, 190; Vatican City, 1957).

Rodulf Glaber, *Rodulfus Glabri Historiarum libri quinque (Five Books of the Histories)*, ed. and trans. J. France (Oxford, 1989).

Sacrorum conciliorum nova et amplissima collectio, ed. G. D. Mansi, 57 vols (Paris and Arnhem, 1901–27).

Thietmar of Merseburg, *Ottonian Germany: The Chronicon of Thietmar of Merseburg*, ed. and trans. D. A. Warner (Manchester, 1998).

Vita Leonis IX, La vie du pape Léon IX (Brunon, éveque de Toul), ed. M. Parisse (Paris, 1997).

Secondary literature

Aird, W., 'Frustrated Masculinity: The Relationship between William the Conqueror and his Eldest Son', in D. M. Hadley, ed., *Masculinity in Medieval Europe* (London, 1999), 39–55.

Asad, T., 'Medieval Heresy: An Anthropological View', *Social History*, 11 (1986), 345–60.

Barthélemy, D., *L'an mil et la paix de Dieu: La France chrétienne et féodale, 980–1060* (Paris, 1999).

——, *La mutation de l'an mil: a-t-elle eu lieu? Servage et chevalrie dans la France des Xe et XIe siècles* (Paris, 1997).

——, 'Le paix de Dieu dans son contexte (989–1041)', *Cahiers de civilisation médiévale*, 40 (1997), 3–35.

——, *La société dans le comté de Vendôme: de l'an mil au XIVe siècle* (Paris, 1993).

——, 'La mutation féodale: a-t-elle eu lieu?', *Annales: Economies, sociétés, civilisations*, 47 (1992), 767–77.

Bartlett, R., *The Making of Europe: Conquest, Colonisation and Cultural Change, 950–1350* (Harmondsworth, Middx, 1993).

Benson, R. L., *The Bishop-Elect: A Study in Medieval Ecclesiastical Office* (Princeton, NJ, 1968).

Bisson, T., 'Medieval Lordship', *Speculum*, 70 (1995), 743–59.

——, 'The Feudal Revolution', *PP*, 142 (1994), 6–42, and responses by D. Barthélemy and S. White in *PP*, 152 (1996), 196–205, 205–23, and by T. Reuter and C. Wickham in *PP*, 153 (1997), 177–95, 196–208. Bisson replies to all in *PP*, 155 (1997), 208–25.

Bloch, M., *Feudal Society*, trans. L. A. Manyon (Chicago, 1961).

Blumenthal, U.-R., *Gregor VII. Papst zwischen Canossa und Kirchenreform* (Darmstadt, 2001).

——, 'Pope Gregory VII and the Prohibition of Nicolaitism', in Frassetto, *Medieval Purity and Piety*, 239–67.

——, *The Investiture Controversy: Church and Monarchy from the Ninth to the Twelfth Century* (Philadelphia, 1988).

Bonnassie, P., *From Slavery to Feudalism in South-Western Europe* (Cambridge, 1991).

Bowman, J. A., 'The Bishop Builds a Bridge: Sanctity and Power in the Medieval Pyrenees', *Catholic Historical Review*, 88 (2002), 1–16.

Brooke, C., *The Medieval Idea of Marriage* (Oxford, 1989).

Brown, E. A. R., 'The Tyranny of a Construct: Feudalism and Historians in Medieval Europe', *American Historical Review*, 79 (1974), 1063–88, repr. in L. K. Little and B. Rosenwein, eds, *Debating the Middle Ages: Issues and Readings* (Oxford, 1998), 148–69.

Brown, P., *The Body and Society: Men, Women and Sexual Renunciation in Early Christianity* (London, 1988).

Callahan, D., '*Ecclesia Semper Reformanda*: Clerical Celibacy and Reform in the Church', in Frassetto, *Medieval Purity and Piety*, 377–88.

Canning, J., *A History of Medieval Political Thought, 300–1450* (London, 1996).

Capitani, O., 'Esiste un'età gregoriana? Considerazione sulle tendenze di una storiografia medievistica', *Rivista di storia e letteratura religiosa*, 1 (1965), 454–81.

Clanchy, M. T., *From Memory to Written Record: England, 1066–1307*, 2nd edn (Oxford, 1993).

Constable, G., *The Reformation of the Twelfth Century* (Cambridge, 1996).

——, 'Past and Present in the Eleventh and Twelfth Centuries: Perceptions of Time and Change', in *L'Europa dei secoli XI e XII fra novità e tradizione sviluppi di una cultura* (Miscellanea di centro di studi medioevali, 12; Milan, 1989), 135–70; repr. in his *Culture and Spirituality in Medieval Europe* (Aldershot, Hants., 1996).

Cowdrey, H. E. J., *Pope Gregory VII, 1073–1085* (Oxford, 1998).

——, 'Pope Gregory VII and the Chastity of the Clergy', in Frassetto, *Medieval Purity and Piety*, 269–302.

——, 'The Papacy, the Patarenes and the Church of Milan', *TRHS*, 5th series, 18 (1968), 25–48.

Cushing, K. G., 'Events that Led to Sainthood: Sanctity and the Reformers in the Eleventh Century', in R. Gameson and H. Leyser, eds, *Belief and Culture in the Middle Ages: Essays Presented to Henry Mayr-Harting* (Oxford, 2001), 187–96.

——, *Papacy and Law in the Gregorian Revolution: The Canonistic Work of Anselm of Lucca* (Oxford, 1998).

Dachowski, E., '*Tertius est optimus*: Marriage, Continence and Virginity in the Politics of Late Tenth- and Early Eleventh-Century Francia', in Frassetto, *Medieval Purity and Piety*, 117–29.

Debord, A., 'The Castellan Revolution and the Peace of God in Aquitaine' in Head and Landes, *Peace of God*, 135–64.

de Jong, M., '*Imitatio morum*: The Cloister and Clerical Purity in the Carolingian World', in Frassetto, *Medieval Purity and Piety*, 49–80.

Douglas, M., *Purity and Danger: An Analysis of the Concepts of Pollution and Taboo* (London, 1966).

Duby, G., *The Knight, the Lady and the Priest*, transl. B. Bray (Chicago and London, 1983).

——, *The Three Orders: Feudal Society Imagined* (Chicago, 1980).

——, *The Chivalrous Society*, trans. C. Postan (London and Berkeley, CA, 1977).

——, *La société aux XIe et XIIe siècles dans la région mâconnaise* (Paris, 1953).

Elliott, D., *Fallen Bodies: Pollution, Sexuality and Demonology in the Middle Ages* (Philadelphia, PA, 1999).

——, *Spiritual Marriage: Sexual Abstinence in Medieval Wedlock* (Princeton, NJ, 1993).

Elze, R., 'Das *sacrum palatium Laterenense* im 10. und 11. Jahrhundert', *Studi*

Gregoriani, 4 (1952), 27–54.

Erdmann, C., *The Origin of the Idea of Crusade*, trans. J. W. Baldwin and W. Goffart (Princeton, NJ, 1977).

Fabre, P., *Etude sur le liber censuum de l'église romaine* (Paris, 1892).

Fliche, A., *La Réforme grégorienne*, 3 vols (Spicilegium sacrum Lovaniense, études et documents, fasc. 6, 9, 13; Paris, 1924–37).

Frassetto, M., ed., *Medieval Purity and Piety: Essays on Medieval Clerical Celibacy and Religious Reform* (New York, 1998).

Geary, P., *Phantoms of Remembrance: Memory and Oblivion at the End of the First Millennium* (Princeton, NJ, 1994).

——, *Living with the Dead in the Middle Ages* (Ithaca, NY, 1994).

Gilchrist, J. T., *Canon Law in the Age of Reform, Eleventh and Twelfth Centuries* (Variorum, Collected Studies Series, CS406; Aldershot, Hants., 1993).

Goetz, H.-W., 'Protection of the Church, Defense of the Law, and Reform: On the Purposes and Character of the Peace of God, 989–1038', in Head and Landes, *Peace of God*, 259–79.

Golinelli, P., *'Indiscreta sanctitas': Studi sui rapporti tra culti, poteri e società nel pieno medioevo* (Istituto Storico italiano per il medio evo, studi storici, fasc. 197–98; Rome, 1988).

Head, T., 'The Judgment of God: Andrew of Fleury's Account of the Peace League of Bourges', in Head and Landes, *Peace of God*, 219–38.

Head, T. and Landes, R., eds, *The Peace of God: Social Violence and Religious Response in France around the year 1000* (Ithaca, NY, 1992).

Howe, J., *Church Reform and Social Change in Eleventh-century Italy: Dominic of Sora and His Patrons* (Philadelphia, PA, 1997).

Iogna-Prat, D., *Order and Exclusion: Cluny and Christendom Face Heresy, Judaism and Islam (1000–1150)* (Ithaca, NY, 2003).

——, 'The Dead in the Celestial Bookkeeping of the Cluniac Monks around the year 1000', in L. K. Little and B. Rosenwein, eds, *Debating the Middle Ages: Issues and Readings* (Oxford, 1998), 240–62.

Jestice, P., *Wayward Monks and the Religious Revolution of the Eleventh Century* (Leiden, New York and Cologne, 1997).

Krautheimer, R., *Rome: Profile of a City, 312–1308* (Princeton, NJ, 1980).

Landes, R., 'The Fear of an Apocalyptic Year 1000: Augustinian Historiography, Medieval and Modern', *Speculum*, 75 (2000), 97–145.

——, 'Between Aristocracy and Heresy: Popular Participation in the Limousin Peace of God, 994–1033', in Head and Landes, *Peace of God*, 184–218.

Le Goff, J., *The Medieval Imagination* (Chicago, 1988).

Lemarignier, J.-F., *Le gouvernement royal aux premier temps capétiens (987–1108)* (Paris, 1965).

Leyser, C., 'Masculinity in Flux: Nocturnal Emission and the Limits of Celibacy in the Early Middle Ages', in D. M. Hadley, ed., *Masculinity in the Middle Ages* (London, 1999), 103–20.

——, 'Custom, Truth and Gender in Eleventh-Century Reform', *Studies in Church History*, 34 (1998), 75–91.

——, 'Cities of the Plain: The Rhetoric of Sodomy in Peter Damian's *Book of Gomorrah*', *Romanic Review*, 86 (1995), 191–211.

Leyser, H., *Medieval Women: A Social History of Women in England, 450–1500* (London, 1995).

Leyser, K. J., 'Concepts of Europe in the Early and High Middle Ages' *PP*, 137 (1992), 25–47.

——, 'The Ascent of Latin Europe', repr. in his *Communications and Power in Medieval Europe: The Carolingian and Ottonian Centuries* (London, 1992), 215–32.

——, 'On the Eve of the First European Revolution', *Communications and Power in Medieval Europe: The Gregorian Revolution and Beyond* (London, 1992), 1–19.

——, 'The Polemics of the Papal Revolution', in his *Medieval Germany and Its Neighbours, 900–1250* (London and Rio Grande, 1982), 138–60.

——, *Rule and Conflict in an Early Medieval Society: Ottonian Saxony* (London and Rio Grande, 1975).

Logan, F. D., *A History of the Church in the Middle Ages* (London, 2002).

Loud, G., *The Age of Robert Guiscard: Southern Italy and the Norman Conquest* (Harlow, Essex, 2000).

Lynch, J. H., *The Medieval Church: A Brief History* (London and New York, 1992).

Mackinney, L. C., 'The People and Public Opinion in the Eleventh-Century Peace Movement', *Speculum*, 5 (1930), 181–206.

Magnou-Nortier, E., 'The Enemies of the Peace: Reflections on a Vocabulary, 500–1100', in Head and Landes, *Peace of God*, 58–79.

McLaughlin, M., 'The Bishop as Bridegroom: Marital Imagery and Clerical Celibacy in the Eleventh and Early Twelfth Centuries', in Frassetto, *Medieval Purity and Piety*, 209–38.

McNamara, J., 'The *Herrenfrage:* The Restructuring of the Gender System, 1050–1150', in C. Lees, ed., *Medieval Masculinities: Regarding Men in the Middle Ages* (Minneapolis, 1994), 3–29.

Miller, M. C., 'Masculinity, Reform, and Clerical Culture: Narratives of Episcopal Holiness in the Gregorian Era', *Church History*, 72/1 (2003), 25–52.

——, 'Clerical Identity and Reform: Notarial Descriptions of the Secular Clergy in the Po Valley, 750–1200', in Frassetto, *Medieval Purity and Piety*, 305–35.

——, *The Formation of a Medieval Church: Ecclesiastical Change in Verona, 950–1150* (Ithaca, NY, 1993).

Milo, Y., 'Dissonance Between Papal and Local Reform Interests in Pre-Gregorian Tuscany', *Studi Medievali*, ser. 3, 20 (1979), 69–86.

Moore, R. I., *The First European Revolution, c.970–1215* (Oxford, 2000).

——, 'Property, Marriage and the Eleventh-Century Revolution: A Context for Early Medieval Communism', in Frassetto, *Medieval Purity and Piety*, 179–208.

——, 'Literacy and the Making of Heresy, c.1000–1150', in L. K. Little and B. Rosenwein, eds, *Debating the Middle Ages* (Oxford, 1998), 363–75.

——, 'Heresy, Repression and Social Change in the Age of the Gregorian Reform', in S. L. Waugh and P. D. Diehl, eds, *Christendom and Its Discontents: Exclusion, Persecution and Rebellion, 1000–1500* (Cambridge, 1996), 19–46.

——, 'Postscript: The Peace of God and the Social Revolution', in Head and Landes, *Peace of God*, 308–26.

——, *The Formation of a Persecuting Society* (Oxford, 1987).

——, *The Origins of European Dissent* (Oxford, 1985).

——, 'Duby's Eleventh Century', *History* 69 (1984), 36–49.

——, 'Family, Community and Cult on the Eve of the Gregorian Reform', *TRHS*, 5th series, 30 (1980), 49–69.

Nelson, J. L., 'Society, Theodicy and the Origins of Heresy', *Studies in Church History*, 8 (1972), 65–77.

Paxton, F. S., 'History, Historians and the Peace of God', in Head and Landes, *Peace of God*, 21–40.

Payer, P., *Sex and the Penitentials: The Development of a Sexual Code, 550–1150* (Toronto, 1984).

Poly, J.-P. and Bournazel, E., *The Feudal Transformation, 900–1200* (New York, 1991).

Remensnyder, A., 'Pollution, Purity and Peace: An Aspect of Social Reform Between the Late Tenth Century and 1076', in Head and Landes, *Peace of God*, 280–307.

Reuter, T., *Germany in the Early Middle Ages, c.800–1056* (London, 1991).

——, 'The "Imperial Church System" of the Ottonian and Salian Rulers: A Reconsideration', *JEH*, 33 (1982), 347–74.

Reynolds, R. E., 'The Subdiaconate as a Sacred and Superior Order', in his *Clerics in the Early Middle Ages: Hierarchy and Image* (Aldershot, Hants., 1999), 1–39.

——, 'The Organization, Law and Liturgy of the Western Church, 700–900', in *The New Cambridge Medieval History*, vol. 2: *c.700–900*, ed. R. McKitterick (Cambridge, 1995), 587–621.

——, '"At Sixes and Sevens" – and Eights and Nines: The Sacred Mathematics of Sacred Orders in the Early Middle Ages', *Speculum*, 54 (1979), 669–84; repr. in his *Clerics in the Early Middle Ages: Hierarchy and Image* (Aldershot, Hants., 1999).

Reynolds, S., *Fiefs and Vassals: The Medieval Evidence Reinterpreted* (Oxford, 1991).

Robinson, I. S., *Henry IV of Germany, 1056–1106* (Cambridge, 1999).

——, *The Papacy, 1073–1198: Continuity and Innovation* (Cambridge, 1990).

——, 'The Friendship Network of Pope Gregory VII', *History*, 63 (1978), 1–23.

——, *Authority and Resistance in the Investiture Contest* (Manchester, 1978).

Rosenwein, B. H., *Negotiating Space: Power, Restraint, and Privileges of Immunity in Early Medieval Europe* (Manchester, 1999).

——, *To Be the Neighbor of St Peter: The Social Meaning of Cluny's Property* (Ithaca, NY, 1989).

Rubenstein, J., 'Liturgy Against History: The Competing Visions of Lanfranc and Eadmer of Canterbury', *Speculum*, 74/2 (1999), 279–309.

Ryan, J. J., *St Peter Damiani and His Canonical Sources: A Preliminary Study in the Antecedents of the Gregorian Reform* (Toronto, 1956).

Somerville, R., 'The Councils of Pope Gregory VII', in *La riforma gregoriana e 'Europa'* (Studi Gregoriani, 13; Rome, 1989), 123–49.

Southern, R. W., *Western Society and the Church in the Middle Ages* (Harmondsworth, Middx, 1970).

——, *The Making of the Middle Ages* (London, 1953).

Stafford, P., *Unification and Conquest: A Political and Social History of England in the Early Middle Ages* (London, 1989).

Stock, B., *The Implications of Literacy: Written Language and Models of Interpretation in the Eleventh and Twelfth Centuries* (Princeton, NJ, 1983).

Swanson, R. N., 'Angels Incarnate: Clergy and Masculinity from Gregorian Reform to the Reformation', in D. M. Hadley, ed., *Masculinity in Medieval Europe* (London, 1999), 160–77.

Tellenbach, G., *Church, State and Christian Society at the Time of the Investiture Contest*, trans. R. F. Bennett (Oxford, 1940).

——, *The Church in Western Europe from the Ninth to the early Twelfth Century* (Cambridge, 1993).

Toubert, P., *Les structures du Latium médiéval: Le Latium meridional et la Sabine du IXe siècle à la fin du XIIe siècle*, 2 vols (Bibliothèque des écoles françaises d'Athènes et de Rome, 221; Rome, 1973).

van Houts, E., *Memory and Gender in Medieval Europe, 900–1200* (Basingstoke, Hants., 1999).

Violante, C., *La pataria milanese e la riforma ecclesiastica* (Rome, 1955).

Vogel, C., *Medieval Liturgy: An Introduction to the Sources* (Washington, DC, 1986).

White, S., 'Feuding and Peace-Making in the Touraine Around the Year 1100', *Traditio*, 42 (1986), 195–263.

——, 'The Politics of Exchange: Gifts, Fiefs and Feudalism', and 'From Peace to Power: The Study of Disputes in Medieval France', in E. Cohen and M. de Jong, eds, *Medieval Transformations: Texts, Power and Gifts in Context* (Leiden, 2001), 169–88; 203–18.

Whitton, D., 'Papal Policy in Rome, 1012–1124', D. Phil thesis (Oxford, 1980).

Woody, K. M., '*Sagena piscatoris*: Petrus Damiani and the Papal Election Decree of 1059', *Viator*, 1 (1970), 33–54.

Zema, D. B., 'Economic Reorganization of the Roman See during the Gregorian Reform', *Studi Gregoriani*, 1 (1947), 137–68.

INDEX

Abbo of Fleury 60, 113
abbots 50, 94, 129, 144
Adalbero of Laon 50
Adversus simoniacos (Against the Simoniacs) 96, 99
agni immaculati 113
Alberic, Prince of Rome 20, 22, 61
Alexander II, Pope 34, 74, 76, 77, 78, 97, 98, 106, 122, 130, 131, 132, 150
anarchy 25, 42, 44, 46, 144
Andrew of Fleury 50-1
apostles 7, 18, 22, 55, 95
Apostolic See 24, 61, 80
    see also Roman papacy
Ariald 74, 102, 103
aristocracy 17, 46-7, 49, 96, 100, 111, 112, 139, 140, 141, 143, 144, 147, 148, 150, 151, 155, 156, 160
aristocratic family 22, 139, 141, 142, 144, 148
Augustine 96, 114
avarice 104, 117

bellatores 35, 50, 146
Benedict of Aniane 12, 15
Benedict VIII, Pope 62-3, 99
bishops 12, 13, 14-15, 39, 50, 52, 59, 69, 93, 94, 96, 97, 99, 100, 104, 107, 115, 119, 120, 121, 122, 125, 127, 130, 131, 132, 133, 148, 150
    see also clergy; clerical orders
Bourges, Council of (1031) 97, 99, 106, 128
boycott decrees 101, 104, 117, 118, 161

canon law 31, 64, 67, 68, 69, 71, 75, 78, 79, 85, 98
cardinals 19
cardinal-bishops 19, 70, 72

cardinal-deacons 19
cardinal-priests 19, 69
Carolingian empire 10-11, 42, 46, 141
Carolingians 10, 25, 31, 45, 140, 142, 149
castellans 42, 52, 140, 144
celibacy 15, 35, 40, 98-9, 115, 124, 146, 151, 152
    see also chastity; virginity
Charlemagne 10
    see also Carolingians, Carolingian empire
chastity 95, 98-9, 103, 105, 121, 122, 124, 128, 147, 151
child oblation 16
Christianity 7-9, 57
Christian society 2, 3, 42, 78, 107, 133, 147, 153, 156-7, 160, 161
Church 1, 7-26, 29-32, 29, 51, 52, 55-9, 60, 65, 70, 71, 78, 84, 104, 105, 106, 112, 115, 117, 119, 141, 143, 144, 146, 147, 148, 149, 150, 151, 153, 154, 155, 156, 160-1
clergy 1, 9, 26, 30, 36, 41, 44, 49, 50, 67, 71, 95, 100, 104, 107, 111, 116, 117, 129, 130, 133, 147, 152, 157
    see also bishops; deacons; priests; subdeacons
clerical celibacy 15, 141
clerical concubinage 5, 34, 67, 78, 100, 103, 119, 120-5, 161
clerical discipline 111
clerical marriage 5, 31, 34, 67, 73, 74, 79, 80, 95, 98, 100, 103, 105, 107, 119, 120-5, 147, 148, 150, 160, 161
clerical office 18-19
clerical orders 12, 13
clerics 116
    see also clergy
Cluny 16, 17, 23, 59-60

confession 13, 28, 156
consanguinity 48, 122, 149–50
consecration 14
councils 39, 65, 67, 83–4, 98, 99, 100, 111
courtly culture 139
Crescentians 22, 61–2, 63
curia 81–3

De ordinando pontefice 64, 69, 119
De privilegio Romanae ecclesiae 74–6
deacons 13, 18, 99
    see also clergy; clerical orders
Dictatus papae 79
Donation of Constantine 58, 61
Duby, G. 51, 140, 145, 148, 151

ecclesiastical hierarchy 35, 43, 122, 123
ecclesiastical property 34, 40, 43–4, 48, 77, 82
Elne-Toulouges, Council of (1027) 41, 44, 48, 149
emperor 13, 63–4, 72, 79, 95, 161
    see also lay rulers
England 11, 92, 130, 144, 145
Ermengol of Urgell 93, 95
Eucharist 120, 121
excommunication 39, 40, 48, 57

feudal revolution 3–4, 39, 42
fideles santi Petri 43, 74, 101, 140, 155
Fleury 59–60
Flodoard 20
France 10, 11, 13, 125, 144
Fulbert of Chartres 25, 143

Gelasius I, Pope 57
gender 123, 152
Gerard of Cambrai 50
Gerbert of Aurillac (Sylvester II, Pope) 25, 60
Germany 10, 11, 79, 84, 142
gifts 46–7, 48
Gregorian reform 33–4, *et passim*
Gregorian revolution 34
Gregory I, Pope 8, 58, 96, 114

Gregory VI, Pope 63–4, 66, 73, 119
Gregory VII, Pope 33–4, 36, 78–80, 81, 82, 83, 84, 98, 99, 100, 101, 102, 104, 105, 106, 107, 111, 117, 118, 119, 120, 124–5, 128, 129, 140, 155–6, 161

hagiography 94, 111
Henry II, Emperor 62, 65, 92, 97, 99
Henry III, King and Emperor 63–4, 65, 67, 68, 69, 72, 92, 93, 150
Henry IV, King and Emperor 33, 35, 68, 72, 76, 77, 80, 81, 100, 106, 111, 118, 129, 142, 161
heresy 31–2, 51, 75, 104, 105
hierarchy 151
Hildebrand 66, 68, 70, 72, 73, 74, 75, 76, 78, 82, 84, 120, 133
    see also Gregory VII, Pope
Hugh of Cluny, Abbot 101, 154
Humbert of Silva-Candida 33, 34, 68, 73, 76, 77, 96, 98, 101, 106, 118, 119, 128

immunity 59–60
incest 44, 49, 122, 147, 149, 150, 152
inheritance 46, 139, 140, 141, 144, 145, 148, 151
Investiture Controversy 107
Italy 11, 79, 81, 92, 93, 144
iuvenes 146

John Gualbertus 14, 91, 111, 131
John XII, Pope 20–1, 61
John XIX, Pope 60, 62, 63

kings 10–11, 13, 64, 106, 129, 130, 143, 148, 153, 161
knights 140, 141, 144, 146, 155, 156

laboratores 34, 49, 146
laity 9, 20, 47, 49, 50, 111, 116, 150
Lanfranc of Bec and Canterbury 25, 34, 77, 92
Latin Christendom 80, 81, 82, 85
Latin Europe 9–12, 25, 26, 160

see also individual countries;
  Western Europe
lay aristocracy 5, 139, 153, 154, 155, 156,
  161
  see also aristocracy
lay investiture 5, 80, 95, 98, 105-7, 119,
  128-30, 160
lay rulers 1
legates 66, 84-5, 112, 116
Leo I, Pope 56-7, 59, 71, 75
Leo IX, Pope 5, 15, 33, 34, 36, 49, 65-8,
  74, 82, 83, 95, 99, 107, 125-8, 131
Liprand 102
liturgical cursing 45
liturgy 8-9, 18-20
Liudprand 20
lordship 4, 42, 142, 144, 146

malae consuetudines 3, 42, 141
marriage 139, 141, 142, 143, 145, 146,
  147-51
married clergy 5, 98, 99, 100, 102, 126, 131
  see also clerical concubinage; clerical
  marriage
masculinity 123-4, 152-3
material renewal 91-5
Marozia 20, 21, 61
Matilda of Tuscany 80, 100, 124, 155
Milan 74-5, 77, 94, 102, 106
militia Christi 17
milites 39, 50, 51, 141, 155
millennia 25, 30, 49, 92
monasteries 8, 12, 15-17, 25, 46, 59, 60,
  91, 92, 132, 146, 154
monastic conversion 154-5
monasticism 15
money 34, 41
monks 8, 17, 92, 115, 130, 131, 132, 133,
  144, 153, 154, 155
Moore, R. I. 35, 36, 50, 116, 144, 145, 147
mutation de l'an mil (transformation of
  the year 1000) 3-4, 36-7, 44, 140

Nicholas II, Pope 34, 68, 70, 71, 72, 73,
  74, 75, 76, 77, 99, 120, 121, 122,
  149, 161

nobility 26, 46, 100
  see also aristocracy
Normans 67-8, 73, 74, 81

obedience 118, 124, 125
Odilo of Cluny 17, 62, 91
oratores 34, 50, 146
Orderic Vitalis 15, 126
ordination 14, 96, 118
Ottonians 10, 32

papal authority 4, 55-64, 71-6, 78-9
Papal election decree (1059) 70-2
papal elections 69-70, 72
papal government 81-5
  see also canon law; councils; legates
papal primacy 74-6, 84
Pataria 51, 74, 77, 94, 100, 102-4, 117
pauperes 42, 43
Pavia, Council of (1022) 99, 120
peace councils 39-42, 43, 44, 45, 47-9, 50
peace leagues 43, 50, 51
peace of God 2, 3, 4, 31, 37, 39-52, 143,
  160, 161
peasants 9, 39, 44, 46, 50
penance 41, 48, 67, 112, 156
penitentials 98, 112
Peter Damian 25, 33, 66, 67, 68, 70, 72,
  73, 74, 75, 76, 77, 92, 96, 115,
  117-18, 119-20, 121-4, 128, 129,
  130, 131, 132, 133, 150, 153
Philip I, King of France 129, 150
pilgrimage 18, 22, 23, 31
plenitudo potestatis 56
polemic 34, 112, 160
  see also rhetoric
pollution 2, 111-17, 125-8, 132
pope 18, 19-24, 56-9, 69-70, 78
  see also individual popes; Roman
  papacy
populus 40, 44, 47, 50, 51, 161
potentes 42, 43
power 35, 46-7, 104, 113, 115, 143, 144,
  151, 152, 153
priests 8, 13-14, 41, 48, 69, 96, 99, 105,
  114, 119, 120, 121, 122, 124, 130

see also clergy; clerical orders
primogeniture 46, 145, 146, 151, 152
privileges 23-4, 59, 60, 102
propaganda 112
see also rhetoric
property 16-17, 23, 46-7, 48, 51, 74, 97,
99, 113, 141, 143, 147, 148, 151
see also ecclesiastical property
purity 2, 47, 111-17

Ramihrd 104, 118
rape 119
reform agenda 30-1, *et passim*
reform councils 73-4, 98, 99, 126, 149,
150
reform historiography 29-39
relics 22, 31, 39, 40, 42, 44, 45, 47, 93, 94
religion 4, 7-9, 44
religiosity 7-8
revolution 2, 4
Rheims, Council of (104) 15, 67, 95,
125-8, 149
rhetoric 111-33, 160
ritual purity 114
Robert Guiscard 67, 72, 74, 146
Rodulf Glaber 24, 34, 42, 49, 92, 117
Roman families 20-2, 61-3
Roman papacy 1, 4, 17-24, 25, 55-86, 161
Rome 17-22, 30, 59, 61-2, 65, 81
Romuald 91, 96, 132
Rule of St Benedict 15
rulers 86

sacraments 13, 40, 96, 97, 98, 112, 118,
122, 131, 147
see also confession; Eucharist;
ordination; penance
saints 17, 22, 31, 40, 42, 43, 47, 93, 94,
102, 112-13
Salians 10
sanctity 101-2, 130, 132
schism 11, 76, 77
sex 49, 113, 114
sexual activity 115, 120, 124

sexual behaviour 35, 48, 147
sexual hierarchy 35, 146
sexual morality 99
simony 5, 31, 34, 44, 49, 63, 66, 67, 74,
77, 79, 80, 93, 95-8, 99, 104, 105,
107, 117-20, 122, 125, 126, 128,
130, 132, 160, 161
social order 34, 36, 47, 50, 111, 118, 146,
148, 153
social transformation 3, 36-7, 111, 116
societas christiana 1, 4, 5, 24
society 1-5, 24, 26, 35, 36, 37, 45, 49-50,
52, 112, 115, 139, 140, 151, 160, 161
sodomy 49, 122, 125, 127, 128
Stephen IX, Pope 66, 68, 70, 72, 73
subdeacons 13, 18, 99, 115
see also clergy; clerical orders
Sutri, synod of (1046) 63-4

theft 49, 119
Theophylact 20, 22, 61-2, 63
Thietmar of Merseburg 32
three orders 34, 50
see also bellatores; laboratores;
oratores
transformation 36-7, 44, 55, 65-81, 114
see also mutation; social
transformation
tuitio 59
Tusculans 61-3

'unreformed Church' 32, 161
Urban II, Pope 79, 80-1, 82, 83, 84, 113,
130, 156

Vallombrosans 91, 100, 130-3
violence 25, 41, 42, 143
virginity 113, 115, 146, 151

war 42-3, 52, 139, 140, 155
Western Europe 9-12, *et passim*
William I, King 77, 101, 146, 149
women 16-17, 41, 98, 112, 120, 122-4,
142, 148, 151